America's Crisis of Values

America's Crisis of Values

REALITY AND PERCEPTION

WAYNE BAKER

PRINCETON UNIVERSITY PRESS

PRINCETON AND OXFORD

Published by Princeton University Press, 41 William Street, Princeton, New Jersey 08540
In the United Kingdom: Princeton University Press, 3 Market Place,
Woodstock, Oxfordshire OX20 1SY

Library of Congress Cataloging-in-Publication Data

Baker, Wayne E.
America's crisis of values : reality and perception / Wayne Baker.
p. cm.
Includes bibliographical references and index.
ISBN 0-691-11794-2 (cl : alk. paper)
1. Social values—United States. 2. Social ethics—United States. 3. United States—Social conditions. 4. United States—Moral conditions. I. Title.
HN79.M6B35 2005
303.3′72′0973—dc22
2004044536

British Library Cataloging-in-Publication Data is available
This book has been composed in Goudy
Printed on acid-free paper. ∞
pup.princeton.edu
Printed in the United States of America
1 3 5 7 9 10 8 6 4 2

To the memory of my parents,
Wendell Hayes Baker and
Evelyn Cotton Baker

✶ Contents ✶

✶ *List of Illustrations* ✶

Figures

TABLES

✻ *Acknowledgments* ✻

COLLEAGUES, FRIENDS, AND FAMILY enabled the writing of this book. Rob Faulkner slogged through two rough drafts, offering comments, ideas, and references. Lance Sandelands read an early draft, gave comments and ideas, and urged me to develop the psychological story more explicitly. I thank Paul DiMaggio for his abiding interest in this project and his encouragement at key points. I thank him and John Evans for comments on my analysis of the Culture War thesis (chapter 3 here).

My appreciation goes to Gene Fisher for technical advice, Howie Becker for critical comments, Allan Schnaiberg and Tom Caprel for penetrating questions, Aaron Cicourel for insights on cognitive science, Evelyn Caprel for information on character education programs, and Greg Prena for endorsing the project. Ron Inglehart, chief architect of the World Values Surveys, provided guidance and advice for working with these data. The article we co-authored in the *American Sociological Review*'s special millennial issue is a basis of chapter 2 here. Fred Block, Leslie Brothers, Jay Demerath, and Alan Wolfe offered sage advice on various themes and topics in the book. Senior Associate Librarian Jo Ann Sokkar at the Kresge Library provided expert (and fast) literature search services.

I thank many current and former colleagues at the University of Michigan for their suggestions and support, including Mary Yoko Brannen, Paula Caproni, Taylor Cox, Jane Dutton, Fiona Lee, Ann Chih Lin, Günter Müller-Stewens (who visited us from the University of St. Gallen), David Obstfeld, Rick Price, Bob Quinn, Nejat Seyhun, Jim Walsh, Janet Weiss, Joe White, and George Widmeyer. I thank Chris Marquis, Kevin Kuan, Ping Wu, and Masahiko Aida for research assistance. I am grateful to Lisa Leneway and Matt Grossman for helping me collect and analyze data on best-selling nonfiction books, and to the Undergraduate Research Opportunities Program (UROP) at the University of Michigan for supporting them.

The University of Michigan Business School and the Institute for

Social Research provided institutional support, excellent support staff, and a collegial environment in which to work.

I am indebted to my editor at Princeton, Ian Malcolm, for seeing the promise in the kernel of an idea, and for sheparding the manuscript through the publication process. I thank Sophia Efthimiatou, Ian's editorial assistant, for handling the preparation of the manuscript for production. I thank Anita O'Brien for copy editing. I am grateful to the three anonymous reviewers of the manuscript for their close reading and detailed comments, and for helping me avoid or correct problems of analysis and exposition.

My custom is to save the most important acknowledgment for last. I acknowledge with love my wife, Cheryl, and thank her for unremitting faith in this endeavor and steadfast support of the project through all its phases. Every day with Cheryl and our dear son, Harrison, is a blessing.

America's Crisis of Values

✶ CHAPTER ONE ✶

A Question of Values

THIS BOOK IS AN ATTEMPT to regard old questions about moral values from a new angle. By doing so, I hope to clarify the widespread perception at the turn of the millennium of an American crisis of values.

I chose the words "perception" and "American crisis of values" intentionally. I use "perception" because I do not begin this treatise with the assumption that there *is* a crisis, only that many Americans *perceive* a crisis—real or not. The reality of a crisis and the perception of a crisis are separable questions. For example, it is possible that many Americans believe society is divided when it comes to the most important values when it is not. I use "American crisis of values" rather than "a crisis of American values" because the discourse about moral crisis covers a much wider range of values than the five that make up the core values of the American ideology (liberty, egalitarianism, individualism, populism, and laissez-faire[1]). Thus, I will explore the question of values over a broad moral territory, including traditional values, secular values, religious values, family values, economic values, and others.

In this introductory chapter, I briefly describe the perception of a crisis of values in America, citing some of the leading voices in public and intellectual debates, as well as the voice of the American people heard through national surveys and studies. Next, I present three ways to think about a crisis of values: as a loss over time of traditional values, as an unfavorable comparison to the value systems of other societies, and crisis as a division of society into opposed groups based on competing moral visions. These are, respectively, the trend hypothesis, the comparative hypothesis, and the distribution hypothesis. I introduce these hypotheses here as an overview but reserve their theoretical justification and empirical testing for later chapters. Finally, I discuss the concept of America as an "imagined community" and consider what a crisis of values means for the twin problems that confront the imagined community of a nation-state: the problem of legitimacy and the problem of social integration. I conclude this chapter with an overview of the book.

The Widespread Perception of Crisis

The perception of an American crisis of values is real; scholars, journalists, politicians, and other participant-observers of American culture have chronicled it for some years. Popular versions include Allan Bloom's indictment of American education in *The Closing of the American Mind;* the caustic effects of runaway individualism described by Robert Bellah and associates in *Habits of the Heart*, a theme reiterated by Francis Fukuyama in *The Great Disruption;* William Bennett's remedial moral education program in *The Book of Virtues* designed to lift America out of "moral poverty"; Robert Hughes's acerbic account of the "fraying" of America in *Culture of Complaint;* John Miller's condemnation in *Egotopia* of the physical and moral "ugliness" of America's consumer society; the loss of virtues and character, portrayed variously by Gertrude Himmelfarb in *The De-Moralization of Society*, Richard Sennett in *The Corrosion of Character*, and James Davison Hunter in *The Death of Character;* and Robert Putnam's "bowling alone" metaphor of America's declining social capital and his call for civic reengagement.[2] "Americans once proudly emphasized their uniqueness," observes Seymour Martin Lipset, "their differences from the rest of the world, the vitality of their democracy, the growth potential of their economy. Some now worry that our best years as a nation are behind us."[3] America, it seems, has fallen from grace.

There does not appear to be a lack of hard evidence of the decline of American society. For example, in *The State of Americans*, Urie Bronfenbrenner and associates review a mass of statistical data and paint a portrait of "societal chaos" in America.[4] Other attempts to chart the course of American society reveal the same trends, such as those reported in The Index of Leading Cultural Indicators, an effort to track the moral and ethical trends of our times much as the government's Index of Leading Economic Indicators tracks economic trends.[5] This cultural index is a composite of twenty-two different trends in American society, including measures of political participation, trust in others and confidence in the federal government, church membership, participation in voluntary groups, violent crime, and family statistics. The statistics used in this index are consistent with those reported in sociological analyses of census and other data, such as reported in *State of the Union*, edited by Reynolds Farley.[6] (Recent reversals of some of these trends are typically dismissed as misleading or simply too modest to indicate true reversals.[7]) To these telling statistics one can add any number of sad and tragic events from the closing years of the century, ranging from the impeachment of President Bill Clinton for lying under oath about his sexual relations with Monica Lewinsky to the massacre at Columbine High School in Littleton, Colorado, where students Eric Harris and Dylan Klebold murdered thirteen and wounded twenty-three more.

For many, such statistics and events represent the descent of American society into moral confusion, perhaps even moral anarchy. It is a question of values. Values are concepts people use to make choices, to decide courses of action, to explain and justify behaviors, to judge and to be judged. Values are "modes of organizing conduct," defines Robin Williams, emotionally invested "principles that guide human action."[8] My main concern is *moral values*—fundamental values about right and wrong, good and evil, noble and base—that live in the hearts of people and are embodied in institutions.[9] Moral values form "the core of the individual's internalized conscience."[10] Violations of moral values evoke shame, remorse, and guilt in the offender who holds them. And because they represent central values of society, violations of moral values invoke strong sanctions from the community—censure, ostracism, condemnation, and punishment in many and varied forms. It is this capacity—the will to make moral judgments and to invoke strong sanctions—that many social critics claim Americans have lost.

Bronfenbrenner and associates conclude their book with the grave interpretation that "values commonly judged as 'good' seem in decline, including honesty, a sense of personal responsibility, respect for others anchored in a sense of the dignity and worth of every individual."[11] Similarly, Bennett and associates argue that America has "experienced an astonishing degree of social regression." Today, they conclude, "[l]arge segments of America are characterized by moral confusion, indolence, indifference, and distraction."[12] Bennett sounds a dire warning in a 1995 Heritage Foundation address: "Current trends in out-of-wedlock births, crime, drug use, family decomposition, and educational decline, as well as a host of other social pathologies, are incompatible with the continuation of American society as we know it. If these things continue, the republic as we know it will cease to be."[13] He repeats the warning in his 1998 best seller, *The Death of Outrage*, lamenting President Clinton's misconduct, the decline of America's values, and the nation's incapacity to make moral judgments.[14] America, he says, has lost its "moral compass."[15] The lost compass is a common metaphor in popular literature. For example, Stephen Covey asserts, "Our moral compass is thrown off, and we don't even know it. The needle that in less turbulent times pointed easily to 'true north'—or the principles that govern in all of life—is being jerked about by the powerful electric and magnetic fields of the storm."[16]

Most Americans seem to agree, as reported in various national surveys and studies conducted from the mid-1990s through 2003. In 1993 and 1994, for example, 62 percent of Americans reported that "Americans are greatly divided when it comes to the most important values." Men and women felt exactly the same way; African Americans were only slightly more likely than whites to feel that the American people are greatly divided when it comes to the most important values (69 versus 60 percent, respectively).[17] In 1995 about 86 percent of Americans agreed that "there was a time when people in this country felt they had more in common and shared more values than Americans do today."[18] The 1996 Survey of American Public Culture reported that 90 percent of Americans felt that the country was not improving overall; 52 percent said the country was actually in decline.[19] Almost 90 percent of middle-class Americans feel that "it has become much harder to raise children in our society," reports Alan Wolfe in his 1998 Middle Class Morality Project, and 67 percent say that, "compared to twenty years ago, Americans have become more selfish."[20] A Pew survey of religion and public life, conducted in spring 2001, found that 55 percent of Americans felt that religion was "losing its significance" as an influence on American life. This figure dropped to 12 percent in mid-November 2001, two months after the September 11, 2001, terrorist attacks, but rose again to 52 percent in March 2002, six months after the attacks.[21] In the same March 2002 survey, three of four Americans said "no" in response to the question, "Do you think people in general today lead as good lives—honest and moral—as they used to?" The same proportion of Americans said "no" to the question, "Do you think that young people today have as strong a sense of right and wrong as they did, say, fifty years ago?" And, in a May 2003 Gallup Poll, 77 percent of Americans rated the "overall state of moral values in this country today" as "only fair" or "poor."[22] In the same poll, 67 percent of Americans said they "think the state of moral values in the country" is "getting worse."

These private feelings of decline, discord, and division are given public voice by those who believe America is engaged in a "culture war" over its future. Sociologist James Davison Hunter came up with the first systematic statement of the culture war thesis.[23] Many resonated with the statement and made it part of everyday discourse. For example, at the 1992 Republican National Convention, Pat Buchanan proclaimed, "There is a religious war going on in this country. It is a culture war as critical to the kind of nation we shall be as the Cold War itself, for this war is for the soul of America." Buchanan's claim cannot be dismissed as mere hyperbole or conservative political rhetoric; it represents a major and pervasive theme in discourse about American society. "Images of U.S. society as polarized into warring moral camps are increasingly evoked by political leaders, media pundits, and scholars alike," observe Nancy Davis and Robert Robinson.[24] Indeed, about 1,500 articles referring to the American culture war appeared in the media between 1993 and 1996,[25] as well as countless references to the culture war on talk radio and television and in political speeches, public debates, and everyday conversations.

The perception of a "crisis of values" is clear and widespread; the causes of the perception are not. We are experiencing, conclude Bronfenbrenner and associates, "nothing less than a transformation of America's culture by forces not well understood, in directions many of its people do not want."[26] Understanding these not-well-understood forces is a goal of this book. Rather than adding my voice to the din of alarm and concern about the symptoms of America in decline, I report what Americans actually say about moral values. I explore the murky realm of underlying causes of the perception of a crisis of values. By doing so, I hope to provide a fresh explanation of the root causes of the question of values in American society. Following Max Weber and Clifford Geertz, I view this as an exercise of interpretation. As Geertz argues, "man is an animal suspended in webs of significance he himself has spun. I take culture to be those webs, and the analysis of it to be therefore not an experimental science in search of law but an interpretive one in search of meaning."[27] My objective, therefore, is to interpret the changing webs of significance spun of values in American culture.

Three Ways to Think About a Crisis of Values — Loss, Unfavorable Comparison, and Division

The various social critics I cited above are an eclectic mix of perspectives, levels of analysis, and foci of interest. Some are empiricists, analyzing and interpreting data, while others are theorists or social commentators. Some focus on symptoms; others focus on underlying causes. Despite its variety, three key themes run through this literature: three ways to think about America's crisis of values. I describe each theme below, which I formulate as hypotheses and test empirically in later chapters.

The first way to think about the crisis of values is a loss over time of traditional values, and with it the capacity or will to make moral judgments. What are traditional values? Many societies have existed in the course of human history; some historic "traditions" would not qualify as "traditions" in America today. For example, as Ronald Inglehart and I wrote, "Infanticide was common in hunting and gathering societies, but became rare in agrarian societies; homosexuality was accepted in some preindustrial societies; and women are believed to have dominated political and social life in some preindustrial societies."[28] We note, however, that data on preindustrial societies nonetheless reveal some common characteristics that can be considered traditional values: the importance of religion and God; absolute standards of good and evil; the importance of family life; deference to authority; the dominance of men in social, political, and economic life; and intolerance of abortion, divorce, euthanasia, and suicide.[29] The opposite of these traditional values are secular-rational values, sometimes called "modern" or "postmodern" values.[30] Here, "secular" means nonreligious, while "rational" refers to the "rationalization of all spheres of society" (as Weber put it), including the use of reason, logic, science, and means-end calculations rather than religion or long-established customs to govern social, political, and economic life.[31] (This use of "rational" does not imply that traditional values are "irrational.") Secular-rational values include the lack (or low levels) of religious beliefs and beliefs in the importance of God; relative standards of good and evil; gender equality; lack of deference to authority; and acceptance of abortion, divorce, euthanasia, and suicide.

Traditional values and secular-rational values are the poles of a single fundamental dimension of cultural variation, as extensive research using the World Values Surveys has shown.[32] If American society has lost its traditional values, then we should observe a significant movement along this dimension. This movement would correspond to the "secularization"[33] of culture in America. I call this the trend hypothesis of the crisis of values, for it represents the replacement over time of traditional values by secular-rational values.

The second way to think about the crisis of values is to compare American society with other societies. An unfavorable comparison would contribute to the perception of crisis in America. Indeed, many of the worries and fears about America arise in comparisons with other societies. The basis of comparison takes various forms, ranging from economic performance to social statistics to moral values. As Lipset notes, "The American difference, the ways in which the United States varies from the rest of the world, is a constant topic of discussion and in recent years, of concern. Is the country in decline economically and morally? Is Japan about to replace it as the leading economic power? Why does the United States have the highest crime rate, the most persons per capita in prison? Does the growth in the proportion of illegitimate births of single-mother families reflect basic changes in our moral order? Why is our electoral turnout rate so low?"[34] Another expression of unfavorable comparison is trepidation about the Americanization of the world—the "contamination" of other cultures by the importation of certain American values, especially the capitalist values of individualism, secularism, and crass consumerism. The deleterious cultural effects of American capitalism are sometimes called the Coca-Colaization or the Hollywoodization or the McDonaldization of society.[35]

An examination of the effects of American society on other cultures is outside the purpose and scope of this book. Rather, I compare the American value system with the value systems of other societies around the world. An unfavorable comparison would mean that America is similar to societies with secularized value systems and different from societies with traditional value systems. Moreover, the paths of value change for America and other societies on the road to secularization would converge over time around secular-rational values, and diverge from the paths of societies with traditional values. I call this the comparative hypothesis of crisis because it locates the perception of a crisis of values in cross-cultural similarities and differences.

Note that both the trend and comparative hypotheses are indications of a crisis of values from a particular point of view—the traditionalist's view of the values inherent in a good society. From this perspective, loss of traditional values is cause for moral alarm, and cross-cultural comparison is unfavorable if it reveals that America's value system is different from that of societies with traditional values and similar to that of societies with secularized values. But the case could be made—and has been made, as I discuss in chapter 4—that secular-rational values are superior to and more desirable than traditional values. For example, secular-rational values may be considered freedom from the tyranny of religion, the triumph of reason over superstition, and the right to make personal choices about how to lead a good and virtuous life. By framing the trend and comparative hypotheses from the traditionalist's view, I am not taking sides in the moral debate about America's crisis of values. Rather, I am expressing the crisis in its own terms, that is, in the language and logics that prevail in discourse about America's crisis of values (such as in the sources cited in the section above).

The third way to think about the crisis of values is the division of society into opposed groups with irreconcilable moral differences. This view is expressed in the popular theory that America is engaged in a "culture war" between two opposed moral camps with incompatible views of the American way of life. The strong form of the culture war thesis contends that the outcome of the conflict will be the "domination of one cultural and moral ethos over all others."[36] Competing *moral visions* are the source of the presumed conflict. Moral visions reside over attitudes or religious values; they are fundamental beliefs about the *location* of moral authority: the "transcendental sphere" versus the "mundane sphere."[37] The former locates the source of moral values and moral judgment outside the self in God (religion) or society; the latter locates the source of moral values and moral judgment in the self. To use more popular terms, we can think of the two moral visions as *absolutism* versus *relativism*.

The culture war thesis presupposes the polarization of society into two opposed moral groups. "The polarization is most conspicuous in such hotly disputed issues as abortion, gay marriage, school vouchers, and prayers in public schools," says Gertrude Himmelfarb. "But it has larger ramifications, affecting beliefs, attitudes, values, and practices on a host of subject ranging from private morality to public policy, from popular culture to high culture, from crime to education, welfare, and the family."[38] Proponents of the polarization thesis argue that it pervades all levels, from social attitudes to religion to the moral visions of absolutism versus relativism. If so, then we should observe two distinct groups based on differences in moral visions, religious values, and social and political attitudes. I call this the distribution hypothesis because it locates the perception of a crisis of values in the existence of a bimodal distribution of the American people.

Each hypothesis—crisis as loss of traditional values, crisis as unfavorable comparisons with other societies, or crisis as division into opposed groups—is distinct from the others but could operate in tandem. For example, there could be a shift away from traditional values (trend hypothesis) and convergence with rational-secular societies (comparative hypothesis), or a shift away from traditional values (trend hypothesis) for one part of society while the other part retains its traditional values, splitting America in two (distribution hypothesis). If at least one hypothesis were true, however, it would be a threat to the validity of the popular image of America as a national community.

Threats to America as an Imagined Community

A nation-state is an "imagined community."[39] It is the popular self-consciousness of belonging to a people. America, for example, is a nation-state in part because Americans imagine it so. This popular national self-consciousness, notes Jürgen Habermas, creates "a relation of solidarity between persons who had previously been strangers to one another."[40] Of course, most Americans are strangers interpersonally: The typical American (like the typical citizen of any nation-state) has personal relationships with or close interpersonal knowledge of only a small fraction of one's fellow citizens.[41] The "relation of solidarity" is not interpersonal; it is a creative act of the imagination. For all societies except America, the solidarity of a nation-state is rooted in common ancestry, language, religion, history, customs, traditions, and territory. This cultural heritage, says Habermas, produces "the consciousness of belonging to 'the same' people, and makes subjects into citizens of a single political community—into members who can feel responsible *for one another*. The nation of the *Volksgeist*, the unique spirit of the people—the first truly *modern* form of collective identity—provided the cultural basis for the constitutional state."[42] National identity helped to solve the twin problems of legitimation and social integration. Historically, the legitimation problem arose from the loss of religion as the basis of the political authority of the state (e.g., the divine right of kings); the integration problem arose from the loss of social ties caused by economic modernization, urbanization, and geographic and occupational mobility.[43] The nation-state addressed these problems by using national identity as an abstract form of social integration and combining it with democratic participation. This process "generated a new level of legally mediated *solidarity* via the status of citizenship while providing the state with a secular source of *legitimation*."[44]

It follows that the absence of a common cultural heritage would impede the formation of a unified nation-state. For example, the creation of a European nation-state confronts this problem. A European self-consciousness would have to transcend the diverse cultural heritages of the European Union (EU) members.[45] Admitting new members in 2004—Slovenia, Poland, Hungary, Slovakia, Lithuania, and others—aggravates the problem of integration. Not only are their cultural heritages quite different from those of the original EU members, but these differences are increasing. As I show elsewhere, the value systems of the original EU members and the new members are not converging. "In fact, there is a widening cultural divide that economic integration may not be able to overcome."[46]

The historic role of a common cultural heritage in the development of virtually every nation-state, along with the struggles of the EU to find an alternative mode of legitimation and form of social integration, illuminate the deviant case of the American nation-state. Observers from Alexis de Tocqueville onward have observed that America is deviant, "exceptional"—qualitatively different from other societies.[47] One qualitative difference is that the foundation of the imagined community of America is *not* a shared cultural heritage rooted in common ancestry, history, religion, language, and so on. Instead, the American nation is founded, as Habermas says, on "a civil religion."[48] "Born out of revolution," writes Lipset, "the United States is a country organized around an ideology which includes a set of dogmas about the nature of a good society. . . . As G. K. Chesterton put it: 'America is the only nation in the world that is founded on a creed. That creed is set forth with dogmatic and even theological lucidity in the Declaration of Independence. . . .'"[49] I discuss the details of "American exceptionalism" in other chapters; for now, the important point is that the imagined community of the United States is based on a set of *ideas* and *values* with as much legitimating and integrating force as religion.

It is this civil religion or ideology that is threatened by a loss of traditional values, unfavorable comparisons with other societies, or a split into opposed moral groups (the trend, comparative, and distribution hypotheses). Each is a threat to the imagined community of America; each undermines the American mode of legitimation and form of social integration. Indeed, the threat is greater for a society based on a cultural heritage of ideas than for one based on a cultural heritage of common ancestry, history, religion, and language. A crisis of values is a direct assault on the ideological core of the imagined community of America.

The crisis of values as a threat to America as an imagined community is a complement to Robert Putnam's thesis of the loss of "social capital" as the cause of the collapse of community.[50] Putnam focuses on only one side of the community question, as Amitai Etzioni notes in his criticism of Putnam's massive compendium of decline, *Bowling Alone: The Collapse and Revival of American Community*.[51] Putnam's side is community as a social network of affect-laden relationships among people. For him, the American crisis is real, and it comes from falling levels of social and civic engagement—the actual disintegration of the social network. For example, Americans are participating in fewer voluntary associations, having fewer family dinners, socializing less often, voting less often, and even bowling alone rather than in leagues.

Putnam's "bowling alone" metaphor and social disintegration thesis have captured popular and media attention. Though Putnam's thesis and evidence have been called into question,[52] most of his critics concede he has a valid point.[53] But community is more than a social network, Etzioni argues; it is also a "commitment to a set of shared values, norms, and meanings."[54] The second side of community is particularly important for America because a common ideology, rather than common ancestry, history, religion, and language, forms the foundation of the American imagined community. "Being an American," observes Lipset, "is an ideological commitment."[55] This book examines this second side of community: the extent to which Americans do or do not share the same values, norms, and meanings.

Taken together, Putnam's analysis of social capital and my analysis of values, norms, and meanings cover both sides of the community question. If I find evidence for at least one of the three hypotheses (trend, comparative, and distribution) and Putnam's thesis is correct, then America faces a double threat: the loss of the community's social bonds *and* the loss of the community's ideas. The widespread perception of crisis would be real.

Conclusion

This introductory chapter is an orientation to the widespread perception of a crisis of values in America and to the analysis in this book. After citing some of the main voices in the discourse about moral crisis, I presented an overview of three ways to think about a crisis of values: as a loss over time of traditional values (trend hypothesis), as an unfavorable comparison to other societies (comparative hypothesis), and as a division of society into opposed moral groups (distribution hypothesis). Finally, I introduced the concept of America as an "imagined community"—the popular self-consciousness of an American people. Unlike other nation-states, the American collective consciousness is not based on common ancestry, history, religion, and language; rather, it is based on a set of ideas—the American ideology or "civil religion." Given the ideological basis of American society, a crisis of values is especially threatening to the popular image of the nation as one community, creating a problem of legitimacy and a problem of social integration.

The next two chapters test the three hypotheses. These tests are a means to an end, not the end itself. That end is understanding.

Proper treatment of social problems follows proper diagnosis. As Joseph Nye writes in his introduction to *Why People Don't Trust Government*, "Many people are proposing a wide variety of remedies for the current discontent with government. But some remedies may prove feckless or even counterproductive unless we have a better understanding of causes."[56] Expand Nye's phrase "discontent with government" to include discontent with social, political, and economic institutions—that is, with American society itself—and we see the real reasons for investigating the origins and causes of a crisis of values.

Chapter 2, "America's Values in Global Context," tests the trend and comparative hypotheses, using data from multiple waves of the World Values Surveys. These surveys are the largest systematic attempt ever made to document attitudes, values, and beliefs around the world. As detailed in the appendix, these surveys include over sixty-five societies on all six inhabited continents, covering roughly 75 percent of the world's population. There are, of course, other sources of good data, and I use some of them here. However, for various reasons, these sources are less appropriate than the World Values Surveys for exploring the issues in this book.[57] The World Values Surveys provide an unprecedented opportunity to compare America's values with those of a wide range of societies, as well as to assess the loss of traditional values over time. As we shall see, America's value system exhibits both stability and change. Thus, this chapter concludes with a discussion of why some values change and others stay the same.

Chapter 3, "Culture War," tests the distribution hypothesis. While the unit of analysis in chapter 2 is the nation-state, here the unit of analysis is the individual. I examine the moral visions, religious beliefs, and social attitudes of the American people over time, using data from multiple waves of the World Values Surveys. I also discuss key findings from other studies of the culture war hypothesis, based on different sources of data. This chapter provides the most comprehensive empirical test of the culture war thesis yet available, examining the polarization of moral visions, religious-moral beliefs, and social attitudes, as well as the actual linkages across the three levels.

In addition, I go beyond the usual definition of the American culture war as a bimodal distribution of moral visions, beliefs, and attitudes to explore the connection between the two sides of community—shared values and social bonds. I investigate the link between moral visions and indicators of social capital: interpersonal trust, confidence in the nation's institutions, frequency of attendance at religious services, participation in voluntary organizations, and political action.

Chapter 4, "Dynamics of Crisis," provides a new interpretation of the perception of a crisis of values. I review some of the main theories used to explain patterns in America's political and religious history, including theories of political cycles, critical elections, critical realignments, the so-called Great Awakenings, and "supply side" explanations of religious change. I derive five propositions from this review, which are used to guide the interpretation. Unlike the previous chapters, this chapter is necessarily more speculative in nature. No opinion poll extends back far enough in time to test the interpretation. I believe the interpretation is reasonable because it is consistent with the five propositions I develop from the review, consistent with the empirical findings presented in chapters 2 and 3, and consistent with additional analyses of the survey data I conduct in this chapter to explore key points. The overall result explains why Americans perceive a widespread crisis of values.

Chapter 5, "The Search for Meaning," is the book's conclusion. I discuss America's unique mixed value system and some of the cultural contradictions it contains. I describe how Americans who have internalized the cultural contradictions of America's mixed value system experience cognitive dissonance—a personal experience of crisis caused by conflicting principles—and use this dissonance to stimulate thinking about the purpose and meaning of life. I examine some other expressions of the search for meaning in American life, such as rising spirituality and interest in the amalgamation of cultural elements known as the "New Age" movement. Next, I focus on the theme of absolutism in America, describing how this moral vision plays a special role in the preservation of the nation's imagined community. Without this role, it would appear as if the moral core of what it means to be American had been lost—metaphorically, it would seem as if the nation had lost its guiding light. Finally, I assess the possibility of and obstacles to a synthesis of the cultural contradictions contained in the nation's mixed value system—an integration of opposites that would resolve the widespread perception of a crisis of values. The chapter ends with a summary of fifteen key findings from the empirical analyses presented throughout the book.

Appendix A contains detailed information about the World Values Surveys, sampling, and the measures used in this study. All tables with statistical results are provided in appendix B. Figures are presented in each chapter. All references are in the notes, which appear at the end of the book. Many notes contain substantive material, such as detailed discussion or amplification of points made in the text itself.

✱ CHAPTER TWO ✱

America's Values in Global Context

THE PERCEPTION OF an American crisis of values may arise from a loss of traditional values, unfavorable comparisons with other societies, or the division of America into two opposed moral camps. As discussed in chapter 1, evidence supporting one or more of these hypotheses would indicate a threat to the imagined community of America. This chapter tests the first and second hypotheses—the trend and comparative hypotheses—using data from multiple waves of the World Values Surveys.* These surveys are the largest systematic attempt ever made to document values, beliefs, and attitudes around the world (see appendix A for description and details). These data provide an unprecedented opportunity to compare America's values with a wide range of societies, as well as to evaluate the possible loss over time of traditional values.

This chapter begins with a framework for understanding and measuring cultural variation and change. This framework, grounded in a wealth of prior research, arrays values along two dimensions: a continuum of traditional versus secular-rational values, and a continuum of survival versus self-expression values. These dimensions make it possible to locate each society on a global map of cross-cultural variation, showing the location of the United States and sixty-four other countries, and to track the trajectories of these societies over time. Next, I analyze the separate and joint effects of economic development and religious-cultural heritage on a society's location on the global cultural map. I then test the trend hypothesis by examining the location and movement of America along the first dimension of cultural variation, traditional versus secular-rational values. If Amer-

*Parts of this chapter are excerpted or revised materials from Ronald Inglehart and Wayne E. Baker, "Modernization, Cultural Change, and the Persistence of Traditional Values," *American Sociological Review* 65 (2000):19–51.

ica has lost its traditional values, we should see a significant shift away from traditional values to secular-rational values. I test the comparative hypothesis by examining the location of the United States relative to other societies, as well as "the company it keeps"—proximity to societies with similar value systems. Finally, I address the question of why values change—or stay the same—over time. Both sides of this question must be answered to understand America's value system. With the global analysis from this chapter in hand, we then proceed to chapter 3, where I test the distribution hypothesis—the possibility that Americans are divided into two opposed moral camps.

Two Dimensions of Cultural Variation and Change

There is no agreed upon framework for analyzing cultural variation and change. Therefore, a reasonable strategy is to use one that is well-developed, tested, and validated—especially in cross-cultural research. A grounding in cross-cultural research is important for theoretical and measurement validity; it is also important for the specific need to test the comparative hypothesis, and for the general need to remove (as much as possible) the cultural blinders that come with analyzing one's own society. A cross-cultural perspective allows one to stand outside and look in, examining cultural variation and change in the United States without the strictures of ethnocentrism.

Prior research with the World Values Surveys has identified distinctive value orientations within and across societies. For example, Ronald Inglehart analyzed aggregated national-level data from the forty-three societies included in the 1990–1991 World Values Survey, finding large and coherent cross-cultural differences.[1] Two key dimensions emerged from this analysis: a continuum of traditional versus secular-rational values and a continuum of survival versus self-expression values. Inglehart used these two dimensions to construct a global map of cross-cultural variation,[2] and to demonstrate how the worldviews of the peoples of various societies differed systematically across a wide range of social, religious, and political values, norms, and beliefs. The two dimensions can be used to track the trajectories of societies over time, as Inglehart and I did in our analysis of data from three waves of the World Values Surveys: 1981, 1990–1991, and 1995–1998.[3] These dimensions have been replicated and revalidated in the analysis of the 1999–2001 wave of the World Values Surveys, based on seventy-eight societies.[4] They appear to be quite robust.

Inglehart and I constructed measures of cross-cultural variation that can be used with all three waves of the World Values Surveys, at both the individual level and the national level. Starting with the variables identified in the analysis of the 1990–1991 surveys, we selected variables that not only tapped these two dimensions, but also had been utilized in the same format in three waves of the World Values Surveys. Originally, Inglehart used factor scores based on over twenty variables from the 1990–1991 surveys, but we reduced this number to ten items to minimize problems of missing data (if one variable were missing, we would lose an entire nation from the analysis). Table 2.1 shows how these ten items tap the traditional/secular-rational dimension and the survival/self-expression dimension, using a factor analysis of the World Values Survey data aggregated to the national level.[5] Table 2.2 shows the results from a factor analysis of the same variables using the individual-level data. As expected, the factor loadings here are lower than at the national level where much of the random measurement error normally found in survey data cancels out. Nonetheless, these items produce two clear dimensions with a basic structure very similar to that found at the national level.[6]

Table 2.3 presents the results from a factor analysis of 24 items, which include the 10 items in the scales used here. Comparing tables 2.2 and 2.3 provides more evidence of the validity of the ten-item scales. For example, the ten items load on the two factors in the same pattern, and almost all of the factor loadings are close to the original values based on the twenty-four items. Further, the traditional/secular-rational dimension based on five items is almost perfectly correlated ($r = .95$) with the factor scores from the comparable dimension based on twelve variables; similarly, the survival/self-expression dimension based on five variables is almost perfectly correlated (r = .96) with the survival/self-expression dimension based on twelve variables. Because the original twenty-four-item scales and the ten-item scales are very highly correlated, the ten-item scales are a more parsimonious way of measuring the same two underlying dimensions.

A broad range of values and meanings are associated with the traditional/secular-rational values dimension. For example, table 2.4 presents twenty-four additional variables included in the World Values Survey that are closely correlated with this dimension. Examining the variables included in this table, along with those in the factors themselves (tables 2.1–2.3), demonstrates that the traditional/secular-rational values dimension represents many of the values, beliefs, and meanings that are said to be in decline in America by many of the social critics I discussed in chapter 1. For example, traditional values include strong beliefs in the importance of God, the importance of religion, regular church attendance, and a great deal of confidence in the country's churches; one who holds traditional values gets comfort and strength from religion and describes oneself as "a religious person." Absolute (versus relative) standards of morality is a traditional value. Though religion is a prominent feature, deference to God, fatherland, and family are all closely linked. Family values is a major theme. For example, children should learn obedience and respect, and a main goal in life is to make one's parents proud—one must always love and respect one's parents, no matter how they behave. Conversely, parents must do their best for their children even if their own well-being suffers. Secular-rational values emphasize the opposite positions on all these topics.

Generally, people in traditional societies idealize large families, and they actually have them; societies with traditional values have high fertility rates, while societies with secular-rational values have low fertility rates.[7] In preindustrial societies, the family is crucial to survival. Accordingly, societies at the traditional pole of this dimension reject divorce and take a prolife stance on abortion, euthanasia, and suicide. The people of traditional societies favor more respect for authority. They take protectionist attitudes toward foreign trade and feel that environmental problems can be solved without international agreements. They accept national authority passively—they seldom or never discuss politics. People of traditional societies emphasize social conformity rather than individualistic striving, support deference to formal authority, and have high levels of national pride and a nationalistic outlook. Secular-rational values emphasize the opposite preferences.

A wide range of values and meanings are associated with the survival/self-expression dimension. Table 2.5 shows thirty-two additional variables that are closely correlated with it. The survival/self-expression dimension taps a syndrome of trust, tolerance, subjective well-being, political activism, and self-expression that emerges in postindustrial societies with high levels of physical security and the satisfaction of material needs. This dimension relates to what Robert Fogel in *The Fourth Great Awakening* calls "spiritual" or "immaterial" needs, and the "spiritual capital" or resources required for the journey of self-realization. Once material needs are satisfied and their future provision taken for granted, concerns turn to "the struggle for self-realization, the desire to find a deeper meaning in life than the endless accumulation of consumer durables and the pursuit of pleasure, access to the miracles of modern medicine, education not only for careers but for spiritual values, methods of financing an early, fruitful, and long-lasting retirement, and increasing the amount of quality time available for family activities."[8] John Dewey and Richard Rorty call this journey of self-realization "a particularized creative process of individual growth."[9]

One of the main components of this cultural dimension is the polarization between materialist and postmaterialist values. Extensive evidence indicates that these values tap an intergenerational shift from emphasis on economic and physical security toward increasing emphasis on self-expression, subjective well-being, and quality of life concerns.[10] This cultural shift is found throughout advanced industrial society; it seems to emerge among birth cohorts that have grown up under conditions in which one can take survival for granted. These values are linked with the emergence of growing emphasis on environmental protection, the women's movement, and rising demands for participation in decision-making in economic and political life. During the past twenty-five years, these values have become increasingly widespread in almost all advanced industrial societies for which extensive time-series data are available.

At the other extreme, people in societies shaped by insecurity and low levels of well-being tend to emphasize economic and physical security above all other goals, and to feel threatened by foreigners, by ethnic diversity, and by cultural change. This leads to an intolerance of homosexuals and other outgroups, an insistence on traditional gender roles, and an authoritarian political outlook. When survival is uncertain, cultural diversity seems threatening. When there isn't "enough to go around," foreigners are seen as dangerous outsiders who may take away one's sustenance. Societies that emphasize survival values show low levels of subjective well-being, low levels of interpersonal trust, and intolerance of outgroups. They exhibit little support for gender equality or for environmental activism; they emphasize materialist values, have relatively high levels of faith in science and technology, and are favorable to authoritarian government. Self-expression values emphasize the opposite positions on these topics.

Global Cultural Maps

Taken together, the two dimensions produce global cultural maps, as shown in figures 2.1a and 2.1b. Figure 2.1a is based on the second and third waves of the World Values Surveys (1990–1991 and 1995–1998). Figure 2.1b includes the fourth wave (1999–2001). The vertical axis of each map represents traditional values versus secular-rational values. The horizontal axis depicts survival values versus self-expression values.[11] The boundaries around groups of countries in these maps are drawn using Samuel Huntington's cultural zones as a guide.[12]

Cross-cultural variation is highly constrained. As shown in tables 2.1 and 2.2, if the people of a given society place strong emphasis on religion, then it is possible to predict that society's relative position on many other topics, from attitudes toward abortion, level of national pride (highly religious nations rank high on national pride),

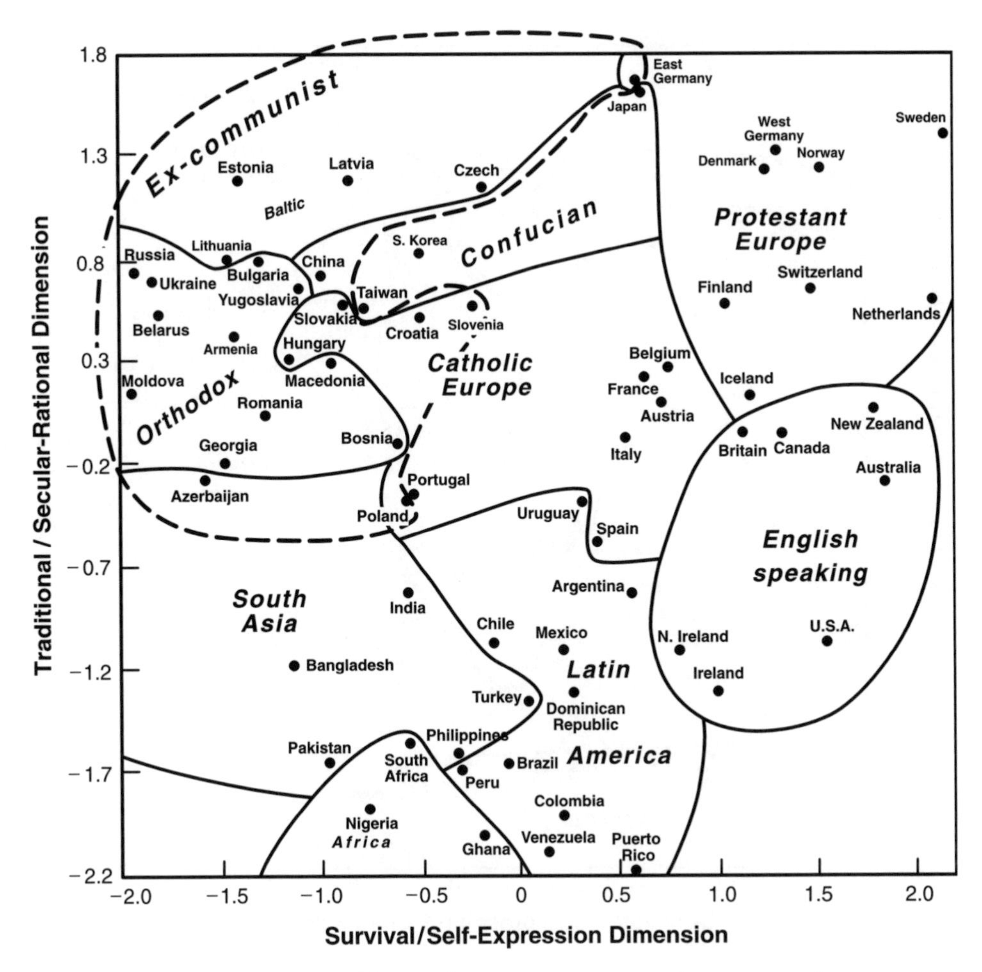

Figure 2.1a. Locations of sixty-five societies on two dimensions of cross-cultural variation: World Values Surveys, 1990–1991 and 1995–1998.

Source: Inglehart and Baker, "Modernization," p. 29, fig. 1.

Note: The scales on each axis indicate the country's factor scores on the given dimension. The positions of Colombia and Pakistan are estimated from incomplete data.

the desirability of more respect for authority (religious nations place much more emphasis on respect for authority), to attitudes toward child-rearing. The second dimension reflects another wide-ranging but tightly correlated cluster of variables involving materialist values (such as maintaining order and fighting inflation), postmaterialist

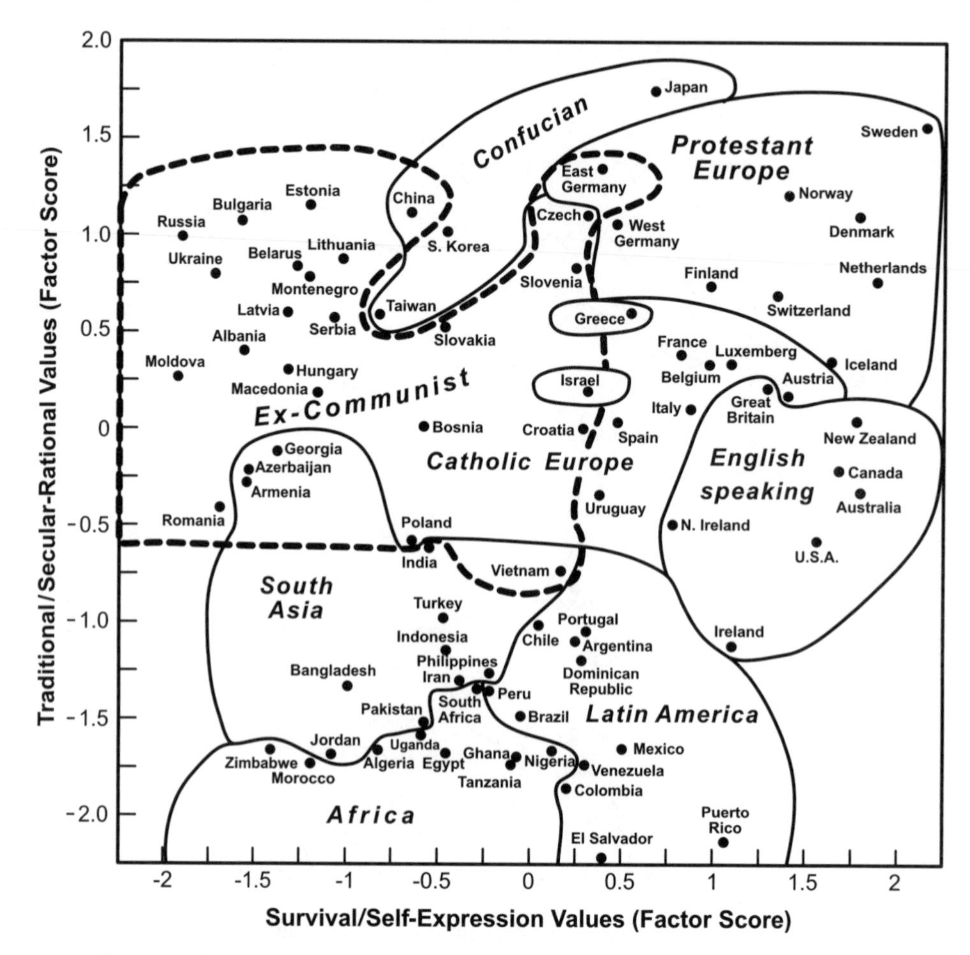

Figure 2.1b. Locations of eighty-one societies on two dimensions of cross-cultural variation: World Values Surveys, 1990–1991, 1995–1998, and 1999–2001.

Source: Inglehart and Norris, *Rising Tide*, p. 155, fig. 7.1.

values (such as freedom and self-expression), subjective well-being, interpersonal trust, political activism, and tolerance of outgroups (measured by acceptance or rejection of homosexuality, which is a sensitive indicator of tolerance toward outgroups in general).

Economic development seems to have a powerful impact on values. The value systems of rich countries differ systematically from those of poor countries. Figures 2.1a and 2.1b reflect a gradient from

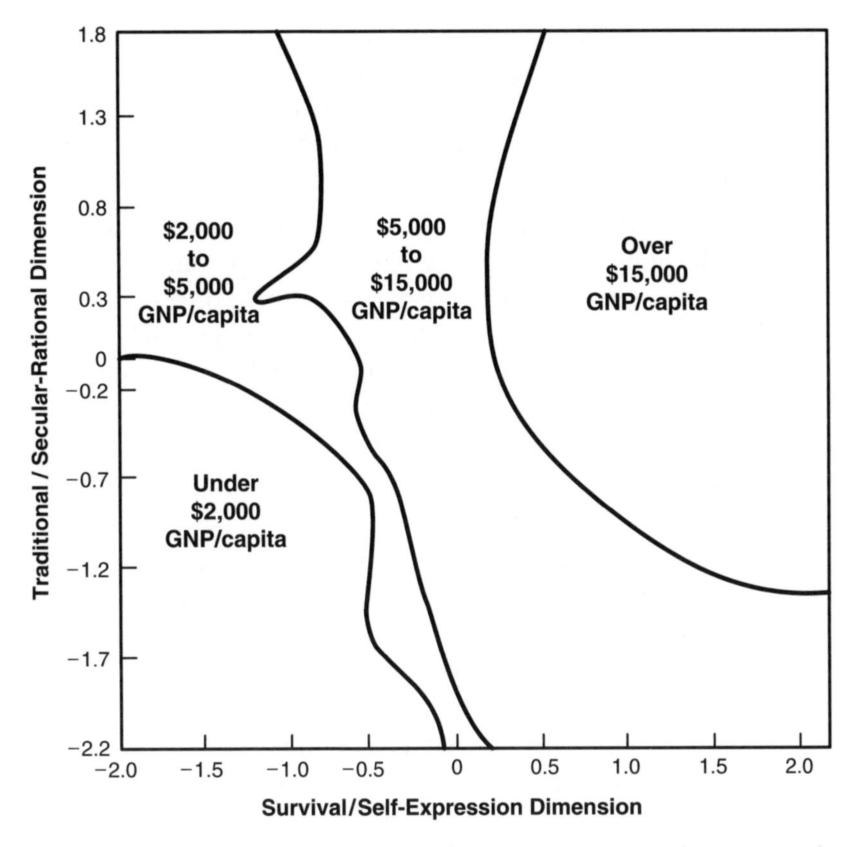

Figure 2.2. Economic zones for sixty-five societies on two dimensions of cross-cultural variation.

Source: Inglehart and Baker, "Modernization," p. 30, fig. 2. GNP per capita is based on the World Bank's Purchasing Power Parity estimates as of 1995, in U.S. dollars. World Bank, *Development Report* New York: Oxford University Press, 1997.

Note: All but one of the 65 societies show in this figure fit into the economic zones indicated here; only the Dominican Republic is mislocated.

low-income countries in the lower left quadrant, to rich societies in the upper right quadrant. Figure 2.2 redraws figure 2.1a, showing the economic zones into which sixty-five societies fall. All nineteen societies with an annual per capita gross national product over $15,000 rank relatively high on both dimensions and fall into a zone in the upper right-hand corner. This economic zone cuts across the boundaries of the Protestant, ex-Communist, Confucian, Catholic, and

English-speaking cultural zones. All societies with per capita GNPs below $2,000 fall into a cluster at the lower left of figure 2.2, located in an economic zone that cuts across the African, South Asian, ex-Communist, and Orthodox cultural zones. The remaining societies fall into two intermediate cultural-economic zones. Economic development seems to move societies in a common direction, regardless of their cultural heritage. Nevertheless, distinctive cultural zones persist, two centuries after the industrial revolution began.

GNP per capita is only one indicator of a society's level of economic development. As Marx argued, the rise of the industrial working class was a key event in modern history. Furthermore, the changing nature of the labor force defines three distinct stages of economic development: agrarian society, industrial society and postindustrial society.[13] Thus, another set of boundaries could be superimposed on societies in figure 2.1a: Societies with a high percentage of the labor force in agriculture would fall near the bottom of the map, societies with a high percentage of industrial workers would fall near the top, and societies with a high percentage in the service sector would be located near the right-hand side of the map.

The traditional/secular-rational dimension is associated with the transition from agrarian society to industrial society. Accordingly, this dimension shows a strong positive correlation with the percentage in the industrial sector ($r = .65$) and a negative correlation with the percentage in the agricultural sector ($r = -.49$), but it is only weakly linked with the percentage in the service sector ($r = .18$). Thus, the shift from an agrarian mode of production to industrial production seems to bring a shift from traditional values toward increasing rationalization and secularization. Nevertheless, a society's cultural heritage also plays a role. Thus, all four of the Confucian-influenced societies have relatively secular values, regardless of the proportion of their labor forces in the industrial sector. The former Communist societies also rank relatively high on this secularization dimension, despite varying degrees of industrialization. Conversely, the historically Roman Catholic societies display relatively traditional values when compared with Confucian or ex-Communist societies with the same proportion of industrial workers.

The survival/self-expression dimension is linked with the rise of a service economy. It shows a .73 correlation with the relative size of the service sector, but it is unrelated to the relative size of the industrial sector ($r = .03$). While the traditional/secular-rational values dimension and the survival/self-expression values dimension reflect industrialization and the rise of postindustrial society, respectively, this is only part of the story. Virtually all of the historically Protestant societies rank higher on the survival/self-expression dimension than do all of the historically Roman Catholic societies, regardless of the extent to which their labor forces are engaged in the service sector. Conversely, virtually all of the former Communist societies rank low on the survival/self-expression dimension. Changes in GNP and occupational structure have important influences on prevailing worldviews, but traditional cultural influences persist.

Religious traditions have an enduring influence on contemporary value systems, as Weber, Huntington, and others have argued.[14] Scholars from many disciplines have observed that distinctive cultural traits endure over long periods of time and continue to shape a society's political and economic performance.[15] As demonstrated in this chapter, evidence from the World Values Surveys supports Huntington's argument that the world is divided into cultural zones that are still powerful today, despite the forces of economic modernization.[16] It is important to recognize that the effects of religious heritage concern the religion that historically dominated a nation, *not* the religious composition or practices of a nation today. The Netherlands, for example, historically was a Protestant country, but if we examined church attendance for Protestants and Catholics, we might conclude that it is a Catholic nation today (Dutch Catholics tend to go to church, while attendance for Dutch Protestants is very low). Protestantism originally dominated the United States, and this heritage continues to exert its influence today, even though over time America has become a religiously diverse nation. Protestantism is still the "deep structure" of American culture today.[17]

A society's culture reflects its entire historical heritage. For example, a central historical event of the twentieth century was the rise and fall of a Communist empire that once ruled one-third of the world's population. Communism left a clear imprint on the value systems of those who lived under it. East Germany remains culturally close to West Germany despite four decades of Communist rule, but its value system has been drawn toward the Communist zone. And although China is a member of the Confucian zone, it also falls within a broad Communist-influenced zone. Similarly Azerbaijan, though part of the Islamic cluster, also falls within the Communist super-zone that dominated it for decades.

The influence of colonial ties is apparent in the existence of a Latin American cultural zone. Former colonial ties also help account for the existence of an English-speaking zone. Geographically, they are halfway around the world, but culturally Australia and New Zealand are next-door neighbors of Great Britain and Canada. The impact of colonization seems especially strong when reinforced by massive immigration from the colonial society—thus, Spain, Italy, Uruguay, and Argentina are all near each other on the border between Catholic Europe and Latin America: The populations of Uruguay and Argentina are largely descended from immigrants from Spain and Italy.

How "Real" Are the Cultural Zones?

Are the cultural zones real? The boundaries in the global cultural map (e.g., fig. 2.1a) could have been drawn in other ways because these societies have been influenced by a variety of factors. Thus, some of the boundaries overlap others. For example, the ex-Communist zone overlaps the Protestant, Catholic, Confucian, Orthodox, and Islamic cultural zones. Similarly, Britain is located at the intersection of the English-speaking zone and Protestant Europe. Empirically, it is close to the English-speaking societies, and so Inglehart and I included it in that zone. But with only slight modification, we could have drawn the borders to put Britain in Protestant Europe, for it is also culturally close to those societies.

Reality is complex. Britain is both Protestant and English-speaking, and its empirical position reflects both aspects of reality. Similarly, we have drawn a boundary around the Latin American societies that

Huntington postulated to be a distinct cultural zone. All ten of these societies show relatively similar values in global perspective, but with only minor changes, we could have defined a Hispanic cultural zone that included Spain and Portugal, which empirically also resemble Latin American societies. Or we could draw a boundary that included Latin America, Catholic Europe, the Philippines, and Ireland in a broad Roman Catholic cultural zone. All of these zones are conceptually and empirically justifiable.

The global cultural map is based on similarity of basic values—but it also reflects the relative distances between these societies on many other dimensions, such as religion, colonial influences, the influence of Communist rule, social structure, and economic level. The influence of many different historical factors is summed up quite well by the two cultural dimensions on which this map is based, but because these various factors do not always coincide neatly, there are some obvious anomalies. For example, East Germany and Japan fall next to each other: Both are highly secular, relatively wealthy, and have high proportions of industrial workers. A Confucian heritage shaped Japan while Protestantism shaped East Germany (though interestingly, when the Japanese first drew up a Western-style constitution, they chose a German model). Despite such anomalies, societies with a common cultural heritage generally *do* fall into common clusters. At the same time, their positions also reflect their level of economic development, occupational structure, religion, and other major historical influences. Thus, their positions on this two-dimensional space reflect a multidimensional reality—and this remarkable socioeconomic-cultural coherence reflects the fact that a society's culture is shaped by its entire economic and historical heritage.

Modernization theory implies that as societies develop economically, their cultures tend to shift in a predictable direction, and the World Values Surveys data fit the implications of this prediction. Economic differences are linked with large and pervasive cultural differences (see fig. 2.2). Nevertheless, we find clear evidence of the influence of long-established cultural zones. Using data from the latest available survey for each society, we created dummy variables to reflect whether a given society is predominantly English-speaking, ex-

Communist, and so on for each of the clusters outlined in fig. 2.1a. Empirical analysis of these variables shows that the cultural locations of given societies are far from random (see table 2.6). Eight of the nine zones outlined on figure 2.1a show statistically significant relationships with at least one of the two major dimensions of cross-cultural variation. (The sole exception is the Catholic Europe cluster: It is fairly coherent but has a neutral position on both dimensions.)

Do Cultural Zones Reflect Only Economic Differences?

Does economics alone explain values? For example, do the societies of Protestant Europe have similar values simply because they are rich? The influence of economic development is pervasive. GDP per capita shows a significant impact in five of the eight analyses based on traditional/secular-rational values, and in *all* of the analyses based on survival/self-expression values (table 2.6). The percentage of the labor force in the industrial sector seems to influence traditional/rational-secular values even more consistently than does GDP per capita, showing a significant impact in seven of the eight analyses. The percentage of the labor force in the service sector has a significant impact in five of the eight analyses predicting survival/self-expression. (Note that the relationship between these values and the size of the service sector resembles a J-curve, with the impact of the service sector growing stronger as it increases; consequently, we use the square of the percentage in the service sector in these analyses.)

Nevertheless, a society's religious heritage makes an independent contribution to its position on the global cultural map. As table 2.6 demonstrates, the impact of a society's historical-cultural heritage persists when we control for GDP per capita and the structure of the labor force. Thus, the ex-Communist variable shows a strong and statistically significant impact on traditional/secular-rational values, controlling for economic development. The secularizing effect of Communism is even greater than that of the size of the industrial sector and almost as great as that for GDP per capita. The ex-Communist dummy variable also has a strong significant ($p < .001$) negative impact on survival/self-expression values. Similarly, the Protestant Europe dummy variable has strong and significant impacts on both of these major cultural dimensions. English-speaking culture has a strong and significant impact on the traditional/secular-rational dimension: Controlling for level of development, it is linked with a relatively *traditional* outlook. But although the English-speaking societies are clustered near the right-hand pole of the survival/self-expression dimension, this tendency disappears when we control for the fact that they are relatively wealthy and have a high proportion of the work force in the service sector. All but one of the dummy variables for cultural zones in table 2.6 show a statistically significant impact on at least one of the two dimensions. The sole exception is the African group, which forms a tight cluster but contains only three cases, so this variable is unlikely to explain much variance.[18]

When we combine the clusters shown on figure 2.1a into broader cultural zones with large sample sizes, we generate variables having even greater explanatory power. Figure 2.3 indicates that the Catholic societies of Eastern Europe constitute a distinct subcluster of the Catholic world—midway between the West European Catholic societies and the Orthodox societies. (Figure 2.1a merges these Eastern and Western clusters into one Catholic Europe zone.) The Latin American cluster is adjacent to the two Catholic groups so we combine all three of these groups to form a broad Roman Catholic "superzone." Two other historically Catholic societies, the Philippines and Ireland, are also nearby and thus can also be merged into the Catholic zone. Similarly, Protestant Europe and most of the English-speaking zone can be merged into a broad historically Protestant zone. Each of these two new zones covers a vast geographic, historical, and economic range, but each reflects the impact of a common religious-historical influence, and each is reasonably coherent in global perspective.

More detailed analyses, which control for the structure of the work force and simultaneously test the influence of various cultural zones, provide additional support for the conclusion that economics *and* cultural heritage matter: Economic development systematically influences a society's value system, *and* a Protestant or Catholic or Confucian or ex-Communist heritage also exerts a persistent and pervasive influence on values. Tables 2.7a and 2.7b show the results of analyses of cross-national differences in traditional/secular-rational values and survival/self-expression values as measured in sixty-five societies (using the latest available survey for each country). For both dimensions, we find that real GDP per capita (using data from the Penn World tables) and the structure of the work force play major roles. However, the percentage enrolled in primary, secondary, and tertiary educational levels has surprisingly little impact on either dimension.[19] The percentage employed in the *industrial* sector has a major impact on traditional/secular-rational values, while the percentage in the *service* sector has a major impact on survival/self-expression values.

The people of poorer societies and societies with a high proportion in the agrarian sector tend to hold traditional values, while the people of richer societies and societies with a high proportion of the labor force in the industrial sector tend to hold secular-rational values. But a given society's historical heritage also has an important influence on the contemporary values and behavior of its people, even when we control for economic level and occupational structure.[20] Tables 2.7a and 2.7b indicate that other cultural variables also show significant relationships with traditional/secular-rational values, but they overlap with, and tend to be dominated by, the three cultural indicators included here. For centuries, Confucian societies have been characterized by a relatively secular worldview, and they remain so today. Communist regimes made major efforts to eradicate traditional religious values, and they seem to have had some success. But historically Roman Catholic societies proved relatively resistant to secularization, even after controlling for the effects of economic development and Communist rule.

Modernization theory holds that the process of economic development and the rise of the industrial sector are conducive to a secular-rational worldview. As model 6 in table 2.7a demonstrates, when we control for a society's cultural heritage, the impacts of GDP per capita and industrialization are significant. Model 6 explains most of the cross-national variation in traditional/secular-rational values with five variables. Models 3, 4, and 5 demonstrate that each of the three

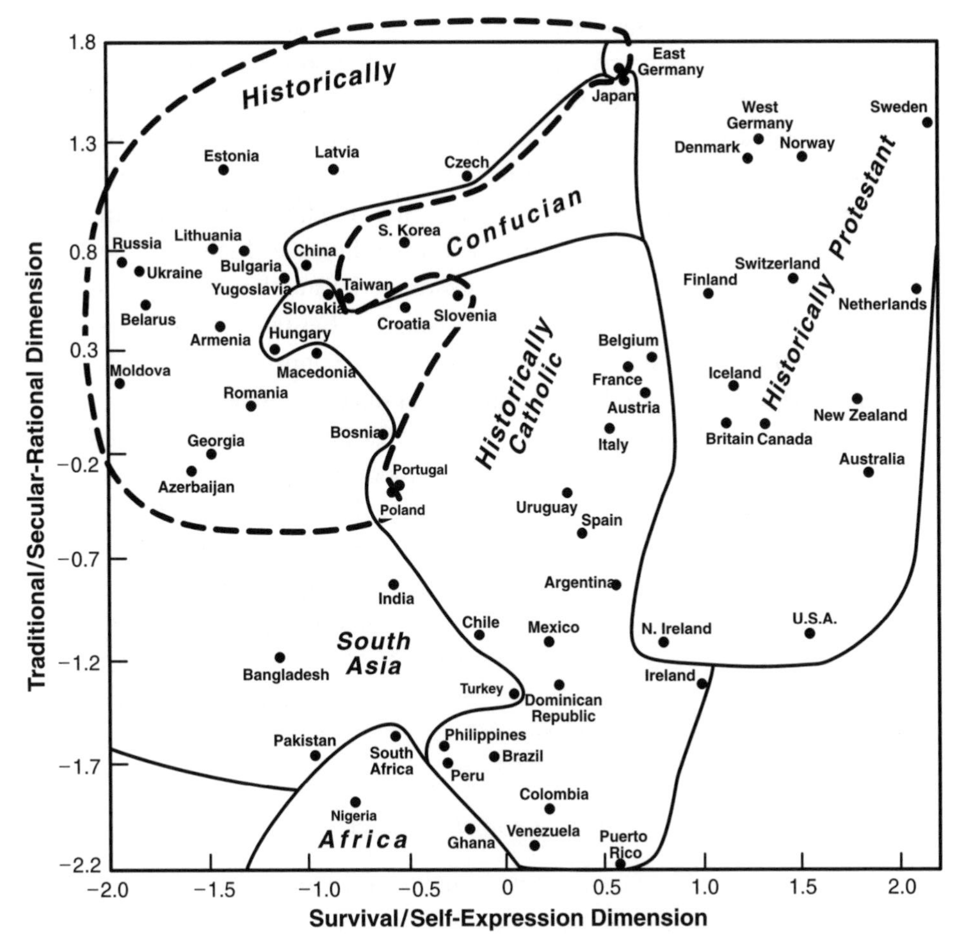

Figure 2.3. Historically Protestant, historically Catholic, and historically Communist cultural zones in relation to two dimensions of cross-cultural variation.

Source: Inglehart and Baker, "Modernization," p. 35, fig. 3.

cultural variables makes a substantial contribution to the percentage of variance explained, with the Confucian variable making the largest contribution. Including all three cultural indicators increases the percentage of explained variance from 42 percent to 70 percent: A society's heritage makes a big difference.

The indicators of economic modernization (GDP per capita and relative size of the service sector) in model 1 explain 63 percent of the cross-national variation in survival/self-expression values. The percentage of the population enrolled in primary, secondary, and tertiary education and the untransformed percentage employed in the service sector do not have significant explanatory power. Nevertheless, three cultural variables do show significant effects: A Protestant cultural heritage is associated with the syndrome of high levels of trust, tolerance, well-being, and postmaterialism that constitutes self-expression values; an Orthodox religious heritage and a Communist historical heritage both show a *negative* impact on these values, even after controlling for differences in economic level and social structure. Each cultural factor adds to the percentage of variance explained (models 3, 4, and 5 in table 2.7b), with the ex-Communist variable making the greatest contribution by itself, but with the Orthodox variable making a substantial supplementary contribution. Including all three cultural indicators in the equation increases the percentage of variance explained in survival/self-expression values from 63 percent to 84 percent (model 6). Thus, a combination of economic and cultural indicators explains considerably more than the economic indicators alone.

America Is an Outlier

America is an affluent society, with high percentages of its workforce employed in the industrial and service sectors. Protestantism is the nation's historical cultural heritage. And it is primarily an English-speaking country. If America followed the general patterns described above, it should be a secular nation with strong self-realization values. The evidence above shows that societies with high levels of GDP per capita, high percentages of their workforces in the industrial and service sectors, and a Protestant cultural heritage tend to be located in the upper right-hand section of the map—a combination of secular-rational and self-expression values (see fig. 2.3). English-speaking Protestant societies tend to be somewhat more traditional, but they are still located in the same general region as their non-English-speaking Protestant neighbors.

Like other economically developed, Protestant, English-speaking societies, America tends to have self-expression values. Unlike these societies, however, America's values are much more traditional. Among wealthy nations, only Ireland is more traditional, but its values stem from a Catholic heritage (as noted above, Catholic societies in general tend to have traditional values). Thus, America is an outlier on the global cultural map: an unusual combination of traditional values and self-expression values (see fig. 2.3).

Understanding America's outlier status is a major theme in this book. In the rest of this chapter, we continue this journey by testing the trend hypothesis, examining America's location and movement over time on the traditional/secular-rational dimension. After that, we compare and contrast the nation's value system with other societies, testing the comparative hypothesis. Finally, we address the question of why values change or stay the same over time. Both sides of this question must be answered to understand America's value system.

Loss of Traditional Values

Has America lost its traditional values? The global cultural maps (figs. 2.1a, 2.1b, and 2.3) show that America at the turn of the millennium has one of the most traditional value systems in the world. America's values are more traditional than any other wealthy society, with the exception of Ireland, as well as more traditional than almost all other societies covered in the World Values Surveys. The nation's location on the traditional/secular-rational dimension ranks it alongside the traditional value systems common in developing and low-income societies. Despite those who chide Americans for losing their traditional values, such as the many voices cited in chapter 1, Americans have some of the highest levels of religious beliefs, conservative family values, absolute moral standards, national pride, and other traditional values (see tables 2.1–2.4 for a long list of values, beliefs, and meanings associated with traditional values).

The trend hypothesis is about change over time. The global cultural maps show us where America was at the turn of the millennium, not where it came from nor the path from origin to destination. For instance, America's value system appears to be quite traditional, but it still could be less traditional than it once was. Puerto Rico's position on the map relative to America's, for example, shows that there is enough room for a change in values that would be perceived as a loss of traditional values. If America had started where Puerto Rico is now, then America's value system would have become noticeably less traditional over time.

The time-series data provided by the World Values Surveys allow us to examine change for the United States and thirty-seven other societies that have data from at least two time points. The map in figure 2.4 shows that America's value system in 1995 was as traditional as it was in 1981.[21] Results from the 1999–2001 wave of the World Values Surveys show that America's values become somewhat less traditional in 2000, but the difference between 1995 and 2000 is small.[22] Moreover, this fourth wave shows that the United States in 2000 remains in about the same location relative to other societies, even though more countries were included in this wave.[23] There is no linear trend upward or downward from 1981 to 2000. The slope of a line fit to these time points is not significantly different from a flat line. In contrast, America's location on the survival/self-expression dimension exhibits a significant and strong—almost perfect—linear trend toward self-expression values from 1981 to 2000.[24]

The years from 1981 to 2000 are a relatively short time span to conclusively evaluate trends, but the lack of a linear trend along the traditional/secular-rational dimension is striking: Americans appear to have a stable traditional value system over this time span.[25] This stability is even more striking in comparative perspective: America has retained its traditional values while virtually *all* of its peers are losing their traditional values. Other economically developed, Protestant, English-speaking societies (Britain, Canada, Australia) already were less traditional than the United States in 1981, and since then each has moved even further away from traditional values. Similarly, all economically developed, Protestant, non-English-speaking societies (Sweden, Norway, Denmark, Switzerland, East

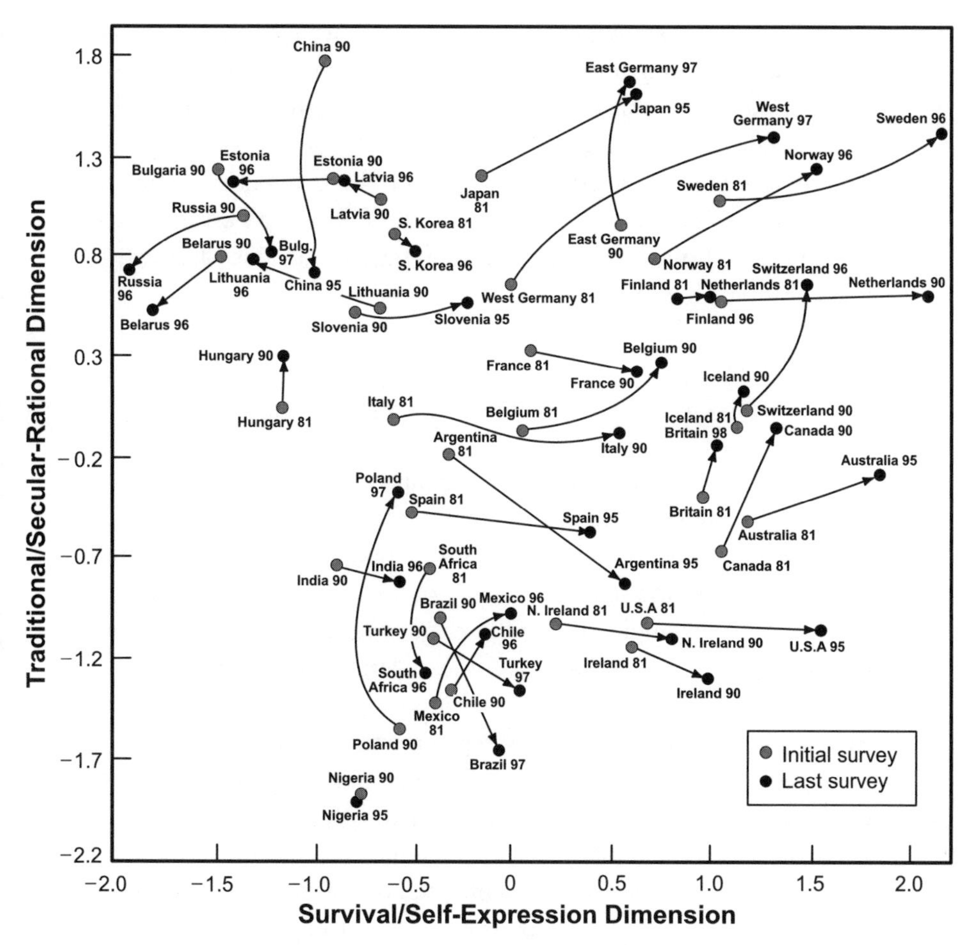

Figure 2.4. Change over time in location on two dimensions of cross-cultural variation for thirty-eight societies.

Source: Inglehart and Baker, "Modernization," p. 40, fig. 4.

and West Germany, Iceland, Netherlands) were much less traditional than the United States in 1981, and all but the Netherlands have continued to become even more secular-rational over time.

Overall, there is little empirical support for the trend hypothesis. The values of Americans are much more traditional than *all* other economically developed Protestant nations, more traditional than virtually all wealthy nations in general, and more traditional than just about all other societies as well. America's traditional values have remained comparatively stable over time, remarkably resistant to the forces of secularization that have precipitated a loss of traditional values in almost all other economically developed societies. This evidence largely eliminates one of three hypotheses about America's crisis of values: The perception of America's crisis of values cannot be linked to an actual loss of traditional values during the years observed here.[26]

Unfavorable Comparisons with Other Societies

On what basis should America be compared with other societies? Comparisons have been made on many dimensions: economic performance, political systems, patriotism, human rights, social and health statistics, and so on. On many of these dimensions, America fares well. For example, during the years of Japan's record economic growth, America's economy was compared unfavorably with the Japanese "economic miracle." American companies raced to scuttle their standard business practices, replacing them with Japanese business practices. However, now that Japan languishes in the economic doldrums, its reversal of fortune is matched with a reversal of advice: Japan, some say, must copy American values, such as individualism, equality, freedom, and fairness to lift itself out of the crisis.[27] Beyond the Japanese-American comparison, the end of the Cold War is widely viewed as a decisive victory for American principles.[28] For yet another example, consider the results of a 1995 cross-national study of patriotism by the National Opinion Research Center (NORC). Comparing America with twenty-two other nations, Tom Smith and Lars Jarkko report that Americans are the world's most patriotic people.[29] For instance, 90 percent of Americans say they would rather be citizens of the United States than of any other country.

Values are the focus of this comparative analysis. As I discussed in chapter 1, a cross-cultural comparison of America would be unfavorable if it revealed that America's value system is different from societies with traditional values and similar to societies with secular values. This definition of unfavorable takes the traditionalist's view of the values inherent in a good society. Of course, the case can be made (see chapter 4) that secular-rational values are superior to and more desirable than traditional values. However, I frame the comparative hypothesis from the traditionalist's view because it dominates the moral debate about America's crisis of values. As we shall see later in this chapter, the traditionalist's view dominates because it helps to preserve the ideological core of America's imagined community.

The World Values Surveys permit the comparison of the value system of the United States with the value systems of a large number of other societies, examining similarities and differences along two dimensions of cultural variation. As demonstrated above, the global cultural maps show that America is an exceptional case: traditional values combined with self-expression values. Moreover, this exceptional mix of traditional and self-expression values has become even more unusual over time. America's already traditional values have remained relatively stable during the same period in which the nation traveled continuously along the survival/self-expression dimension. The 2000 World Values Surveys show that America moved even farther since 1995 toward the self-expression pole.[30] Today, America is a society with traditional values in which self-realization plays an increasingly prominent role.

How does America's value system and the path it has taken compare with those of other societies? Some societies have more traditional values, while a few others have more self-expression-oriented values, but no other society is as traditional *and* as self-expression-oriented as America. In other words, there is no other society located below *and* to the right of the United States on the global cultural maps. This is true for every global cultural map shown in this chapter, including the map that contains the fourth wave (1999–2001) of the World Values Surveys (fig. 2.1b). None of the eighty other societies on this map is located below and to the right of the United States.[31]

Thirty-one of eighty nations on the latest global cultural map (fig. 2.1b) are more traditional than the United States. All of these nations, however, are poor or developing societies from Africa, South Asia, or Latin America, with the exception of Ireland. But, as noted above, the source of Ireland's traditional values is a Catholic religious-cultural heritage. America's peers on the traditional/secular-rational dimension—those that are more or less as traditional as the United States—include Turkey, Vietnam, India, Poland, Romania, and Northern Ireland. Among these, only Northern Ireland would otherwise be compared with the United States, due to their similar levels of economic development and their English-speaking and historically Protestant heritage. Nonetheless, the source of Northern Ireland's traditional values is different: this society has witnessed a true culture war—a brutal clash based on religious differences—that has led to sustained political unrest and organized violence.[32]

At the same time, America has become one of the most self-expression-oriented nations in the world. As the fourth wave of the World Values Surveys shows, only seven nations are more self-expression oriented: Sweden, Netherlands, Australia, Denmark, New Zealand, Canada, and Iceland. America's peers on the survival/self-expression dimension (those that are more or less as self-expression oriented as the United States) are Austria, Norway, Switzerland, New Zealand, Canada, and Iceland. All of these are economically advanced democracies and, with the exception of Austria, share a common historically Protestant heritage.

Focusing on religion—the biggest component of the traditional/secular-rational dimension (tables 2.1–2.3)—underscores American exceptionalism. For example, America has the highest level of attendance at religious services, compared to almost all advanced industrial democracies (see table 2.8). In 1995, for example, 55 percent of Americans reported that they attended religious services at least once a month. Of nineteen other economically advanced democracies, only three report higher levels—Ireland, Northern Ireland, and South Korea. When asked to rate the importance of God in their lives, using a 10-point scale, 50 percent of Americans say "10"—the highest score possible. No other economically advanced democracy reports a higher percentage (see table 2.9). The 2000 World Values Survey of the United States shows that religious beliefs and practices have gotten stronger since 1995. Sixty percent of Americans in 2000 reported that they attended religious services at least once a month, and 58 percent rated the importance of God in their lives as "10." Similarly, 63 percent of respondents to my 2003 Detroit Area Study, a representative survey of the three million adults (eighteen and older) living in the three-county Detroit metropolitan region, rated the importance of God in their lives as "10." Finally, a comprehensive "religiosity scale," composed of five measures of religious beliefs and practices, demonstrates that America remains one of the most religious nations on earth. Using the latest data for all nations in the four waves of the World Values Surveys, Inglehart and Norris report that only nineteen of seventy-five nations rate higher than the United States on this religiosity scale—and all of these nations are poor or developing countries, such as Uganda, Nigeria, El Salvador, Iran, Egypt, Brazil, Turkey, and the Dominican Republic.[33] The only exception is Ireland, which rates somewhat higher than the United States. Religion continues to figure prominently in American society. "God-talk," says Phyllis Tickle, suffuses American culture, conversation, and conduct.[34]

Taken together, these findings demonstrate that traditional values persist in America, even though these typically decline as societies shift from an agrarian to an industrial (and postindustrial) economy. There is little empirical support for the comparative hypothesis. America compares favorably with secularized postmodern societies because, unlike them, it has retained traditional values. Moreover, the path of value change for America has *not* converged over time around other societies with secular-rational values, and it has *not* diverged from the paths of societies with traditional values. This evidence largely eliminates the second of three possible explanations of America's crisis of values: The perception of a crisis of values cannot be linked to unfavorable comparisons with the value systems of other societies.

In total, the evidence presented above fails to support two of three hypotheses about America's crisis of values: the trend hypothesis (loss of traditional values) and the comparative hypothesis (unfavorable comparisons with other societies). In the process of testing these two hypotheses, we have seen that America's value system is an unusual combination of traditional values and self-expression values. This combination makes it an outlier in the world community. Over time, America has become even more of an outlier as its traditional values remain virtually unchanged but it continues to move toward self-realization values. Understanding the causes of this unusual value system is the subject to which we now turn.

Why Have Some Values Changed and Others Stayed the Same?

America's value system exhibits both stability and change: America retains its traditional values as it adopts other values that emphasize self-expression, subjective well-being, and quality of life. An explanation must account for both phenomena: Why have some values changed while others have stayed the same? In this section, I develop an answer to this question for the relatively short twenty-year period of observation covered in this chapter. In chapter 4, I fold this explanation into an argument about the dynamics of crisis in American history and in world history.

As we have seen in this chapter, the World Values Surveys demonstrate that a society's location on both dimensions of cultural variation reflects two forces: economic development and religious-cultural heritage. Generally, economic development propels societies in roughly the same predictable direction: from traditional values to secular-rational values, and from survival values to self-expression values—that is, toward the upper right corner of the global cultural map (fig. 2.4). Nonetheless, different societies follow different trajectories—even when subject to the same forces of economic development—because situation-specific factors also shape how a particular society develops. In next section, I argue that America's outlier position on the global cultural maps is an outcome of its unique cultural heritage. This unique heritage contributes to the nation's location on both dimensions. It retards movement toward secular-rational values, counteracting the usual effect of economic development on this dimension. And it accelerates America's shift to self-expression values, boosting the usual effect of economic development on this dimension. As we shall see, this argument actually *confirms* the theory that a society's value system reflects both economic development and cultural heritage, even though America's outlier value system violates some of the general patterns observed in the World Values Surveys.

The Persistence of Traditional Values in America

The basic values of individuals tend to become fixed by the time they reach adulthood and remain fairly stable throughout the life course. The experiences of members of a generation in adolescence and early adulthood forge a common outlook and collective identity that persist throughout the life cycle, as Karl Mannheim, José Ortega y Gassett, and others have argued.[35] Thirty years of Eurobarometer data support this view, demonstrating that the basic values of younger cohorts are quite different from those of older cohorts, and that these intergenerational differences persist as cohorts age.[36] Given the stability of basic values by generation, values in a society change through the process of intergenerational replacement: When younger cohorts' formative experiences are significantly different from older cohorts', values change as the younger groups replace the older ones. As we shall see, however, America's traditional values tenaciously resist this mechanism of value change. America has maintained a traditional value system over time *despite* big differences in the formative experiences of various generations.

Theoretically, rising levels of existential security are the key factor underlying intergenerational value change. During the twentieth century, the formative experiences of the younger generations in industrial societies have differed from those of older ones—survival has been increasingly secure, and a growing segment of the younger generation has come to take survival for granted. A country's GDP per capita is a rough indicator of the degree to which survival is secure, but war, disease, crime, and other factors also are significant. The best indicator of existential security during one's formative years is the country's life expectancy from 1900–1910 (during the childhood of the oldest respondents in the World Values Surveys) to the present. Although we do not have time-series data for most of these countries, we do know that life expectancies were relatively low at the start of this century and have risen dramatically in all societies that have experienced economic growth, improved diet and improved medical care, and related factors. Even in the United States (already the richest society on Earth), life expectancy in 1900 was only forty-eight years, and today it is seventy-six years. Societies with high life expectancies today tend to be societies that have experienced relatively large increases in existential security since 1900.

Thus, we would expect to find strong correlations between a given society's life expectancy and the size of the intergenerational value differences in a society. We do. Intergenerational value differences are greatest in societies with the highest life expectancies. Across sixty-one societies, the correlation of 1995 life expectancy and the size of the intergenerational difference in traditional/secular-rational values is .56, significant at the $p < .001$ level; and the correlation of life expectancy and the size of the intergenerational difference in survival/self-expression values is .41, also significant at the $p < .001$ level.

Figure 2.5 shows the level of traditional/secular-rational values among seven birth groups, born during the seventy-year span from 1907 to 1976. A graph that attempted to depict the age differences among sixty-some societies would be unreadable. To convey the overall pattern in parsimonious fashion, these societies are grouped into four categories, based on their economic histories during the twentieth century: (1) The "advanced industrial democracies" have 1995 per capita GNPs over $10,000 (based on World Bank purchasing power parity estimates). These countries experienced substantial economic growth during the twentieth century (which is the main reason why they are rich)—according to data from the Penn World tables, their real mean per capita GNP in 1992 was 7.0 times higher than it was in 1950. (2) The "ex-Communist societies" experienced even faster economic growth during most of this period—their mean real per capita GNP in 1992 was 13.1 times higher than in 1950—but they have experienced major economic reversals in recent years.

(3) The "developing societies" include all non-Communist countries with real per capita GNP from $5,000 to $10,000 per year—their mean per capita GNP in 1992 was 4.7 times higher than in 1950. (4) The "low-income societies" include all countries with a real per capita GNP below $5,000—a group that experienced the least long-term growth, with real per capita GNP in 1992 being only 2.0 times higher than in 1950.[37]

As figure 2.5 indicates, the young are markedly less traditional than the old in the advanced industrial democracies and in the ex-Communist societies. But this holds true only in societies that have experienced substantial economic growth since 1950. The steep slope indicates that younger groups have much more secular-rational world-views than do older groups in both capitalist and ex-Communist industrial societies. The slope is less steep in developing societies, and in low-income societies the young and the old are about equally likely to hold traditional values.

A graph for the United States only, constructed to match figure 2.5, shows that the values held by cohorts born in the early part of the century are not dramatically different from the values held by cohorts born in the late part of the century (see fig. 2.6). Even though the formative experiences of American cohorts are quite different—consider, for example, the experiences of those who came of age in the Great Depression versus the experiences of the post–World War II cohorts—Americans of all ages tend to have traditional values. Indeed, the American pattern is more similar to developing societies than to advanced industrial democracies. The correlation of the line for developing societies (fig. 2.5) and America (fig. 2.6) is .88

The shallow upward slope of the line in figure 2.6 implies that America's traditional values could gradually erode in the future as the less-traditional younger cohorts replace the more-traditional older cohorts. Indeed, this upward slope could explain the small but statistically significant shift toward secular-rational values observed in the 2000 surveys. Note, however, that the positions of the United States on the global cultural map in 1981 and 1995 are not different (fig. 2.4). Further, the results from the 2000 World Values Survey of the United States shows that America remains in about the same lo-

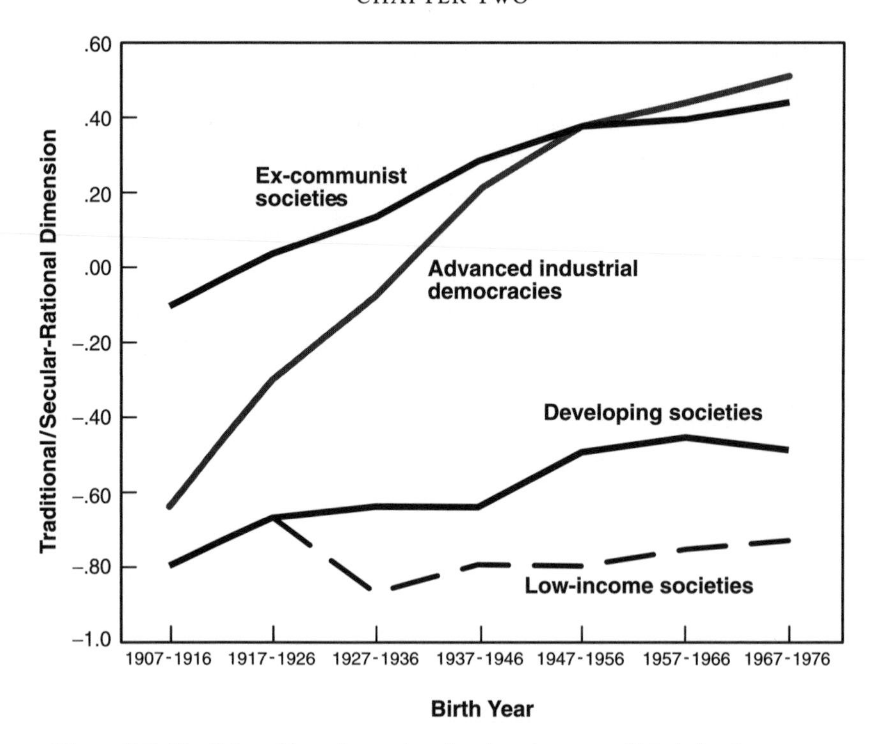

Figure 2.5. Traditional/secular-rational values by year of birth for four types of societies.

Source: Inglehart and Baker, "Modernization," p. 43, fig. 7. Data come from the most recent survey for each country in the World Values Surveys.

Notes: High values on the traditional/secular-rational values scale indicate secularization. Data are weighted to give each society equal weight.

Ex-Communist societies include Armenia, Azerbaijan, Belarus, Bosnia, Bulgaria, Croatia, Czech Republic, Estonia, Georgia, Hungary, Latvia, Lithuania, Macedonia, Moldova, Poland, Romania, Russia, Slovakia, Solvenia, Ukraine, Yugoslavia (N = 15,804).

Advanced industrial democracies include Australia, Austria, Belgium, Canada, Denmark, Finland, France, East Germany, West Germany, Great Britain, Iceland, Ireland, Northern Ireland, Italy, Japan, South Korea, Netherlands, New Zealand, Norway, Portugal, Spain, Sweden, Switzerland, United States (N = 21, 947).

Developing societies include Argentina, Brazil, Chile, Mexico, South Africa, Puerto Rico, Turkey, Uruguay, Venezuela (N = 8,024).

Low-income societies include Dominican Republic, Ghana, India, Nigeria, Peru, Philippines (N = 5,280).

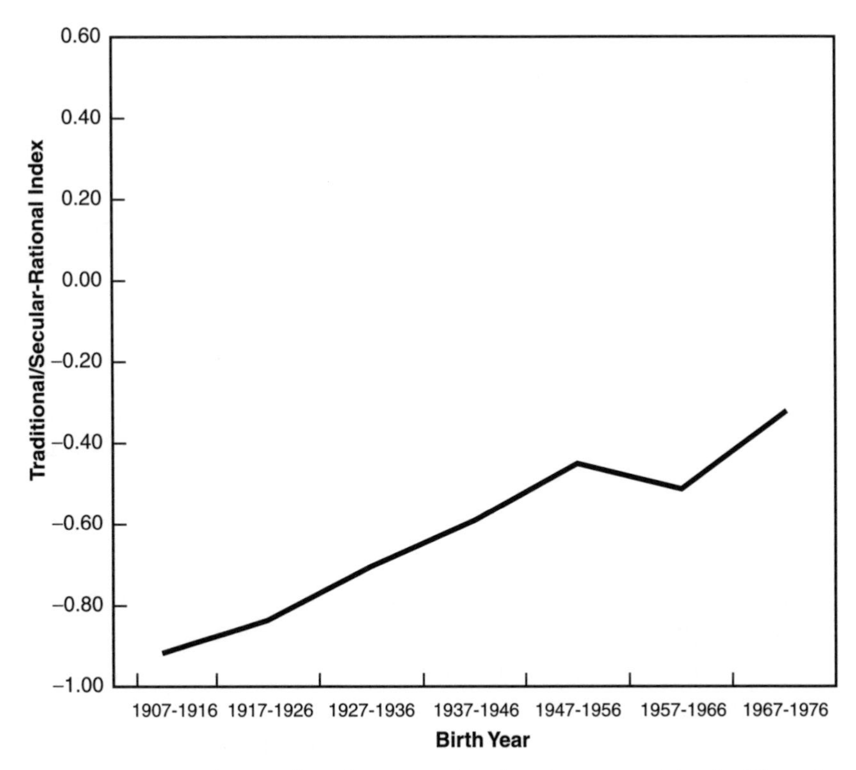

Figure 2.6. Traditional/secular-rational values by year of birth, United States.

Source: World Values Surveys, United States, 1995.

cation relative to other societies.[38] Thus, the traditional values of Americans have remained comparatively stable over a twenty-year period. It is unlikely that America's values will become dramatically less traditional in the foreseeable future.

America's traditional values have resisted the main mechanism of value change operating in the rest of the world—intergenerational replacement. The reason, I argue, is the unique cultural heritage of America. This heritage is strong enough to resist the usual secularizing effect of economic development. What is unique about America's cultural heritage? Observers from Alexis de Tocqueville onward have observed that America is "exceptional"—qualitatively different from other societies.[39] One reason why the United States is qualitatively different from other nations, says John Kingdon, is that Americans "*think* differently."[40] For example, Americans "have a different view of the proper authority, limits, and possibilities of government."[41] Unlike most peoples, Americans have a distinctive distrust of authority and a preference for limited government. Europeans, Canadians, and Japanese, in contrast, put much more emphasis on deference to superiors and obedience to authority.[42] The nation's position as an outlier on the global cultural map is testimony to the fact that Americans think differently.

America is the world's "first new nation," as Lipset puts it. Part of the American way of thinking stems from its revolutionary founding, coupled with radical ideas about the nature of a good society. "Born out of revolution," says Lipset, "the United States is a country organized around an *ideology* which includes a set of dogmas about the nature of a good society. Americanism, as different people have pointed out, is an 'ism' or ideology in the same way that communism or fascism or liberalism are isms. As G. K. Chesterton put it: 'America is the only nation in the world that is founded on a creed. That creed is set forth with dogmatic and even theological lucidity in the Declaration of Independence.'"[43] The American ideology—part of its different way of thinking—can be summarized in five core ideas: liberty, egalitarianism, individualism, populism, and laissez-faire.[44] This set of ideas or ideology, as I describe below, was forged in the nation's beginning and continues to this day, embodied in America's social, political, and economic institutions.

The origins of the American ideology are the early immigrants who dominated American thinking and institutions.[45] "American values," says Kingdon, "are connected to the kinds of people who came here. But the key point is that many of the people who traveled to these shores were systematically and fundamentally different from those who stayed behind in the old countries. They therefore brought ideas about government and politics with them that were systematically different from the ideas of the people who remained."[46] The earliest immigrants were religious exiles, such as the Puritans and the Pilgrims, who fled religious and political persecution in Europe. They imported with them a radical spirit of independence and self-reliance, and an aversion to and distrust of established political and religious authority. For example, the so-called separatists withdrew from and repudiated the Church of England due to disagreements about such issues as religious rituals and state control of religion. Some years later, the Methodists left England because they despised the power of the established Church of England, the taxes they were forced to pay for its maintenance, and the close partnership of church and state.[47]

The Protestants who left Europe were fundamentally different from the Protestants who stayed, and they set up fundamentally different institutions from those they left behind.[48] Indeed, the Puritans' original intention was to found a living model of a new society, one that would "cleanse the churches of Christ throughout the world by restoring them to the purity and simplicity they had known in the days of the Apostles."[49] Church hierarchies dominated European Protestants; American Protestants established local congregational sects. European Protestants were members of churches by birthright; American Protestants became members by acts of choice. European Protestants were expected to obey the clergy, who mediated their relationship with God; American Protestants were expected to obey God through a direct personal relationship. The clergy and schools of European Protestants were paid by the state and subsidized by taxes; the congregations of American Protestants paid the clergy, and their schools were self-funded. Compared to the Protestants of Europe, those who migrated were more individualistic, less obedient to authority, and more skeptical of hierarchy. They also had different views about human nature. European Protestants viewed human beings as innately sinful and weak and consequently were more forgiving and less judgmental about (inevitable) lapses in conduct. American Protestants thought and acted differently. "The American sects," says Lipset, "assume the perfectibility of human nature and have produced a moralistic people."[50] Given these fundamental differences, America should be an outlier in the historically Protestant zone of the global cultural map—and it is (fig. 2.3). America shares a general heritage of Protestantism with other countries, but the American variety is unique.

Those who left for economic reasons joined those who left Europe for religious reasons.[51] These immigrants came to America because it was viewed as the land of economic opportunity, a place to achieve economic success for themselves and their children. Those who migrated in the pursuit of economic gain were generally more individualistic, more antigovernment, more independent, more entrepreneurial, and bigger risk takers than those who stayed behind. Thus, economic immigrants held many of the same values as the religious groups that preceded them, but for different reasons. Together, those who left for religious reasons and those who left for economic reasons contributed to the unique constellation of American values—the American ideology or creed.

But that was a long time ago. How do values originating hundreds of years ago continue to exert influence today? One answer is path dependence.[52] Path dependence means that initial conditions or choices send a system down a path of development that is not easily reversed. Consider, for example, Kingdon's explanation of America's political values and institutions:

> America started down the path of limited government very early. We started with a distinctive distrust of authority, including governmental authority, that sprang from both the values of the immigrants and the pervasive localism of America. Faithful to and believing in that orientation, the founders deliberately built the country's fragmented governmental institutions (separation of powers, checks and balances, bicameralism, federalism) so as to limit government. Their design also contained specified limits on government action, as in the Bill of Rights, to be enforced by independent courts. Now that we have gone down the path of limited government for two centuries, we are extremely unlikely to design a wholly different set of institutions from scratch. . . . Some Americans think that the genius of the founders is their lasting legacy to all of us; others think that we're all stuck with these unwieldly institutions. Either way, there's no turning back."[53]

Path dependence helps to explain why America's traditional values are durable—these values are locked in a system that repeatedly reproduces them. America's founding values were built into early social, economic, and political institutions, which then reinforced and reproduced these values, setting Americans down a path that could not be reversed. There is no turning back for America's traditional values. Change is possible, of course, but barring widespread natural catastrophes, total war, or economic collapse, change tends to be gradual. This view stands in sharp contrast to the fragility of traditional values assumed by the purveyors of America's crisis of values (chapter 1). Those who decry the (presumed) loss of America's traditional values assume that these values will evaporate without constant vigilance and continual intervention. Path dependence ensures that evaporation is unlikely.

Evidence from multiple sources supports the path dependence argument. For example, expressions today of the American ideology and its traditional values are loud and clear. The principal investigators of the 1996 Survey of American Political Culture report "remarkably high levels of support for the 'American creed.'"[54] For example, 92 percent of respondents "agree that children should be taught that 'Our founders limited the power of government, so government would not intrude too much into the lives of its citizens.'" Eighty percent of respondents "expressed a high degree of 'support for our system of government.'" And 96 percent agree with "the principle that 'with hard work and perseverance, anyone can succeed in America' should be taught to children."[55] Furthermore, as mentioned above, the National Opinion Research Center's 1995 cross-national study of patriotism reports that Americans are the world's most patriotic people.

Protestantism still is the "deep structure" of American culture, argues Robert Bellah. The institutionalization of the values associated with the American variety of Protestantism produces and reproduces a culture that is so powerful and monolithic that Bellah brands it a "monoculture."[56] Similarly, Amitai Etzioni calls America the "monochrome" society because its diverse groups actually share the same American values and aspirations.[57] In general, Christianity (especially the Protestant version) is central to the imagined community of America. "The narrative of a Christian America has always had a hold on the collective imagination of Americans," says Diana Eck.

"This narrative moves through every chapter in American history, and it is a story deeply embedded in the subsoil of American consciousness."[58] The persisting force of the nation's Protestant heritage is evident today in the similarity of values for different religious groups in America. As discussed above, the American variety of Protestantism, formed in the nation's infancy, contributes today to the nation's position as an outlier in the historically Protestant zone (fig. 2.3). The institutionalization of the founding values also exerts a homogenizing force on the values of different religious groups. For example, time-series data from the General Social Survey reveals increasing similarity among American Protestants, Catholics, and Jews in their beliefs about an afterlife.[59] Most American Protestants (85 percent) believe in life after death, and their belief has not wavered over the past twenty-five years. In the same period, however, more and more American Catholics, American Jews, and Americans with no religious affiliations have come to believe in life after death—up to the same high level as American Protestants. Evidence from the World Values Surveys shows that American Catholics and American Protestants are adjacent to one another on both dimensions of cultural variation (see fig. 2.7), even though the values of historically Catholic countries and historically Protestant countries are far apart (fig. 2.3). American Catholics share more values with their Protestant compatriots than they do with Catholics in historically Catholic societies (fig. 2.7). America may be the world's "most religiously diverse nation," as Diana Eck argues,[60] but the American experience remakes the basic values of different religious groups into *American* values, even as it tolerates (and sometimes celebrates) differences in specific religious practices and beliefs.

Inglehart and I observed the same homogenizing pattern in other societies. For example, the differences between Catholics and Protestants within other religiously mixed societies are quite small (fig. 2.7), even though historically Catholic and Protestant societies show very distinctive values (fig. 2.3).[61] Surprisingly, this pattern also holds true for the differences between Hindus and Muslims in India, and Christians and Muslims in Nigeria. For example, the values of Nigerian Muslims are closer to those of their Christian compatriots than they are to those of Indian Muslims. Of course, on questions that directly evoke specific Islamic or Christian identity, this would almost certainly not hold true; on the two dimensions of basic values, however, the cross-national differences dwarf the within-nation differences. Despite globalization, the nation remains a key unit of shared experience, with its educational and cultural institutions shaping the values of almost everyone in that society, regardless of religious affiliation. There are built-in limits to the global convergence of national cultures and economies, observes Mauro Guillén, because nations "use their unique economic, political, and social advantages as leverage in the global marketplace."[62] Their behavior reinforces the differences between nations, sending them down unique development trajectories.

America's traditional values are path dependent. These values are incorporated in the nation's institutions and reproduced over time as they are transmitted from generation to generation. This process makes America's traditional values resistant to the changes usually associated with economic development. This, however, is not the entire explanation. Another reason, which I develop next, is the role of America's traditional values in the preservation of America's "imagined community." In chapter 1, I introduced the concept of a nation-state as an "imagined community"—what Jürgen Habermas calls the popular self-consciousness of belonging to the same people.[63] This popular self-consciousness creates "a relation of solidarity between persons who had previously been strangers to one another."[64] Unlike other nations, where this "relation of solidarity" is based on common ancestry, history, language, customs, religion, and so on, the "relation of solidarity" in America is a shared set of ideas or values. As noted in chapter 1, Habermas calls this relation of solidarity America's "civil religion." Ralph Waldo Emerson and Abraham Lincoln labeled it America's "political religion."[65] As Lipset put it, "Being an American . . . is an ideological commitment. It is not a matter of birth. Those who reject American values are un-American."[66]

Americans imagine they belong to the "same people"—an American people—because they believe they share the same values. This

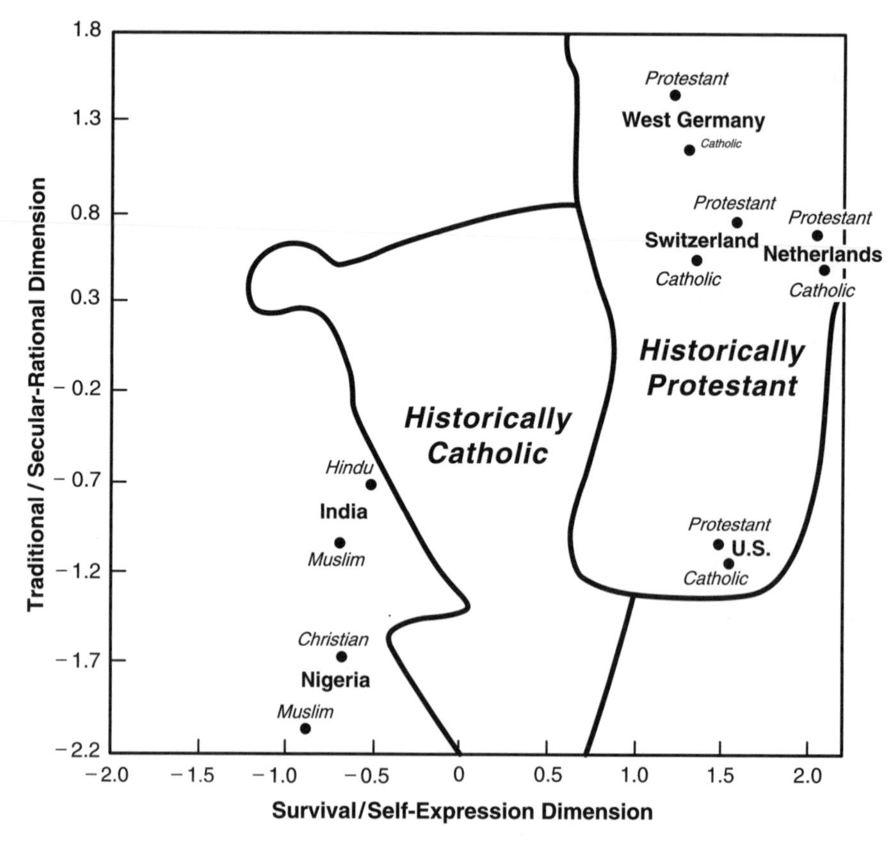

Figure 2.7. Differences between the religious groups within religiously mixed societies on two dimensions of cross-cultural variation.
Source: Inglehart and Baker, "Modernization," p. 37, fig. 5.

imagined relation of solidarity overcomes differences in ancestry and ethnic origin, in religion, in customs, even in language. American national identity is ideological unity within diversity.

America's traditional values—strong beliefs in religion and God, family values, absolute moral authority, national pride, and so on—are fundamental to what it means to be American. Because America's collective identity is founded on values, their preservation is paramount. America would not be America if its people lost their traditional values because this loss would eliminate the foundation of the nation's imagined community. There is no other foundation to fall back on. In contrast, the loss of traditional values in birthright nations is *not* a threat to their imagined communities. Swedes are still Swedish, Japanese are still Japanese, Germans are still Germanic, and Poles are still Polish even though they have shed their traditional values over time (see fig. 2.4). With or without strong traditional values, these nations and others like them still have their common ancestry, history, religion, customs, and language.

Thus, there is a profound need to preserve the traditional values that undergird America's imagined community. This need, I suggest, creates a strong demand for crisis rhetoric, such as vociferous and repeated warnings of a loss of traditional values (even though Americans have not lost them). "Among the great nations of the world," observes John Kenneth Galbraith, "none is more given to introspection than the United States. No day passes without reflective comment—by the press, on radio or television, in an article or book, in compelled or compelling oratory—on what is wrong in the society and what could be improved."[67] This strong demand can be understood by considering together the functions of deviance and rhetoric. One function of deviance, as Emile Durkheim proposed and later sociologists, such as Kai Erikson, developed, is to create "a sense of mutuality among the people of a community by supplying a focus for group feeling. Like a war, a flood, or some other emergency, deviance makes people more alert to the interests they share in common and draws attention to those values which constitute the 'collective conscience' of the community."[68] One function of rhetoric is to place or keep certain topics in mind. It is less about telling people *what* to think than it is telling them what to think *about*.[69] Crisis rhetoric, therefore, serves the valuable social function of keeping America's traditional values in mind, affirming and reinforcing the ideological core of America's imagined community—the values that define "who we are."[70]

The Shift to Self-Expression Values

If path dependence is a major reason why America has retained its traditional values, why has the nation shifted toward self-expression values? Theoretically, change is always possible; path dependence is probabilistic, not deterministic. Realistically, however, some changes are more likely and some changes are less likely. Changes that are *congruent* with the institutionalized values of a nation are more likely to occur than changes that are incongruent with them. For example, socialism and unionism never caught on in America as they did in all other industrialized nations because they are incongruent with American values and institutions. As Lipset summarizes, "The American social structure and values foster the free market and competitive individualism, an orientation which is not congruent with class-consciousness, support for socialist or social democratic parties, or a strong trade union movement."[71]

I argued above that America's cultural heritage is incongruent with the usual secularizing effects of economic development. This heritage enables the nation to resist movement along the traditional/secular-rational dimension. Here, I argue that cultural heritage is also the cause of the nation's location on the second dimension of cultural variation—survival versus self-expression values. However, because America's cultural heritage is *congruent* with the effects of economic development on this dimension, the forces of culture and economics join together and accelerate the shift to self-expression values.

The pursuit of self-realization—"a particularized creative process of individual growth"[72]—is especially congruent with the American cultural heritage. For example, American individualism strongly favors the pursuit of *self*-realization. Belief in the perfectibility of human nature, coupled with the moral charge to pursue perfection,[73] favors undertaking the journey of self-realization in the first place as it disfavors the alternatives of hedonism or nihilism. Belief in laissez-faire favors the use of the market to provide immaterial goods (one reason why Fogel uses the linguistic term "spiritual *capital*" to refer to the resources needed for self-realization) as it disfavors the use of governmental alternatives (e.g., state-sponsored religion, or the provision of psychological counseling through socialized medicine). There is, for example, a market for religion in America, another institution that makes America unique. "A key element in American religious exceptionalism," observe Andrew Greeley and Michael Hout, "is the vigorous competition among religious organizations for members."[74] The rise of "New Age" institutions adds to the intensity of religious competition in America. Traditional religious organizations offer the resources for what Robert Wuthnow calls a "spirituality of dwelling"—sacred places, such as a church, synagogue, or mosque.[75] The new competitors offer the resources to engage in a "spirituality of seeking"—a personal quest for sacred moments and the exploration of new spiritual avenues. The new competitors appear to be winning: the decline of organized religion in America (though it is declining much more slowly in the United States than in other societies) is accompanied by a rise of spiritual concerns and the pursuit of self-realization through personal quests for spiritual insight and fulfillment.[76]

Evidence from the World Values Surveys shows a clear trend toward self-realization in the United States from 1981 to 2000. Other data suggest that this is may be the tail of a longer trend. Figure 2.8 shows a general upward trend over an eighty-year period in self-help and advice books on the national nonfiction best-seller lists.[77] Over several decades, this genre has grown as a percentage of the most popular books sold in America. This cultural indicator indicates growing interest in the goal of self-realization as well as a uniquely American way of pursuing it—personal growth and development through individualized self-study.

Generally, value change along the survival/self-expression dimension occurs through intergenerational replacement, the same mechanism of change along the traditional/secular-rational dimension for most economically advanced democracies (except the United States). We know from the World Values Surveys that material needs start to become satiated in all post-industrial societies; under the conditions of existential security, concerns shift from material needs to immaterial or spiritual needs, such as subjective well-being, self-expression, and the quality and meaning of life.[78] Figure 2.9 shows the levels of survival/self-expression values among seven birth groups in four types of societies. The steepest intergenerational differences occur in advanced industrial democracies and in ex-Communist societies, relatively small intergenerational differences in developing

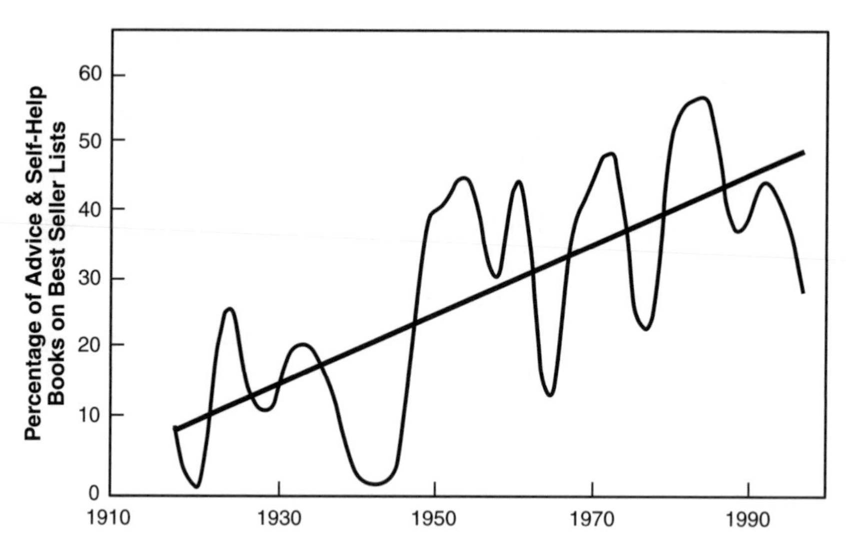

Figure 2.8. Percentage of self-help and advice books on national nonfiction best-seller lists, by year, 1917–1997 (smoothed time-series and best linear fit).

societies, and very little difference is found between the values of older and younger cohorts in the low-income societies. In contrast to figure 2.5, figure 2.9 shows that ex-Communist societies rank much lower than other societies on the syndrome of trust, tolerance, subjective well-being, political activism, and self-expression that constitutes this second major dimension of cross-cultural variation. This pattern may reflect the impact of the collapse of Communism and the experience of economic, political, and social turmoil.[79]

The absence of intergenerational change in low-income societies suggests a continuing emphasis on survival values by the overwhelming majority of their people throughout the past several decades.[80] In the ex-Communist societies, by contrast, successive birth cohorts experienced rising levels of economic security until the collapse of Communism propelled them downward. The low levels of self-expression values found in ex-Communist societies are not solely the result of current economic factors, however. Even in 1981, a decade before the collapse of the Soviet Union, these societies showed lower levels of subjective well-being than societies that had

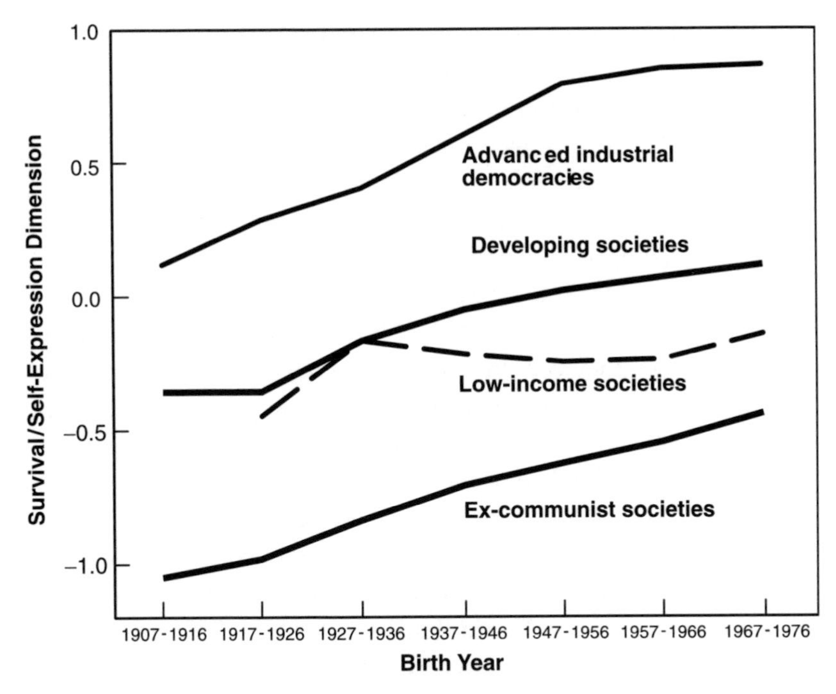

Figure 2.9. Survival/self-expression values by year of birth for four types of societies.

Source: Inglehart and Baker, "Modernization," p. 44, fig. 8. Data come from the most recent survey for each country in the World Values Surveys.

Note: High values on the survival/self-expression values scale indicate high self-expression. Data are weighted to give each society equal weight.

a fraction of their per capita GNP. As the analyses above indicate (tables 2.5 and 2.6), the low levels of self-expression values found in ex-Communist societies persist, even after controlling for economic variables. In part, they may reflect the consequences of living under repressive authoritarian regimes.

Figure 2.10 presents a graph of survival/self-expression values by birth cohort for the United States, constructed to match figure 2.9. It shows a pattern similar to that of all economically advanced democracies. The correlation of the line for the United States (fig. 2.10) and the line for these economically advanced societies (fig. 2.9) is .87. Generally, later American birth cohorts are more oriented to self-expression and less to survival, compared with earlier American cohorts. For example, those who came of age in the Great Depression are more survival oriented than those who came of age after World War II. Note, however, that all American birth cohorts are more self-expression oriented—including the Great Depression cohorts—than their peer cohorts in other advanced industrial democracies. Thus, it appears that the base level for all Americans is more self-expression oriented, regardless of age.

Data from the 2000 World Values Survey show that America has continued its journey away from survival values toward self-expression values, even as the nation retains its traditional values.[81] Like other societies that enjoyed existential security from the date of the first survey (1981) to the date of the latest (2000), Americans have become more and more oriented toward self-realization. Some of this shift comes from the nation's prolonged experience of physical security, peace, and satisfaction of material needs for most people. (The terrorist attacks on the World Trade Center and the Pentagon on September 11, 2001, interrupted America's sense of physical safety, but at least at this writing they do not appear to have had a lasting effect on the nation's values.[82]) But some of the shift also stems from American culture, which accelerates the shift toward self-realization values. Advanced economic development provided the *means*—a surplus of time and money, and freedom from existential worry. But culture supplied the *ends*—the pursuit of self-realization. As I argued above, self-expression is an especially American orientation; it appears to have blossomed in recent years, but it has always been an American preoccupation.

Like all societies, America's location on the two dimensions of cultural variation reflects both economic development and cultural heritage. The nation's trajectory on the global cultural map is unusual because America's combination of economic development and cultural heritage is unusual. America's cultural heritage retards the movement toward secular-rational values that usually accompanies advanced economic development. At the same time, this heritage accelerates the nation's shift toward self-expression values. Self-expression is congruent with the usual effects of economic develop-

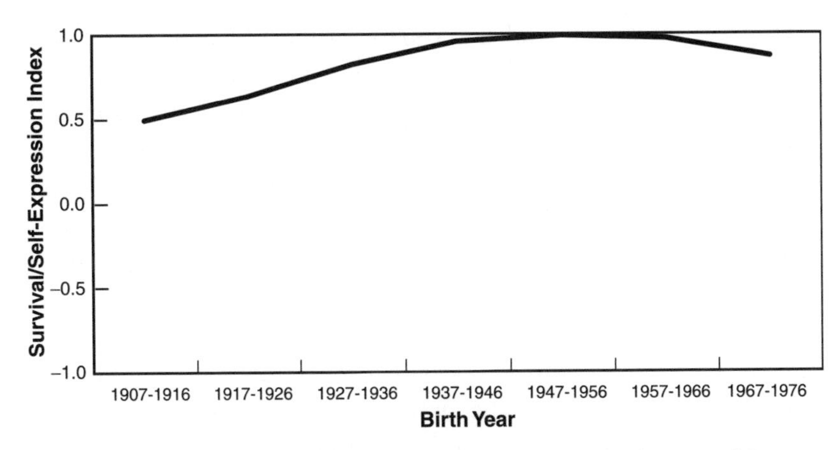

Figure 2.10. Survival/self-expression values by year of birth, United States.
Source: World Values Surveys, United States, 1995.

ment and so the two together propel American society toward the self-expression pole. Secular-rational values are incongruent with the usual effects of economic development and so the two pull in opposite directions, with culture suppressing the secularizing effects of economics.

Conclusion

This chapter tested two of the three hypotheses about the perception of an American crisis of values—crisis as a loss of traditional values, and crisis as unfavorable comparisons to other societies—using data from multiple waves of the World Values Surveys. These are the trend and comparative hypotheses, respectively. The analysis was guided by a framework for understanding and measuring cultural variation and change that is well-grounded in cross-cultural research. This framework arrays values along two dimensions: a continuum of traditional versus secular-rational values, and a continuum of survival versus self-expression values. These dimensions make it possible to locate each society on a global map of cross-cultural variation, as well as to track the trajectories of societies over time.

Substantial changes have occurred in the values and beliefs in the eighty-one societies included in the four waves of the World Values Surveys. These changes are closely linked with the economic changes experienced by a given society: Economic development is associated with predictable shifts from traditional to secular-rational values and from survival to self-expression values. However, cultural heritages leave a durable legacy that continues to differentiate cultural zones across a wide range of social, religious, political, and economic values. The fact that a society was historically Protestant or Orthodox or Confucian or experienced Communist rule gives rise to distinctive value systems that persist even when economic development is held constant. The analyses show that the location and trajectory of societies are a function of economic development and religious-cultural heritage. Both economics and culture explain values and value change.

I tested the trend hypothesis by examining the location and movement of America along the first dimension of cultural variation—traditional versus secular-rational values. If America had lost its traditional values, we should have seen a significant shift away from traditional to secular-rational values. The evidence clearly shows that America is one of the most traditional societies in the world. Moreover, America's traditional values have remained relatively unchanged over two decades. Contrary to the claims of the purveyors of decline (see chapter 1), there is little evidence of a decline of traditional values in the years covered by the World Values Surveys.

I tested the comparative hypothesis by examining the location of the United States relative to other societies, as well as the nation's proximity to societies with similar value systems. America's value system compares favorably with those of other societies. Most advanced industrial and postindustrial democracies have lost their traditional values, becoming secular-rational societies. In contrast, Americans have much more traditional values than the peoples of any comparable advanced industrial democracy, and more traditional values than the peoples of almost *any* society regardless of level of economic development and type of political system. The path of value change for America has *not* converged over time around other societies with secular-rational values, and it has *not* diverged from the paths of societies with traditional values. There is little empirical support for the comparative hypothesis.

America has experienced rapid change along the second dimension of cultural variation—survival versus self-expression values. While Americans have retained their traditional values, they have rapidly lost their survival values in favor of self-expression or self-realization values. I argued that the reason for the nation's dramatic shift on the survival versus self-expression dimension was the same reason the nation resists change on the traditional versus secular-rational dimension: America's cultural heritage. America's cultural heritage is antithetical to the rise of secular-rational values, but favorable to the rise of self-expression values. The loss of traditional values would be a direct assault on the ideological core of the imagined community of America, and so the preservation of traditional values is paramount. At the same time, not only is the postmodern quest for self-realization congruent with American values, the quest itself is an expression of these values. Existential conditions at the end of the twentieth century and turn of the millennium were the fertile soil in which self-realization could flourish.

This chapter analyzed America in global context, treating each nation as a unit of observation. The next chapter examines the variation of values inside American society, analyzing the third of three hypotheses about the perception of an American crisis of values: crisis as division into two opposed moral camps (the distribution hypothesis). This is the popular theory that America is engaged in a "culture war." If true, it would mean that the ideological core of the imagined community of America is split in half, based on incompatible views of the American way of life. Even though Americans have not lost their traditional values, on average, and American society compares favorably with other societies, it is still possible that we will see an internal division. If we do, this would be the explanation of the widespread perception of an American crisis of values.

CHAPTER THREE

Culture War

AMERICA HAS NOT LOST its traditional values, and it does not compare unfavorably with other societies; the evidence in chapter 2 does not support the trend or comparative hypotheses. This chapter explores the distribution hypothesis: the popular theory that America is engaged in a culture war, an apocalyptic vision of Americans taking sides in a battle between incompatible views of the American way of life. Of the three explanations of a crisis of values, this one may be the most devastating. If true, it means that Americans are irreconcilably divided and the inevitable outcome is the defeat of one group of Americans at the hands of another group of Americans.

I begin this chapter by describing the contours of the culture war debate. As we will see, there are two versions of the culture war thesis, the strong and the weak forms. The strong form makes two assumptions. First, it assumes that Americans are polarized into two groups, based on two fundamental moral visions. On one side, moral absolutists believe that morals and moral judgment exist outside the self in God or society; on the other side, moral relativists believe that morals and moral judgment exist only in the self. Second, the strong form assumes that moral visions reside over and influence religious beliefs and social attitudes. For example, people use their moral visions to derive their attitudes on social issues and policies. Advocates of the weak form of the culture war thesis, in contrast, argue that moral visions and social attitudes are loosely coupled if they are coupled at all. According to the weak form, American absolutists and American relativists can share similar moral values and similar social attitudes.

Next, I test both forms of the culture war thesis. This chapter provides the first complete empirical test of the culture war thesis. Prior analyses, which I describe below, have examined the polarization of the American people's social attitudes and religious beliefs. They have not, however, directly measured moral visions. The World Values Surveys provide an unprecedented opportunity to observe moral visions because they include a direct measure of them. The measure of moral visions is not perfect, but it permits the first test of the actual links among moral visions, religious beliefs, and attitudes about social issues and polices.

Finally, the World Values Surveys data allow the exploration of the empirical link between the two characteristics of community I outlined in chapter 1: community as a social network, and community as shared moral values. In particular, we consider the relationship between moral visions and civic engagement, such as political action and participation in voluntary associations, looking for evidence of differences in the forms or types of social capital that may be linked to differences in beliefs about moral authority. As such, this analysis bridges the two sides of the "community question"—Putnam's focus on America's social capital and my focus on America's values.

The Culture War Thesis

America is at war with itself. Once again, Americans are taking sides in a civil war between incompatible views of the American way of life. Once again, two armies are mustered and their ranks are swelling. Once again, the objective is total victory—what James Davison Hunter calls the "domination of one cultural and moral ethos over all others."[1] The outcome is uncertain but the stakes are high: the future of America. This time, however, the civil war is not fought by military armies. It is fought by moral armies. This time, the battlefields are not physical terrain but political, intellectual, and social terrain. The new civil war is a culture war, and the moral armies locked in mortal combat represent the two sides in the eternal conflict over moral authority, absolutism versus relativism.[2] Or so the story goes.

Are Americans really divided into two moral armies engaged in an all-out struggle over the future of America? Many think so. Culture war rhetoric is common in politics, the mass media, and intellectual discourse about the crisis of values in America. Many social scientists believe Americans are engaged in a culture war.[3] Others disagree. The notion of a culture war is nothing more than political or journalistic hyperbole. Rumors of war, they say, are greatly exaggerated.[4] This chapter explores the extent to which there is an empirical basis to the claims made by those who say the culture war is real.

The Polarization Claim

The polarization of moral visions is the first of two claims made by advocates of the culture war thesis. This claim assumes that Americans are divided into two opposing moral camps, based on incompatible beliefs about moral authority.[5] The source of the conflict is competing moral visions. Moral visions are fundamental beliefs about the location of moral authority: the "transcendental sphere" or the "mundane sphere."[6] According to the transcendental view, the source of moral values and moral judgment is located outside the individual in God (religion) or society. In contrast, according to the mundane view, the source of moral values and moral judgment is located in the self. Moral absolutists believe in a universal moral code located in a transcendental sphere; this absolute moral authority is independent and separate from the individuals it governs. This "legalistic" approach, as Joseph Fletcher calls it, applies the same rules and regulations to all people at all times in all situations—no matter what.[7] The true absolutist applies universal principles without deviation and without exception, even if it causes harm or disastrous consequences; absolutists faithfully follow the dictum, "*Fiat justitia, ruat caelum*" (Do the "right" even if the sky falls down).[8] God or society is the final judge of what is right and wrong. For the absolutist, relativism is pathological; it is the essence of evil and the root cause of social problems.

Relativists reject the idea of moral authority located in some transcendental sphere and instead locate the source of moral authority in the individual living in this world—the mundane sphere. Relativists locate moral authority in the self and local situation; the individual is the final judge of what is right and wrong—"the final arbiter of truth."[9] Relativists argue that moral codes can vary from person to person, from time to time, and from situation to situation as people struggle to work out the practical problems of everyday life. Fletcher's *Situation Ethics* is one of the best known (and perhaps most systematically developed) treatments of ethical relativism.[10]

A third approach, opposed to both absolutism and relativism, is *antinomianism*—literally, *against* laws or norms.[11] I put "against" in italics to emphasize the distinction between *anti*nomie (*against* laws or norms) and *a*nomie (*without* laws or norms). The person caught in an anomic situation experiences ambiguity of meaning, conflicting definitions of a situation, and confusion about the right guide to conduct. In contrast, the antinomian deliberately stands *against* law and norms, against *all* guides to conduct, absolutist *or* relativist. Peter Berger defines *nomos* as "a meaningful order."[12] The antinomian *opposes* meaningful order; the person experiencing anomie *searches* for meaningful order. The antinomian is an anarchist who "enters into the decision-making situation armed with no principles or maxims whatsoever, to say nothing of *rules*. In every 'existential moment' or 'unique' situation," Fletcher describes, "one must rely upon the situation itself, *there and then*, to provide its ethical solution."[13]

Relativism is often confused with antinomianism, leading many to assume that relativists take weak moral positions, hold inconsistent attitudes, and display inconsistent behaviors. Consider, for example, a statement by Brent Staples in his *New York Times* review of Alan Wolfe's *One Nation, After All,* a sociological study of two hundred middle-class Americans and their views on morality: "Anything but moral relativists, those interviewed had firm views of right and wrong."[14] Statistical tests of the internal consistency of opinion domains, presented later in this chapter, show that each moral vision produces consistent attitudes. The fact is that both relativism and absolutism are *systems* of ethics; both yield firm views of right and wrong.

Moral visions are not religious beliefs. Some definitions of moral visions mix beliefs about moral authority with religious beliefs. This is an easy mistake to make because those with strong religious beliefs often believe in God as the source of moral authority. But atheists, too, can believe in a transcendental vision: society itself and abstract ideas are other transcendental sources of moral authority.[15] Thus, traditional religious beliefs and absolute moral visions are often related, but they do not have to be.

Absolutism and relativism are worldviews; they are fundamentally different and opposed ways people conceptualize, reason, and talk about life. As such, they are what cognitive linguists call "radial categories."[16] These categories, says George Lakoff, "are the most common of human conceptual categories."[17] Radial categories are basic to the way the human mind works. Given the intensity of the discourse about America's crisis of values, it would be surprising to *not* find radial categories in operation.

Radial categories define both central tendencies (or models) and their variations. To illustrate with a simple example, consider the radial category "harm."[18] The central case is "physical harm," but there are variations that include financial harm, political harm, social harm, psychological harm, and others. For a more complex example, consider the radial category "mother."[19] This radial category includes four submodels: the birth-mother model (the mother who gives birth), the genetic-mother model (the mother who contributes half of a child's genes), the nurturance-mother model (the mother who cares for a child), and the marriage model (the mother who is wife of the father). Due to the complexity of modern life, the category extends to other forms of "mother," such as foster mother, stepmother, and surrogate mother.

Absolutism and relativism are complex categories, with many variations. But the theory of radial categories helps to make sense of this complexity by accounting for both the central tendencies and their variations in the discourse about moral crisis.[20] Despite the complexity and variety, there are only two coherent systems used in moral discourse—absolutism and relativism, as defined above. These are central tendencies, and so we see many variations. The key is that the many variations are related systematically to these two central tendencies. Moreover, these variations can be measured and their coherence analyzed, as presented later in this chapter.

Figure 3.1 presents a simplified illustration of the radial categories of absolutism and relativism, with cases in the domains of religion, politics, and family. Religion is the domain most people think of first

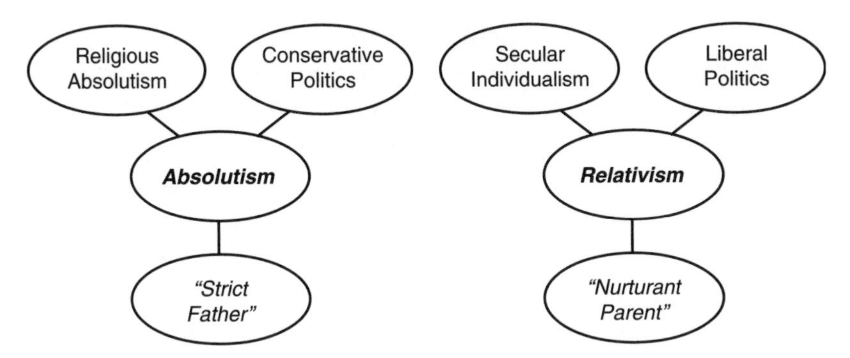

Figure 3.1. Simplified illustration of absolutism and relativism as radial categories.

when they think of absolutism and relativism. Therefore, religious absolutism is the central case for absolutism. There are many forms of religious absolutism, of course, but they have in common a belief in a religious source of transcendental moral authority. Secular individualism is the central case for relativism, stemming from a belief in the self as the ultimate source of moral authority. (Individualism alone is not sufficient for relativism, because individualism can be combined with religious absolutism to form the American Protestant belief in and quest for a direct personal relationship with God.)

The second domain links politics with opposite beliefs about moral authority. Moral reasoning in politics involves only two systems—conservatism and liberalism—even though there are many variations.[21] In *Moral Politics*, George Lakoff argues that these two forms of morality and politics are based on "the common, unconscious, and automatic metaphor of the Nation-as-Family."[22] Thus, ways of thinking in the third domain, family, are metaphors for ways of thinking in the second. Family metaphors are also ways of conceptualizing the first domain, religion (e.g., "God the Father").

Strict Father morality assumes "a universal, absolute, strict set of rules specifying what it is right and what is wrong for all times, all cultures, and all stages of development."[23] According to the Strict Father model, the world is a difficult and dangerous place; it is divided into good and evil.[24] For children to survive in this tough world, the father must teach them right from wrong by using strict rules, punishing transgressions, and rewarding obedience. This approach to childrearing is the only way to develop moral strength, respect for authority, self-discipline, responsibility, and the ability to compete successfully in the world. Children must not be spoiled lest they become dependent for life and never learn moral values. In the domain of politics, Strict Father morality produces conservatism, Lakoff argues. The Strict Father model is the basis of the conservative agenda, including opposition to gay rights (homosexuality threatens the integrity of the family and Strict Father authority), the welfare system (coddling the poor only makes them dependent and lose willpower), and the distribution of condoms to reduce teen pregnancy (because it promotes promiscuity and lack of self-discipline) or clean needles to intravenous drug users to combat AIDS (because it promotes hedonism and avoids punishment for irresponsibility).

In contrast, Nurturant Parent morality "requires that one empathize with and be nurturant toward people with different values than one's own, including moral values," says Lakoff. "This means that one cannot maintain a strict good-evil dichotomy. To be able to see the world through other people's values and truly empathize with them means that you cannot see all people who have different moral values than yours as enemies to be demonized."[25] According to the Nurturant Parent model, the goal of childrearing is for children to be "happy, empathic, able to take care of themselves, responsible, creative, communicative, and fair."[26] Children become so not by responding to rewards and punishments, but through nurturance and empathy, by "being cared for and respected, and through caring for others."[27] In the domain of politics, Nurturant Parent morality produces liberalism, Lakoff argues. This model is the basis of the liberal agenda, such as support of gay rights (all people deserve love, fair treatment, and respect), multiculturalism (for much the same reasons), and a host of social programs designed to support the poor and disadvantaged (all seen as investments in people who deserve empathy and need help).

A few paragraphs cannot convey the depth and breadth of Lakoff's analysis in *Moral Politics*. But they serve to illustrate the point that human thought often relies on a small number of fundamental categories, even though reality is complex, varied, and contradictory.

The absolutism-relativism duality does not oversimplify reality, once we understand that these two systems are radial categories. As radial categories, they show that complexity is ordered around central models, and that variation is systematic—indeed, it is measurable. For example, one can measure the "coherence" of a conceptual system in operation—how consistently people apply one model (absolutism or relativism) across domains. Lakoff notes that political leaders are always trying to get voters to become coherent in their views, applying one model across all domains, rather than using different models in different situations. To what extent, therefore, do moral absolutists apply the absolutist model at home, in religion, and in their politics? To what extent do moral relativists apply the relativist model at home, in religion, and in their politics? These and similar empirical questions are explored later in this chapter.

The Linkage Claim

Tight linkage of social attitudes, religion, and moral visions is the second of two claims made by advocates of the culture war thesis. Indeed, political and religious activists promote tight linkage. For example, consider the comments in a 1999 radio address by Christian radio commentator Charles Colson: "Our culture is embroiled in nothing less than a clash of worldviews, and Christians must stop focusing on social issues one at a time. Instead, we must delve beneath the surface and identify the underlying principles, the broad worldviews, that give rise to social problems in the first place. Otherwise, we may win a few battles, but still lose the war."[28]

The linkage claim is an expression or restatement of the "coherence" question discussed above. Tight linkage implies more coherence; loose linkage implies less coherence. The linkage claim assumes a particular ordering to the coherence of a conceptual system in operation: moral visions → religious beliefs → social attitudes. This ordering suggests a three-level *hierarchy of beliefs*.[29] This hierarchy is illustrated in figure 3.2. Moral visions form the overarching framework. Religious beliefs form the middle level under the framework of moral visions; as Clifford Geertz puts it, religion "objectivizes moral

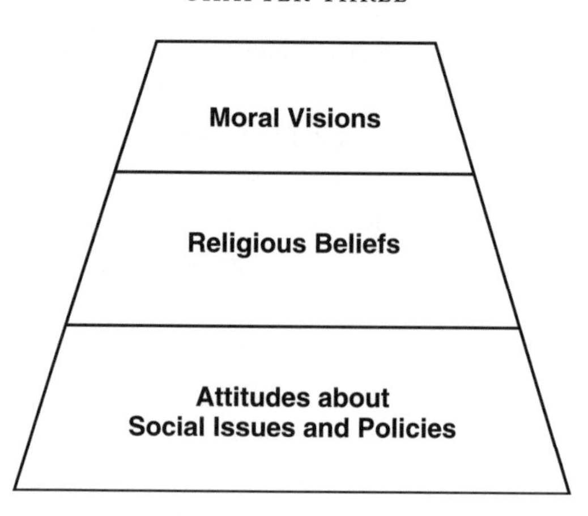

Figure 3.2. The hierarchy of beliefs.

and aesthetic preferences."[30] Religious beliefs, in turn, are the framework for attitudes about contemporary social issues, the bottom level; as Nancy Davis and Robert Robinson argue, "[religious] orthodoxy provides an overarching moral framework from which individuals may derive positions on specific policy-related issues."[31]

Some advocates of the culture war thesis assume that the three levels of the hierarchy of beliefs are tightly coupled. For example, moral visions inform attitudes about social issues and policies.[32] "Because this is a culture war," Hunter argues, "the nub of political disagreement today on the range of issues debated—whether abortion, child care, funding for the arts, affirmative action and quotas, gay rights, values in public education, or multiculturalism—can be traced ultimately and finally to the matter of moral authority."[33] Similarly, Getrude Himmelfarb says that America is one nation split into two cultures, a culture of traditional virtues embattled by a counterculture of loose morals and permissiveness, and that the "ethics gap" between these two cultures cuts across all social and political issues.[34] Many others argue that beliefs about moral authority and social attitudes are indeed tightly coupled.

But some social scientists doubt it. Beliefs about moral authority and social attitudes, they say, are loosely coupled if they are coupled at all.[35] These competing views are sometimes called, respectively, the "strong form" and the "weak form" of the culture war thesis.[36]

The strong form assumes that polarization runs from the top to the bottom of the hierarchy, splitting Americans by moral visions, by religious beliefs, and by social attitudes. In contrast, the weak form of the culture war thesis argues that, even if Americans' moral visions are polarized, religious beliefs and social attitudes need not be. Americans can still find common ground. For some, the weak form seems illogical. How could disagreements about moral authority co-exist with agreement about social attitudes? Yet people can agree on specific social issues and policies and disagree on the moral visions underlying their opinions. This argument is consistent with attitude models in psychology that decompose attitudes into a set of beliefs, each having its own valuation; two people can share an attitude while having different underlying beliefs.[37]

Proponents of the culture war thesis make *empirical* claims about the distribution and interrelationship of America's moral visions, religious beliefs, and social attitudes. For the most part, however, the debate about the culture war has been a war of words, not a war of evidence. As Paul DiMaggio, John Evans, and Bethany Bryson put it, "despite widespread claims and perceptions, little systematic research bears on ideological polarization per se."[38] Many claim the culture war exists and many claim it does not, but most have only eloquent arguments to back their claims. Since the middle 1990s, however, the culture war thesis has attracted the professional interests of empirically minded sociologists and political scientists.[39] Below I summarize the findings from several empirical tests of the culture war thesis, based on measurements of two of the three levels in the hierarchy—religious beliefs and social attitudes. To these studies I add unique data from the World Values Surveys about moral visions. These data permit the first complete empirical test of the polarization and linkage claims.

The Polarization of Americans

Is America a house divided? Several empirical studies of the polarization of social attitudes and religious beliefs in America provide compelling evidence of a general *lack* of polarization among Americans—at least at two of the three levels of the hierarchy of beliefs.[40] Based on analysis of over 20 years of data from the General Social Survey and the National Election Studies, DiMaggio, Evans, and Bryson conclude, "We find no support of the proposition that the United States has experienced dramatic polarization in public opinion on social issues since the 1970s."[41] They investigate the polarization claim by testing it over time in the American population as a whole and for particular subgroups. In the population as a whole, they find that attitudes about race, gender, crime, liberals and conservatives, and sexual morality have become *less* polarized over time; American's opinions about these matters are converging, not separating. The one exception was abortion, where they found some evidence of increasing polarization of attitudes.[42] In subsequent analyses focusing on abortion, John Evans found that the polarization of attitudes about this emotionally charged issue is related to religious traditions. For example, polarization has increased between evangelical Protestants and mainline Protestants.[43]

The attitudes held by members of various subgroups—voters, political activists, college graduates, and young people—have *not* become more polarized over time, compared with the attitudes of the general population. Indeed, DiMaggio, Evans, and Bryson found substantial evidence of *declining* polarization of attitudes by age, education, gender, race, religion, region, and ideology. Increasing polarization occurred only between Republicans versus Democrats, consistent with David King's observation that these two parties have become more extreme over time.[44]

Evans updated the analyses reported in the study by DiMaggio, Evans, and Bryson, adding new data from both the General Social Survey and the National Election Study.[45] These data extend the time series to the year 2000. Overall, Evans' results are the same: There is little evidence of polarization from the early 1970s to 2000. Indeed, with the longer time-series, he observes the continuation of the convergence of attitudes about race, gender issues, crime, and feelings about liberals and conservatives. Consistent with the previous study, the additional data reveal increasing polarization of attitudes about abortion.

In contrast, however, Evans also finds that attitudes about sexuality are becoming more polarized. Finally, the additional data strengthen DiMaggio, Evans, and Bryson's finding of increasing polarization in the political system.

While DiMaggio, Evans, and Bryson examined polarization at the bottom level of the hierarchy of beliefs (fig. 3.2), Nancy Davis and Robert Robinson examined the possibility of polarization at the middle level: American religious life. Using data from the 1991 General Social Survey, they constructed a scale of religious orthodoxy by combining three survey questions about God and the bible. Observing the locations of Americans on this scale, they find that Americans are not divided into two opposed moral camps based on religious beliefs. A key finding is reported in a simple histogram, which illustrates clearly that Americans are *not* divided into two large moral camps based on religious orthodoxy.[46] Rather, most Americans (64.8 percent) reside in the middle, with 21.9 percent at the "religious orthodox" pole and 13.3 percent at the "theological progressive" pole.[47] This clustering of Americans in the middle is particularly striking, given that the diversity of religions in the United States is greater than anywhere else in the world.[48] "Contrary to the 'culture war' metaphors popular in the political arena, the mass media, and academia," argue Davis and Robinson, "we found that most Americans occupy a middle ground between the extremes of religious orthodoxy and moral progressivism."[49]

There are many other ways to examine the question of polarization. My strategy is to build on earlier work by adding analyses of new data and new measures, rather than replicating previous research designs. Therefore, following the analysis in chapter 2, I examine the possibility of polarization along the traditional/secular-rational dimension of cultural variation, using data from World Values Surveys on the United States from 1981 to 2000. This dimension represents the constellations of values associated with absolutism and relativism as radial categories (fig. 3.1). (See tables 2.1–2.4 for the components of the traditional/secular-rational values dimension and the many additional items correlated with it.) An advantage of this measure is that it preserves the separation of levels in the hierarchy of beliefs (fig. 3.2) because it does not include a direct measure of absolutism and relativism. (As I discuss below, the World Values Surveys provide a separate and direct measure of moral visions.)

The traditional pole of this dimension represents the constellation of values associated with absolutism as a radial category, such as strong beliefs in the importance of God, Strict Father morality (e.g., it is more important for a child to learn obedience and religious faith than independence and determination), a strong sense of national pride, and prolife family values (e.g., abortion is never justifiable). The secular-rational pole represents the constellation of values associated with relativism as a radial category. This pole of the continuum emphasizes the opposite of traditional values, such as the absence of beliefs in the importance of God, Nurturant Parent morality (e.g., it is more important for a child to learn independence and determination than obedience and religious faith), a weak sense of national pride, and prochoice family values (e.g., abortion is always justifiable).

The empirical distribution of the traditional/secular-rational dimension does not exhibit polarization in any of the four waves of the World Values Surveys. Figure 3.3 shows that Americans are not divided into a bimodal distribution of traditionalists versus secular-rationalists in any year. Instead, there tends to be considerable consensus among Americans on the traditional/secular-rational dimension in each wave of the World Values Surveys. Moreover, Americans tend to cluster together toward the traditional pole of this dimension. (Comparisons with other societies in the World Values Surveys show that Americans are about one standard deviation below the average for all societies in a given year.) Statistical analysis supports these conclusions.[50]

The lack of polarization of traditional/secular-rational values is consistent with results from other investigations of the polarization claim. Almost all other empirical studies find a lack of polarization of religious beliefs or social attitudes.[51] This evidence, however, does not bear directly on the question of the polarization of moral visions, the top level of the hierarchy of beliefs. Few studies include direct measures of moral visions. An exception is the 1996 Survey of American Political Culture, conducted by the Post-Modernity Project at the University of Virginia.[52] This survey item tapped moral orienta-

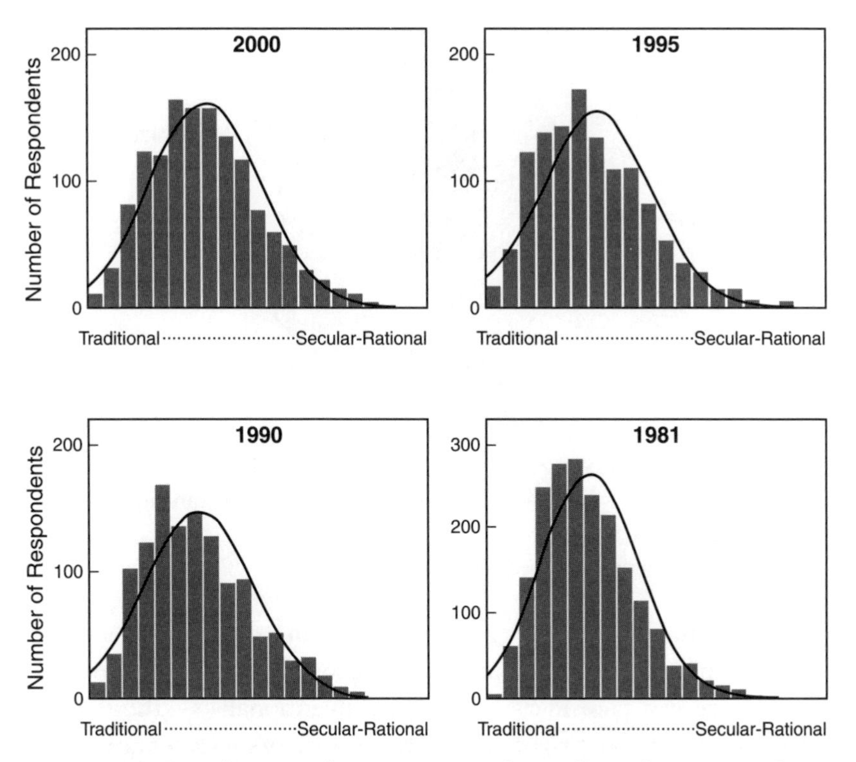

Figure 3.3. Distributions of Americans on the traditional versus secular-rational values dimension, 1981, 1990, 1995, and 2000.

Note: Height of bars in each histogram represents weighted number of cases. Solid line represents normal curve.

tion: "If you were unsure of what was right or wrong in a particular situation, how would you decide what to do?" Respondents chose from five answers: (1) Do what would make you happy (expressivists); (2) Do what would improve your situation (utilitarians); (3) Follow the advice of an authority, such as a parent, teacher, or youth leader (conventionalists); (4) Do what would be best for everyone involved (humanists); (5) Do what God or the scriptures tell you is right (theists). (The labels in parentheses are Hunter's.[53])

Theists are absolutists because they base decisions about right and wrong on a transcendental source of moral authority—God or the scriptures. About one of four Americans is theist, according to these data (see fig. 3.4).[54] Nonreligious sources of absolutism exist, as

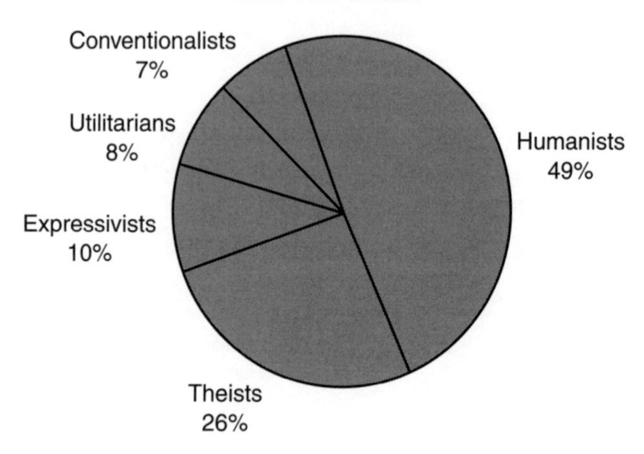

Figure 3.4. Responses of Americans to the question, If you were unsure of what was right or wrong, which would be the most important in deciding what to do?

Source: 1996 Survey of American Political Culture.

Marco Orrù observed. For example, Durkheim believed in society itself as a transcendental source of morals; for Plato, the transcendental source was pure ideas.[55] Hence, conventionalists—those who base decisions about right and wrong on society's representatives—use society itself as an absolute source of moral authority. Combined, theists and conventionalists make up 33 percent of the respondents to the 1996 Survey of American Political Culture.

Expressivists and utilitarians are relativists, because they base decisions about right and wrong on the self. Humanists are probably relativists, because doing what is best for everyone involved is a decision rule that appears to take the local situation into account. However, "for everyone involved" is ambiguous and could include society as a whole; if so, then some humanists base their decisions on society as an absolute source of moral authority. Together, expressivists, utilitarians, and humanists make up 67 percent of the sample, suggesting that two of three Americans are relativists. However, this is likely an overestimate and the actual proportion of relativists is lower, because some undetermined number of humanists relies on an absolute source of moral authority.

The World Values Surveys provide a direct measure of moral visions, allowing the claim of polarized moral visions to be explored at the appropriate level of analysis. Moral visions—beliefs about the ultimate source of moral authority—are indicated by responses to this question: "Here are two statements which people sometimes make when discussing good and evil. Which one comes closest to your own point of view? Statement A—There are absolutely clear guidelines about what is good and evil. These always apply to everyone, whatever the circumstances. Statement B—There can never be absolutely clear guidelines about what is good and evil. What is good and evil depends entirely upon the circumstances at the time." A respondent could (1) agree with statement A, (2) agree with statement B, or (3) disagree with both statements.[56] "Absolutists" are those who chose statement A, "relativists" are those who chose statement B, and "intermediates" disagreed with both statements.

The distribution of the moral visions of Americans at four points in time—1981, 1990, 1995, and 2000—is displayed in figure 3.5. In 1981 Americans' views of moral authority were more relativistic than absolutistic, 60 percent versus 37 percent. Few took the middle position (about 3 percent). By 1990, however, the distribution had shifted toward absolutism, producing an almost even division of the American population into moral absolutists and moral relativists. From 1981 to 1990 the proportion of absolutists grew from 37 to 50 percent, and the proportion of relativists declined from 60 to 45 percent. The change is statistically significant ($p < .001$). This polarized distribution remained about the same through the 1995 and 2000 surveys. Overall, there appears to be an upward trend since 1981 in the proportion of absolutists in America, as shown by the linear regression line in figure 3.5, but most of this change occurred between 1981 and 1990.

Other sources of data support these findings from the World Values Surveys. For example, I found a similar pattern in my 2003 Detroit Area Study: fifty-one percent are absolutists (agree with statement A) and 45 percent are relativists (agree with statement B). Less than 4 percent disagree with both statements. Alan Wolfe reports a roughly 50:50 split in his Middle Class Morality Project, based on intensive interviews with two hundred Americans. In his follow-up survey to the

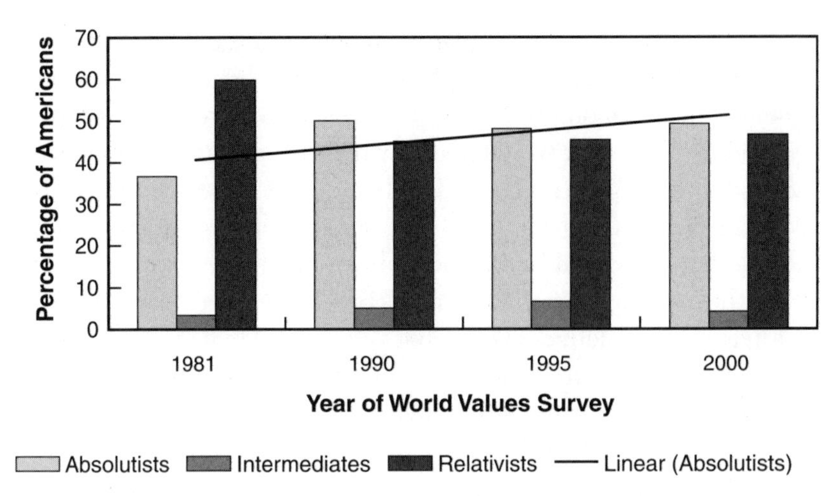

Figure 3.5. Distribution of the moral visions of Americans, by year.
Source: World Values Surveys 1981, 1990, 1995, and 2000.

interviews, he asked a question designed to correspond to the question in the World Values Surveys about moral visions: "To what extent do you agree or disagree with the following statement? America has become far too atheistic and needs a return to strong religious belief." He received nearly the same distribution of responses—almost a 50:50 split.[57] Fifty percent strongly agreed or agreed with the statement; 40 percent disagreed or strongly disagreed; only 10 percent fell in the middle. Wolfe concludes: "Results such as those [obtained in the World Values Survey] were confirmed in our survey, taken after we completed our more in-depth interviews, with each of the people with whom we spoke; half of them, the same percentage as [the World Values Surveys'] believers in absolute moral authority, agreed or strongly agreed with the statement that America has become too atheistic."[58]

Cross-cultural comparisons of the ratio of absolutists to relativists demonstrate once again just how different America's value system is from most of the world. Consider, for example, figure 3.6, which shows the distribution of the ratios of absolutists to relativists in the various societies included in the 1995–1998 World Values Surveys. Societies are ranked by ratio, high to low, so that societies with many absolutists and few relativists are on the left, and societies with few absolutists and many relativists are on the right. Ghana has the highest ratio, almost three absolutists for every relativist (ratio = 2.91 to 1). Ghana's nearest neighbors in figure 3.6 are South Africa, Romania, Georgia, the Philippines, and Nigeria. Most economically developed and historically Protestant societies are located at the other end. The two extremes, based on the 1995–1998 surveys, are the East and West German regions (ratios = 0.18 to 1 and 0.22 to 1, respectively). America has the eleventh highest ratio, with one absolutist for every relativist (ratio = 1.09 to 1). This ratio places the nation closer to poor and developing societies than to most other economically developed, historically Protestant societies (fig. 3.6).

Most societies, in contrast to the United States, have fewer absolutists than relativists. Consider table 3.1, which presents the distribution of moral visions for seventy-nine nations, using the latest data from the four waves of the World Values Surveys. As shown, fifty-seven nations have fewer absolutists than relativists. Nineteen have less than 30 percent absolutists and more than 65 percent relativists. Each of the extremes—Hungary, Sweden, Denmark, and Iceland—has less than 16 percent absolutists and more than 75 percent relativists. Thus, the equal distribution of moral visions in America—one absolutist for every relativist—is one way that the nation is different from most of the world. A second way America is different is that it has one of the highest percentages of absolutists in the world (table 3.1). Only seventeen nations have a greater proportion of absolutists than the United States. All of these societies, such as Morocco, Tanzania, Vietnam, Azerbaijan, Bosnia, and Brazil, are low-income or developing societies, and many suffer from political turmoil and ethnic-racial conflict. As discussed in chapter 2, these conditions almost always produce and reinforce moral absolutism and traditional values. Thus, a third way America is different is that the cause of America's absolutism is different from the causes of absolutism in other societies (see chapter 2). Finally, most other economically developed, historically Protestant countries are much more relativistic than America. Northern Ireland is close to the United States, with 47 percent absolutists and 48 percent relativists (table 3.1), but most have far fewer absolutists and far more relativists

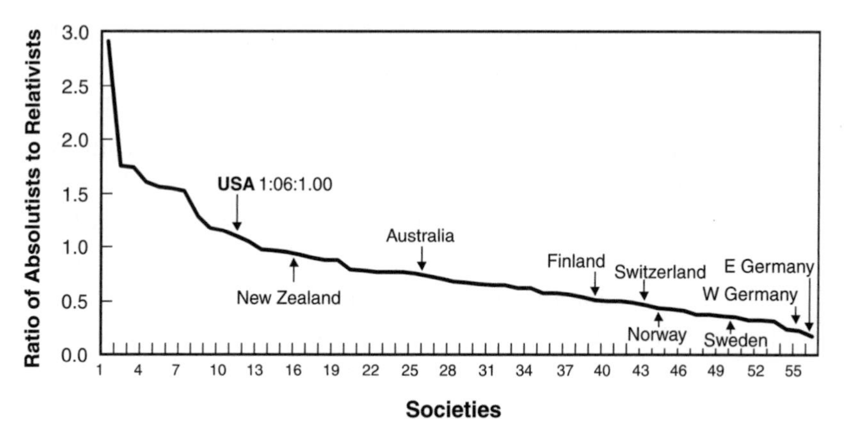

Figure 3.6. Distribution of the ratio of absolutists to relativists in various societies.

Source: World Values Surveys 1995–1998.

than the United States. Thus, the fourth way America is different is that its moral absolutism makes it an outlier among those societies with which it shares the same cultural heritage.

Because I use a single, essentially dichotomous survey item to investigate the polarization claim at the level of moral visions, it is important to address concerns about validity and reliability. There are several justifications for using this measure; taken together, I believe they make a compelling case for using this survey item. Overall, the World Values Surveys measure of moral visions has solid content validity. It focuses directly on the top level of the hierarchy of beliefs (fig. 3.2), and it does not mix religious beliefs (or social attitudes) with moral visions. This measure clearly distinguishes between the two fundamental views of moral authority, absolutism and relativism, but does not restrict consideration to a *specific* source of moral authority (such as God, society, or the self).[59]

More evidence of the validity of this survey item is the host of additional items that are significantly correlated with it ($p < .01$) in theoretically sensible and expected ways. For example, absolutists are more likely than relativists to believe in God, life after death, hell, and heaven; to say that they are religious, that God is important in their lives, and to find comfort in religion; to attend church regularly and to pray; to have confidence in the church and to feel that the church answers questions about moral problems, family life, and social problems, and addresses spiritual needs. (In addition, look ahead to tables 3.3–3.11 to examine the correlations of moral visions with the two cultural dimensions, economic ethics, family/life values, attitudes about the separation of church and state, and social capital.)

Analysts typically resolve the issue of measurement reliability by combining multiple items into a single scale. As I discussed above, Davis and Robinson, for example, constructed a scale of religious orthodoxy by adding together three survey items about religious beliefs.[60] I would prefer, of course, a battery of items on moral visions that could be combined into a single scale. Since such a battery does not exist in the World Values Surveys, the only alternative would be to construct a multiple-item measure of moral authority by combining the absolutism-relativism measure with religious measures or social attitude measures (such as those mentioned in the preceding paragraph). Doing so, however, would confound the various levels of the hierarchy of beliefs, causing the very problems I wish to avoid. It is possible to assess test-retest reliability, using the multiwave design of the World Values Surveys to measure stability over multiple measurements. For example, the correlation of the ratios of absolutists to relativists in the nations included in both the 1981 and 1990 waves is almost perfect ($r = .92$), indicating that the ratios of absolutists to relativists remained stable over this ten-year period in most of the world (coefficient of reliability = .960).[61] (The United States is excluded from the analysis of test-retest reliability.)

It is possible that the essentially dichotomous nature of this measure could create a false appearance of polarization. Jay Demerath and Yonghe Yang, for example, criticize the use of any dichotomous measure because "it is virtually guaranteed to generate polarization when the respondents are asked to identify with one of two opposing ideological positions."[62] Their concern is valid in general, but their guarantee of polarization is not ironclad. Polarized responses would appear as a more or less even split, 50 percent absolutists and 50 percent relativists. This survey question *rarely* generated polarized responses in the four waves of the World Values Surveys. In the 1981–

1982 wave, for example, 25 percent of all respondents were absolutists and 62 percent were relativists; only one society came close to the 50:50 split.[63] Similarly, in the 1995–1998 wave, 35 percent of all respondents were absolutists and 56 percent were relativists. Only ten of sixty-five societies in this wave exhibited polarized responses, one of which was the United States. Finally, analyzing the latest data for all nations included in the four waves of the World Values Surveys (table 3.1) shows that 40 percent of all respondents were absolutists and 55 percent were relativists. Only fifteen of seventy-nine nations exhibited a polarized pattern. Polarized responses are possible with a dichotomous variable, of course, but the question about moral visions is seldom associated with a polarized pattern in the World Values Surveys.[64]

The final—and in some ways most important—justification for this measure is theoretical. This dichotomous survey item was designed purposely to tap a binary model of thinking about moral authority. Every culture develops beliefs about good and evil as its members grapple with the basic problems of human nature, relationships among people, and the relationship between this world and the transcendental world.[65] As I described above in this chapter and elaborate in the next, these beliefs are commonly expressed in a dual conceptual system: transcendental versus mundane moral authority. Indeed, a theologian who was on the original World Values Surveys design team proposed this dichotomous survey item to capture this dual conceptual system.[66] And it is this dual system that is the basis of the culture war argument: a struggle between two competing camps—moral absolutists versus moral relativists.[67] Thus, this survey measure captures the culture war argument in its own terms.

Are Americans polarized? Is the polarization claim of the culture war thesis correct? The research conducted by others and reviewed above shows that Americans' social attitudes and religious beliefs are *not* polarized. Rather, Americans have a lot in common: Americans have similar attitudes about social issues and policies and similar beliefs about religion. Further, most social attitudes are *converging* over time. Not only do Americans have a lot in common, but also their attitudes and beliefs are becoming more alike as time passes. Even Americans' attitudes about homosexuality have become less conservative and more liberal over time.[68] Consistent with the findings of these studies, my analysis of traditional/secular-rational values does not reveal evidence of polarization. Instead, Americans tend to cluster together toward the traditional pole in each of the four waves of the World Values Surveys. Thus, the polarization claim appears to be incorrect at both the bottom and middle levels of the hierarchy of beliefs (fig. 3.2).

At the top level of the hierarchy, however, there is some evidence of polarization. In 1981 there were three relativists for every two absolutists. By 1990 Americans were divided almost evenly into absolutists and relativists. This is a significant change over time. The even split persisted in the 1995 and 2000 surveys. The rarity of this even split of moral visions becomes apparent when we compare the United States with large numbers of other societies. Few societies are as absolutistic as America; few societies have equal numbers of absolutists and relativists. This evidence suggests that Americans may be polarized at the top level of the hierarchy of beliefs. This conclusion must be tempered, however, with knowledge of the possible limitations of using a single dichotomous question about moral visions. And yet it is instructive to note how uniquely Americans respond to a question about good and evil. Every society must grapple with questions about good and evil.[69] When asked to make a choice between two opposing moral positions about good and evil, most people around the world choose a relativistic position. This is especially true for the peoples of rich and historically Protestant societies. Half of all Americans, however, choose absolutism, while the other half choose relativism. Even if Americans' moral visions are not polarized per se, there is decided tendency for Americans to take opposing moral positions. Given the opportunity to choose between two moral opposites, Americans are willing to take sides.

Linkage of the Hierarchy of Beliefs

Culture war advocates claim that social attitudes, religious beliefs, and moral visions are tightly coupled. This is the second of two culture war claims. If true, it means that people base their values and social attitudes on their moral visions; there is, as cognitive linguists put it, "coherence" in their conceptual systems. Prior research has established the link between social attitudes and religious beliefs; knowing a person's religious beliefs and practices lets you predict the person's attitudes about social issues and policies. For example, Davis and Robinson find that the religiously orthodox tend to hold conservative views about sexuality, reproductive rights, and the gendered division of labor.[70] Prior research has not explored the link between moral visions and social attitudes, however, or the link between religious beliefs and social attitudes while controlling for moral visions. Using data from four waves of the World Values Surveys, I explore the connections among all three levels of the hierarchy of beliefs. First, I examine the link between the middle and top levels by predicting moral visions as a function of the two dimensions of cultural variation, controlling for various sociodemographic variables. Second, I consider the link between all three levels by predicting various social attitudes as a function of moral visions and the two dimensions, controlling for the same sociodemographics. These two steps provide the most complete analysis of the linkage claim to date.

As we saw in chapter 2, America is a religious society. It is, Lipset concludes, "the most religious country in Christendom."[71] Do the religious beliefs of absolutists and relativists differ? In theory, they should. Absolutists believe in a transcendental source of morals and moral judgment. This transcendental source is almost always assumed to be God (religion). But, as noted above, nonreligious sources of absolutism exist, such as society or pure ideas. Relativists, in contrast, reject the idea of a transcendental source of moral authority and instead locate the source in the self or local situation. Therefore, relativists should hold weak religious beliefs or be atheists.

The religious beliefs of absolutists and relativists differ, but not always as much as one might expect (see table 3.2). For example, almost 100 percent of absolutists believe in God and almost as many believe in the soul, but generally 90 percent or more of relativists in each year also share these beliefs. Bigger differences between absolutists and relativists appear when we consider other religious beliefs:

beliefs in heaven, life after death, and hell. A large majority of absolutists hold these beliefs; fewer relativists share these beliefs, with the largest differences—at least 20 percentage points—occurring for belief in hell. Even so, at least two-thirds of relativists believe in heaven and life after death, and the majority of relativists also believe in hell. Surprisingly few relativists claim to be atheists (for example, only 1 percent in 1995 and 1.5 percent in 1990).

These simple statistics suggest that the middle and top levels of the hierarchy of beliefs are coupled, but not tightly—absolutists and relativists differ in their views about moral authority, but they share many religious beliefs. This conclusion is supported by the results of a more sophisticated statistical analysis. The chief findings show a significant link between moral visions and religious beliefs. [72] For example, the more important God is in an American's life, the more likely the person is an absolutist. The more religious beliefs an American holds—beliefs in God, the soul, sin, heaven, life after death, hell, and the devil—the more likely the person is an absolutist. The more often an American attends religious services, the more likely he or she is an absolutist. And Protestants are more likely than Catholics to be absolutists. Thus, moral visions and religious beliefs are correlated, as proponents of the culture war thesis have argued but have not measured directly.

To build on the analysis of America's values in global context (chapter 2), I focus on the possible link between moral visions and the two dimensions of cultural variation: traditional versus secular-rational values and survival versus self-expression values. The first dimension represents the religious-moral content of the middle level of the hierarchy of beliefs (fig. 3.2). This dimension captures the constellation of religious and moral values that, according to theory, revolve around the radial categories of absolutism and relativism (fig. 3.1). This dimension does not measure moral visions per se. As such, it preserves the critical distinction between the top and middle levels of the hierarchy of beliefs and permits an analysis of the linkage of the two.

The second dimension of cultural variation does not represent the middle level of the hierarchy—at least as culture war advocates conceive of this level—but including this dimension in the analysis adds a new way to think about links between moral visions and cultural values. "Culture" has many meanings and varieties, as Paul DiMaggio describes.[73] This second dimension captures "culture" as goals and orientations. Self-expression (or survival, its opposite) is a goal that one is oriented to pursue. In contrast, the first dimension—traditional versus secular-rational values—captures what DiMaggio calls the "regulatory" forms of culture, such as norms and conventions, which shape, constrain, and guide behavior. For example, religion prescribes some behaviors and proscribes others. Similarly, family values prescribe and proscribe certain behaviors.

In sum, the combination of the two cultural dimensions establishes destination and journey—goals and the proper routes to them. Consider, for example, Weber's concept of an "economic ethic." As Richard Swedberg summarizes, the economic ethic of a religion (or society) "implies specific evaluative attitudes (or norms)" toward work, occupation, wealth, possessions, trade, finance, and so on.[74] A person who wishes to pursue "self-expression" through work *and* conform to the norms of a religion must choose among occupations that are approved of by the religion, even if the person would experience more self-fulfillment and self-expression in occupations that are disapproved of. Of course, one may deviate from mainstream goals and prescribed routes, and so there is variation along both dimensions among the people of a nation, as we see in this chapter. Further, the two dimensions may be in conflict, specifying contradictory goals and regulations.[75] (I take up the idea of "cultural contradictions" in later chapters.)

Both cultural dimensions are significantly associated with moral visions, controlling for a variety of sociodemographic factors (see table 3.3). Americans who hold traditional values are more likely to be absolutists, while those who hold secular-rational values are more likely to be relativists. Recall from chapter 2 that the traditional/secular-rational dimension captures the importance of religion. Hence, this finding shows that moral visions (the top level of the hierarchy of beliefs) are linked to religious values (the middle level). Survival-oriented Americans are more likely to be absolutists, while those who are oriented toward self-realization are less likely. Americans who hold both traditional and survival values are the most likely to be absolutists; those who hold both secular-rational and self-realization values are the least likely. These findings lend support to the claim of linkage between the top and middle levels of the hierarchy of beliefs.

Are social attitudes related to moral visions and the two cultural dimensions? That is, are all three levels of the hierarchy of beliefs linked? To test the complete linkage claim, I constructed two social attitude scales using variables included in all four waves of the World Values Surveys.[76] An economic ethics scale indicates the extent to which the following acts can be justified: claiming government benefits to which one was not entitled, avoiding a fare on public transportation, cheating on taxes if one has the chance, and accepting a bribe in the course of one's duties. (I call this an "economic ethics" scale because it involves ethical decisions about property and money.) A high score indicates the opinion that these economic acts can be justified; a low score indicates they cannot. The family/life values scale indicates the extent to which prostitution, divorce, euthanasia, and suicide can be justified. (I call this a "family/life values" scale because, from a traditionalist's point of view, prostitution and divorce threaten the integrity of the intact family, while euthanasia and suicide violate the sanctity of life.) A high score indicates the opinion that these acts can be justified; a low score indicates they cannot.

These scales exhibit high to acceptable levels of reliability in each year of the World Values Surveys, based on Cronbach's reliability measure (see table 3.4).[77] This measure also indicates the internal consistency of opinion domains, as DiMaggio, Evans, and Bryson show.[78] As discussed above, cognitive linguists think of consistency as the "coherence" of a radial category. An opinion domain is internally consistent or coherent if respondents tend to report similar answers to the various questions that make up the opinion domain. Contrary to the argument that relativism is not a coherent ethical system, table 3.4 shows that relativists are at least as consistent as absolutists and sometimes even more.[79] Moreover, the internal consistency of the two scales for absolutists and relativists is quite stable between 1981 and 2000.

Theoretically, moral visions can have direct and indirect effects on social attitudes. A direct effect is the unmediated relationship between moral visions and social attitudes, controlling for the two cultural dimensions. An indirect effect is the relationship between moral visions and social attitudes mediated by the cultural dimensions. These possible effects are illustrated in figure 3.7. The horizontal arrow from moral visions to social attitudes shows that the measure of moral visions is expected to have a *negative* direct effect on social attitudes—absolutists believe that the acts in these two scales cannot be justified, while relativists believe that they can. The two arrows from moral visions to the cultural dimensions indicate the *negative* relationships established in the analysis above. As shown in table 3.3, absolutists are less secular-rational (more traditional) than relativists, and they also are more survival oriented (less self-expression oriented) than relativists. The arrows from the cultural dimensions to social attitudes indicate that these dimensions are expected to have *positive* effects on social attitudes: Those who are secular-rational feel that the acts in these scales can be justified, while those who are traditional feel they cannot; those who are self-expression oriented believe these acts can be justified, while those who are survival oriented believe they cannot. Finally, the combined arrows from moral visions to the cultural dimensions and from these dimensions to social attitudes indicate the *indirect* effects of moral visions on social attitudes: Absolutists are more traditional, and those who are more traditional feel that the acts in these attitude scales cannot be justified; similarly, absolutists are more survival oriented, and those who hold these values believe that such acts cannot be justified. Altogether, the *total* effect of moral visions on social attitudes is the sum of the direct and indirect effects.

Attitudes about family/life values clearly follow the pattern in figure 3.7. As shown in tables 3.5 and 3.6, moral visions have a significant direct effect on these social attitudes in each of the four waves of the World Values Surveys: Absolutists tend to feel that prostitution, divorce, euthanasia, and suicide cannot be justified, while rel-

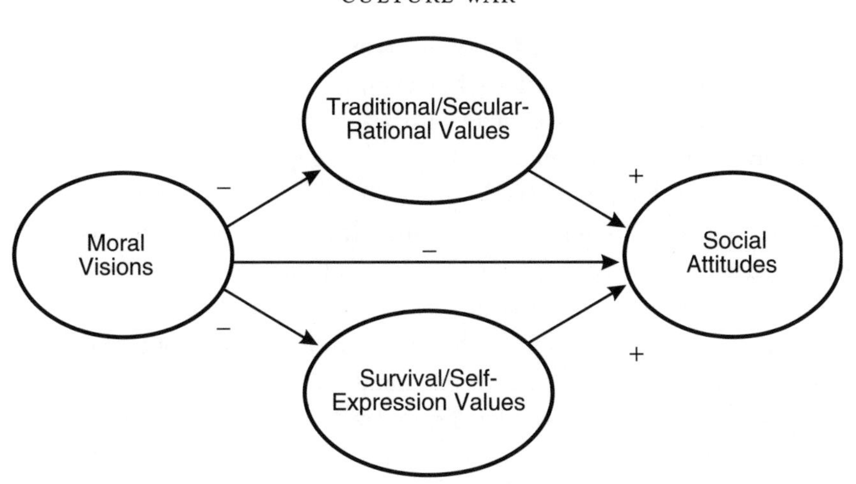

Figure 3.7. Illustration of direct and indirect effects of moral visions on social attitudes.

ativists tend to feel they can. Each of the two cultural dimensions has a positive effect on family/life values in each of the four waves: Those who are secular-rational feel that these acts can be justified; those who are self-expression oriented feel the same way. In contrast, those who hold traditional values feel that these acts cannot be justified; and those who are survival-oriented feel the same way. In total, moral visions have significant direct and indirect effects on attitudes about family/life values (look ahead to table 3.12 for a summary). These effects are quite strong. They do not change much when eight sociodemographic variables are added to the analysis (tables 3.5 and 3.6). Taken together, moral visions, traditional/secular-rational values, and survival/self-expression values explain at least 40 percent of the variation in attitudes about family/life values each year.

Economic ethics are more complicated. As expected, moral visions have a negative direct effect on economic ethics in most years, meaning that absolutists tend to feel that falsely claiming government benefits, avoiding fares, cheating on taxes, and accepting bribes cannot be justified while relativists feel they can. Also as expected, the traditional/secular-rational dimension has a positive effect on these social attitudes—those who are secular-rational feel these economic acts can be justified; those who are traditional feel they cannot. Contrary to expectations, however, the survival/self-expression dimension has a *negative* effect on these social attitudes. Upon reflection, this negative effect makes sense. People whose goal is basic survival would naturally (perhaps necessarily) see these acts as justifiable. Those who are pursuing self-realization have the luxury of considering these economic acts to be unjustifiable.

Because the two cultural dimensions have opposite effects on economic ethics, they tend to wash out the indirect effects of moral visions on these attitudes. On the one hand, the indirect effect of moral visions via traditional/secular-rational values *increases* the total effect of moral visions on economic ethics. On the other hand, the indirect effect via survival/self-expression values *decreases* the total effect of moral visions on these social attitudes (look ahead to table 3.12 for a summary). Overall, the combined impact of moral visions and the two cultural dimensions on economic ethics is small, explaining at most an unimpressive 5 percent of the variation in these social attitudes. The sociodemographic variables explain much more. For example, those who are older, white, female, married, and more educated tend to feel that falsely claiming government benefits, avoiding fares, cheating on taxes, and accepting bribes cannot be justified.

The 2000 World Values Surveys include a new set of measures that permit further exploration of the linkage claim. These items gauge attitudes about the separation of church and state. The nation's founders believed in the separation of these institutions, as I described in chapter 2, and this principle is enshrined in the First Amendment of the U.S. Constitution. Separation of church and state is a contentious issue today, pitting the Religious Right against moral progressives and civil libertarians in debate and litigation about prayer in school, public vouchers to support religious schools, religious symbols in public buildings and places, and so forth. With such prominence in the culture war, attitudes about the separation of church and state should be significantly related to moral visions and the two cultural dimensions.

Absolutists, who locate moral authority in God and believe in universal moral rules, should favor less separation. Relativists, who locate moral authority in the self and believe in circumstantial moral codes, should favor more separation. Given the religious content of the traditional/secular-rational dimension, these values should be closely related to attitudes about the separation of church and state: Those who are closer to the traditional pole should favor less separation, while those closer to the opposite pole should favor more. Those who are self-expression oriented should favor more separation if they interpret it to mean fewer constraints on freedom of expression. Those who are survival oriented should favor less separation if they interpret it to mean greater economic and physical security.

The results support these expectations (see table 3.7). For example, absolutists believe that "it would be better for America if more people with strong religious beliefs held public office" and "politicians who do not believe in God are unfit for public office." Absolutists disagree with the arguments that "religious leaders should not influence how people vote in elections" and "religious leaders should not influence government decisions." Those who hold traditional values express the same views, favoring less separation of church and state, while those with secular-rational values express the opposite views. Those who are survival oriented favor less church-separation, while those who are self-expression oriented favor more separation. Moral visions have both direct and indirect effects on attitudes about church-state separation: Absolutists favor closer ties between religion and politics; absolutists hold traditional values, and those with these values also favor closer ties; and, absolutists are survival-oriented, and those with this orientation also favor closer ties between church and state. Note, however, that the indirect effect of moral visions via the two cultural dimensions is stronger through the traditional/secular-rational dimension than it is through the other dimension (look ahead to table 3.13 for a summary of these effects).

The analyses of the linkage between moral visions and economic ethics, family/life values, and opinions about church-state separation are the first to observe and measure the actual links between moral visions and social attitudes. As discussed above, previous analyses have used religious beliefs as a proxy for moral visions. The findings here demonstrate that moral visions have direct effects on social attitudes as well as indirect effects via the two cultural dimensions. As advocates of the culture war thesis have long argued but have not measured, Americans do tend to use their beliefs about moral authority as a basis of making judgments about social issues and policies. The evidence supports the linkage claim of significant coupling of the three levels of the hierarchy of beliefs. But does it support the claim of tight or loose coupling? Here, the evidence is mixed. The strongest link occurs between moral visions and family/life values; the weakest link occurs between moral visions and economic ethics. The strength of the link between moral visions and attitudes about the separation of church and state falls between these two, but closer to family/life values.[80] I conclude that moral visions and social attitudes are coupled, but the relationships are not strong enough or consistent enough to support the claim of tight coupling. First, the amount of variation in family/life values that is explained by moral visions and the two cultural dimensions is quite good, compared with the results reported in other analyses of social attitudes,[81] but most of the variance is still left unexplained. The same is true for attitudes about church-state separation. Second, the amount of variation explained varies considerably within and across opinion domains. Overall, the evidence does not support the claim of tight coupling.[82] There is a link between moral visions and social attitudes, but it is a loose link.

To this point we have examined the American culture war thesis on its own terms—a crisis of values. Advocates of this thesis make two claims. First, they claim that Americans have become deeply divided, separated into two opposed camps based on irreconcilable differences in beliefs about moral authority. Second, they claim that these moral visions are tightly linked to religious beliefs and social attitudes. The evidence does not support the first claim. The social attitudes, moral values, and religious beliefs of Americans are not polarized; in fact, most Americans share similar attitudes, values, and beliefs. The moral visions of Americans have exhibited a tendency to become polarized over time, creating equal numbers of absolutists and relativists by the year 2000, but this is only a *tendency*—it is not the basis of two morally opposed camps. After all, American absolutists and relativists have a lot in common. Most absolutists and most relativists profess strong religious beliefs; many absolutists and relativists share similar attitudes about social issues and policies. The evidence offers support of the linkage claim, but only its weak version: moral visions are significantly but only loosely linked to social attitudes.

The final exploration of the culture war thesis goes beyond its definition of crisis as a polarized distribution of moral visions, religious-cultural values, and social attitudes. We now turn to examine the connection between moral visions and social capital—interpersonal trust, confidence in the nation's institutions, participation in voluntary organizations, church attendance, and political action. This analysis considers the possibility that absolutists and relativists have different *sources* and *forms* of social capital. For example, do the holders of one moral vision trust people more and institutions less? Do holders of the other moral vision trust people less and institutions more? Do absolutists and relativists belong to different voluntary organizations? Do they both engage in political action? By addressing these questions, we can evaluate the extent to which differences in moral visions are connected to real social structures. Some sociologists argue, for example, that differences in moral visions are meaningful only if they motivate behavior and are connected to actual groups and organizations—what Peter Berger calls a "plausibility structure."[83] As we shall see, moral visions do have a concrete plausibility structure.

The Connection between Social Capital and Moral Visions

There are two sides to community, as discussed in chapter 1. One side is community as a set of shared moral values; the other side is community as a social network of affect-laden relationships among people.[84] The preceding analysis considered the first side. Here, we turn to the second side, considering what is commonly known as "social capital." There are many definitions of social capital.[85] For example, Robert Putnam defines social capital as social and civic engagement, political participation, trust, and confidence. These, he says, are the forms of social capital that America is losing: Americans are becoming more distrustful, losing confidence in the nation's institutions, voting less often, participating in fewer voluntary associations, socializing less often, and even bowling alone rather than in leagues.[86] Putnam's "bowling alone" metaphor and warnings of decline have captured popular, media, and academic attention. His thesis and evidence have been called into question,[87] but most of his critics concede that he has a valid point.[88]

Previous analyses, such as Putnam's, focus on measures of the decline of social capital over time. My focus, in contrast, is the possible connection between moral visions and the sources and forms of social capital. In the process of analysis, however, we shall examine data that bear on the question of decline over time for the American population as a whole, as well as for the subpopulations of absolutists and relativists.

Trust and confidence in institutions may seem like nebulous ideas. Yet trust and confidence are necessary to enter into business contracts, put money in the bank, make investments, pay taxes, adhere to laws and regulations, get an education, take jobs, commit to relationships, plan families, and make long-term life plans. Confidence and interpersonal trust are essential for democracy, and for building large-scale complex organizations.[89]

In 1981, 47 percent of Americans said, "Most people can be trusted." This increased slightly to 50 percent in 1990 and fell to only 36 percent in 1995 and 2000.[90] This generally downward trend mirrors the findings of other opinion polls, such as the National Election Studies and General Social Survey.[91] In general, levels of interpersonal trust do not differ by moral visions, as shown in figure 3.8. In 1981 relativists were slightly more trusting of others ($p < .05$), but the difference is small and disappears after that. For the most part, absolutists and relativists are equally trusting of others, and their levels of trust rise and fall together.

What about confidence in the nation's institutions? The four

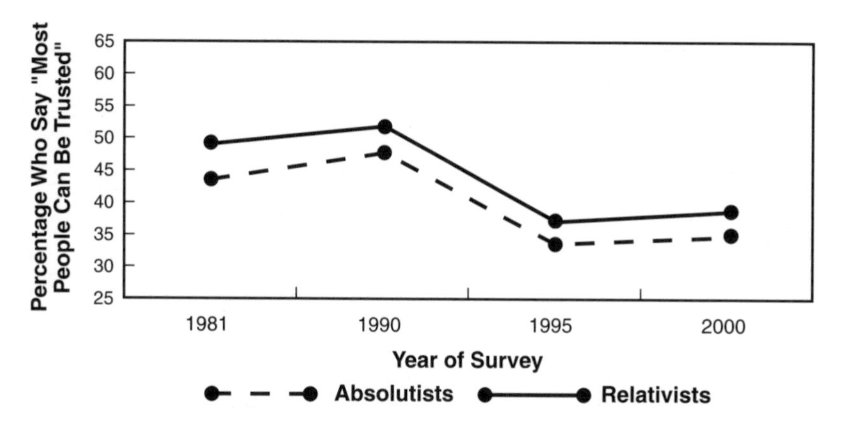

Figure 3.8. Percentage of Americans who say "most people can be trusted," by moral visions, by year.

Source: World Values Surveys 1981, 1990, 1995, and 2000.

waves of the World Values Surveys consistently measured confidence in seven institutions: the church, armed forces, press, labor unions, police, civil service, and major companies. Confidence in these seven institutions exhibits an overall downward trend, consistent with the findings of other studies. Along with declining interpersonal trust, the downward trend in confidence is interpreted as one of the main indicators of America's crisis of values, as I discussed in chapter 1. Unlike interpersonal trust, however, confidence varies considerably by moral visions (see fig. 3.9). In 1981 absolutists had a "great deal" of confidence in an average of 1.8 of these seven institutions; relativists had a great deal of confidence in an average of 1.4 ($p < .001$). Confidence fell nine years later for both groups, but absolutists still had a great deal of confidence in significantly more institutions than did relativists. Tables 3.8 and 3.9 show that the effect of moral visions on confidence is mainly indirect, mediated by the two cultural dimensions (see table 3.12 for a summary of effects). Confidence continued to erode for absolutists, so that by 1995 and again in 2000, there were small differences between absolutists and relativists in the average number of institutions in which they had a great deal of confidence (see tables 3.10–3.11).

More differences appear when we delve beneath the number of in-

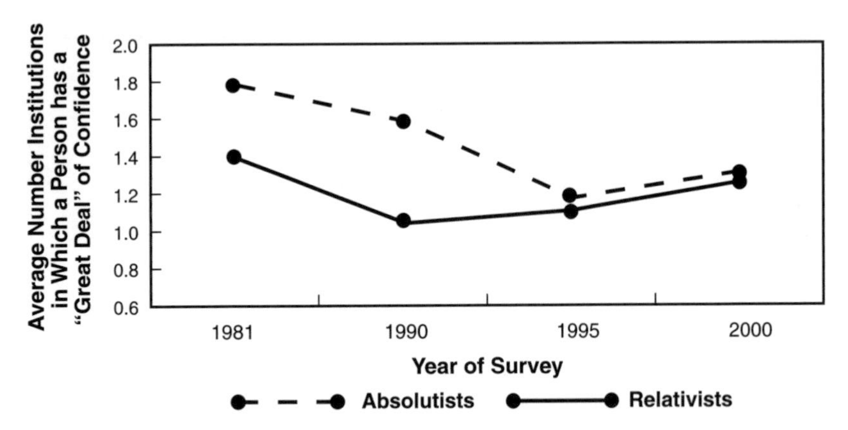

Figure 3.9. Average number of seven institutions in which Americans have a "great deal" of confidence, by moral visions, by year.
Source: World Values Surveys 1981, 1990, 1995, and 2000.

stitutions in which absolutists and relativists have confidence to examine confidence in individual institutions. For example, in 1981 and 1990, absolutists had significantly more confidence in the armed forces than relativists did, though the two groups had about the same confidence in the military by 1995. From 1981 to 1995, absolutists had significantly more confidence in the civil service than relativists did. Most important, absolutists *always* have significantly more confidence in the church than relativists do. This difference is true in each year of the survey, and it is the only remaining difference between absolutists and relativists by 2000. Steadfast confidence in the church is consistent with the absolutist's beliefs about the location of moral authority: Because absolutists believe in the transcendental moral authority of God and religion, they are more likely than relativists to have confidence in religious institutions.

The final tests of the connection between moral visions and social capital examine civic engagement, namely, involvement in voluntary organizations (especially religious organizations) and political action. Observers of American society since Alexis de Tocqueville have remarked upon the American propensity to create and join voluntary groups, organizations, and associations.[92] Some say that this propensity is unique to America, but an analysis of data on thirty-three nations in the 1990–1993 World Values Surveys finds that America's high voluntarism rates are sometimes matched and even surpassed by a few other nations, such as Canada, the Netherlands, and some Nordic countries.[93] Nonetheless, America always ranks the highest when it comes to membership in churches and religious organizations.[94]

Putnam claims that Americans are losing their propensity to join voluntary organizations. He reports declines over time of memberships in a variety of voluntary organizations, such as the Parent-Teacher Association (PTA), church groups, unions, and fraternal and veterans organizations.[95] Lipset, however, notes contradictory trends; according to some polls, "the proportion of people indicating that they have volunteered for charitable, 'social service,' or 'non-profit' organizations has doubled between 1977 and the 1990s."[96] Wolfe argues that middle-class Americans are still joiners; those he interviewed did report a vague sense of declining community involvement around them, but 75 percent of his two hundred interviewees belonged to one or more civic organizations.[97] The appearance of declining social capital, Wolfe argues, may be caused by a shift in the type of organization middle-class Americans now join—from *community* to *workplace* organizations. "To the degree that we look at the place in which people live for evidence of the decline of social capital rather than where they work," Wolfe says, "we may be looking in the wrong place."[98]

The four waves of the World Values Surveys consistently measured involvement in six types of voluntary organizations: religious or church group; sport or recreation organization; art, music, or educational organization; political party; environmental organization; and professional association.[99] These survey items capture participation in different types of voluntary organizations, not the actual number of memberships. For example, a person's membership in, say, two professional associations would be counted as involvement in only one type of voluntary organization, a "professional organization."

Generally, Americans have become more involved over time. In 1981, on average, Americans belonged to 1.3 voluntary organizations. This figure tripled by 1995.[100] In 1995, Americans belonged

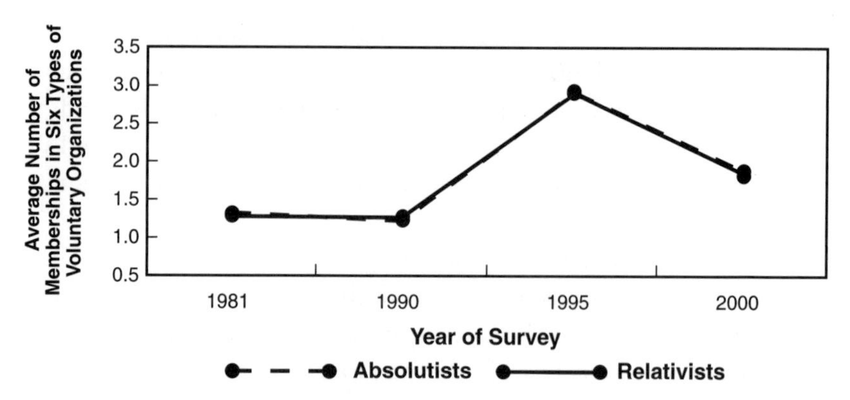

Figure 3.10. Average number of six types of voluntary organizations to which Americans belong, by moral visions, by year.
Source: World Values Surveys 1981, 1990, 1995, and 2000.

to an average of 2.9 types of voluntary organizations per person. Voluntarism fell between 1995 and 2000, but the level in 2000 is still higher than the levels in 1990 or 1981. Absolutists and relativists are equally involved, on average, over the two decades covered by the World Values Surveys (see fig. 3.10). There are no statistically significant differences between absolutists and relativists in any year except 1981 (see tables 3.8–3.12). There are, however, significant and strong differences if we examine only membership in religious or church organizations, one of the six types included in figure 3.10. As shown in figure 3.11, a higher percentage of absolutists than relativists belong to a religious or church organization in every year.

The data in figures 3.10 and 3.11 obscure an important difference between absolutists and relativists in 1981. In 1981, relativists outnumbered absolutists three to two (fig. 3.5). Hence, the sheer volume of voluntary organizations in which relativists were involved in 1981 surpassed the volume by absolutists, simply because there were many more relativists. Similarly, the number of relativists who belonged to a religious or church organization in 1981 outnumbered the number of absolutists who belonged, even though proportionately more absolutists than relativists belonged, simply due to the larger number of relativists overall.[101] The number of absolutists rose and the number of relativists fell between 1981 and 1990, so that by

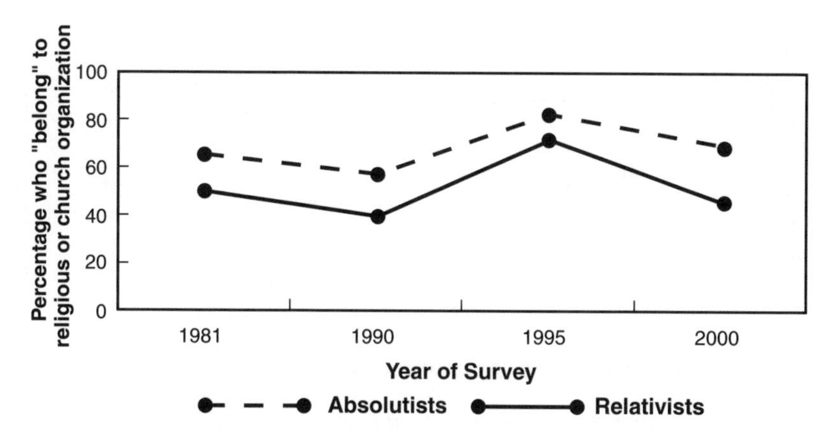

Figure 3.11. Percentage of Americans who "belong to" a religious or church organization, by moral visions, by year.

Source: World Values Surveys 1981, 1990, 1995, and 2000.

1990 (and in 1995 and 2000) there were equal numbers of each category (fig. 3.5).

Frequency of attendance at religious services is dramatically different for absolutists and relativists in every year of the World Values Surveys. As shown in figure 3.12, absolutists always attend services more often than relativists do. Moral visions have a substantial direct effect on frequency of attendance, plus a substantial indirect effect, mediated mainly by the traditional/secular-rational values dimension (see tables 3.8–3.12). Absolutists and relativists may not differ in levels of voluntarism overall, but they do differ dramatically in both membership and frequency of participation in religious organizations.

What about political action? All four waves of the World Values Surveys asked about participation in five political acts: signing a petition, joining in boycotts, attending lawful demonstrations, joining unofficial strikes, and occupying buildings or factories. On average, Americans "have done" or "might do" about 2 of these 5 in 1981; about 2.5 in 1990 and 1995; and about 3 of the 5 in 2000. Signing a petition is the most common political act. Moral visions influence levels of political action: Relativists are more politically active, on average, than absolutists are in each year (fig. 3.13). These are statistically significant differences ($p < .01$). (Since relativists outnum-

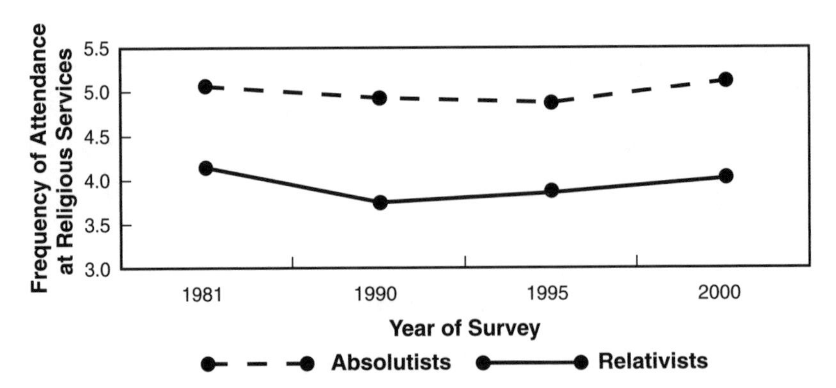

Figure 3.12. Average frequency of attendance at religious services, by moral visions, by year.

Source: World Values Surveys 1981, 1990, 1995, and 2000.

bered absolutists in 1981, the difference between levels of political acts by moral visions in this year is even greater than it appears in fig. 3.13.) Because signing a petition is an item used to construct the survival/self-expression scale, it must be excluded from analyses that include the cultural dimensions. Nonetheless, similar patterns emerge even when only four political acts are included (boycotts, demonstrations, unofficial strikes, and occupying buildings). Absolutists are significantly less likely to engage in these acts (tables 3.8–3.11). The effect of moral visions on political acts, however, is mainly indirect, mediated by the two cultural dimensions (table 3.12). Absolutists tend to hold traditional values, and those with traditional values are significantly less likely to take these political actions. Similarly, absolutists tend to be survival oriented, and those with this orientation are significantly less likely to engage in political acts.

These analyses of the connection between moral visions and social capital—trust, confidence, involvement in voluntary associations, and political activity—reveal that absolutists and relativists have similar *levels* of social capital but different *sources* and *forms* of social capital. Absolutists and relativists are equally likely to say that most people can be trusted; and, by 1995, they had similar levels of confidence in the nation's institutions. Absolutists and relativists are equally involved in voluntary organizations. Compared to relativists,

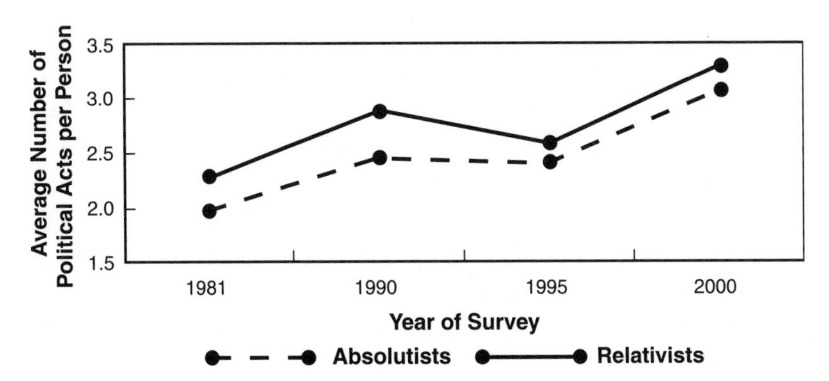

Figure 3.13. Average number of five political acts that Americans "have done" or "might do," by moral visions, by year.
Source: World Values Surveys 1981, 1990, 1995, and 2000.

however, absolutists are more likely to be members of religious organizations and to frequently attend religious services. While absolutists are more active in religious institutions, relativists are more active politically, engaging in more political acts than absolutists.

These findings demonstrate that moral visions animate real behavior and social action, and that they are connected to real groups and organizations. The main differences between absolutists and relativists are related to the content of their moral visions—absolutism leads to more involvement in religious institutions, and relativism leads to more involvement in political action.

Is There An American Culture War—Could There Be?

At best, the evidence considered in this chapter offers only modest support of the thesis of an American culture war. Advocates of the culture war thesis make two claims. The first, the polarization claim, maintains that Americans' social attitudes, cultural-religious values, and moral visions are deeply divided and becoming more divided over time. Generally speaking, they are not. Almost all social attitudes—even about emotionally charged issues such as homosexuality—are not polarized. Moreover, most social attitudes are converging, becoming even more similar over time. The notable exception is attitudes about abortion. Religious values are not polarized. Most Americans are religious centrists, located between the extremes of religious orthodoxy and moral progressivism. Cultural values are not polarized. Most Americans cluster toward the traditional pole of the traditional/secular-rational dimension. There is some evidence of the polarization of moral visions, but this a tendency, not the basis of two morally opposed camps, because absolutists and relativists still have a lot in common.

The second of two claims is tight linkage of the three levels of the hierarchy of beliefs: moral visions are tightly linked to religious beliefs and social attitudes. Generally, they are not. Moral visions are related to religious-cultural values and social attitudes, but these links are moderate to weak. Despite some real differences, absolutists and relativists tend to share similar religious beliefs, cultural values, and attitudes about social issues and policies. Finally, the analysis of moral visions and social capital reveals few differences between absolutists and relativists in their feelings of interpersonal trust, confidence in institutions, or levels of civic engagement. The main difference is their choice of civic engagement: absolutists are more involved in organized religion, and relativists are more involved in political acts. In general, the differences between absolutists and relativists have not coalesced into a "coherent dualist social structure, in which progressives are pitted against traditionalists across a number of different issues."[102]

Even if there were strong support for the claims of the culture war thesis, Jay Demerath and Karen Straight argue that it would not indicate a true cultural war, because America has not suffered the sustained political unrest and organized violence experienced in Northern Ireland, Guatemala, Israel/Palestine, India, and elsewhere: "Compared to most other countries, our religious discord remains generally civil and involves very little serious effort to overturn the constitutionally embedded political system."[103] They are correct, generally, and their argument helps to cool the superheated culture war rhetoric. But it is wise to remember that ideological conflicts have erupted into violence in America's not-so-distant past: during the American Civil War (1861–1865), in which 620,000 Americans were killed and at least as many wounded. The causes of the Civil War were complex, but one of the issues at its heart was the ideological difference about slavery between the North and South. America's cultural tool kit played an important role in the escalation of this difference into sustained military conflict. "A key element in the conflicts that culminated in the Civil War," says Lipset, "was the tendency of both sides to view the other as essentially sinful, as an agent of the Devil."[104] Americans are capable of organized and sustained violence against themselves.

Is there a social issue today like slavery? Some believe abortion is that issue. Abortion is one of the most emotionally charged social issues in contemporary American life. For example, half of all Americans believe that abortion is the same thing as murder, according to the January 1998 CBS News/*New York Times* poll taken on the twenty-fifth anniversary of the U.S. Supreme Court's *Roe v. Wade* decision.[105] Just a week after the twenty-fifth anniversary, one person died and another was seriously injured in the bombing of an abortion clinic in Birmingham, Alabama.[106] This was the first time someone was killed in a clinic bombing. Abortion is a contentious issue, and attitudes about it have become more polarized over time. Violence has erupted many times[107] in the years since the Supreme Court barred the states from banning abortion in its landmark decision on January 22, 1973, but it has not escalated to the scale of a true cultural war as Demerath and Straight define it.

Could the abortion issue turn into sustained civil conflict, as the slavery issue did? Abortion is a moral dilemma, but it lacks a key element present in the case of slavery: a dominant economic basis linked to geographic regions. Slavery was the backbone of the South's largely agricultural economy, in contrast to the industrial and financial economy of the North. "Although the slaveholding planter class formed a small minority of the population," notes Leon Litwak, "it dominated Southern politics and society. Slaves were the largest single investment in the South, and the fear of slave unrest ensured the loyalty of nonslaveholders to the economic and social system."[108] As troubling as abortion may be, and as strong as feelings may run, it is unlikely that the abortion issue will escalate into sustained violent conflict.

Are there other social issues that might? The violent acts of extreme right-wing, antigovernment groups might indicate a threat to political stability. Some analysts view these acts as deplorable but isolated incidents unlikely to evolve into "concerted violence over governmental legitimacy."[109] Others, however, such as the Anti-Defamation League, report "an ever-increasing cross-fertilization between the [right-wing, antigovernment] groups [that] has begun to blur their tactical differences and emphasize the opposition to government that is common to the ideology of every segment of the movement."[110] These "crossovers" are causes for concern because alliances among extremist groups "are likely to energize and strengthen the movement and make it more dangerous."[111]

There are other possibilities, especially when the definition of violence is expanded to include "all forms of intentional harm or injury, including such threats by individuals or groups to another person or persons. [V]iolence includes interpersonal violence (among intimates and strangers) and collective violence (e.g., mob action, hate groups, genocide)."[112] Consider, for example, the prevalence and persistence of race-related hate crimes. The American Civil War ended slavery but not racial animosity. Sixty-one percent of the 7,947 hate-crime incidents reported in the FBI's Uniform Crime Report on Hate Crime, 1995, were motivated by racial hatred.[113] The city of Los Angeles remains racially split years after the 1992 riots, according to a 1997 *Los Angeles Times* poll.[114] For example, 65 percent of the respondents to this survey felt that LA has "remained about same" or is "worse" since the acquittal of four white police officers in the Rodney King beating case sparked the city's riots. Sixty-six percent said race relations were "not good" or "poor." Racial resentment and fear remains a driving force behind America's racial divide, according to research by Donald Kinder and Lynn Sanders.[115] Indeed, states with the largest black populations are more likely to retain the death penalty.[116] Nonetheless, a Gallup poll on race relations in the United States, conducted from December 2002 to February 2003, reports that the majority of Americans (55 percent) feel that the state of race relations is "some-

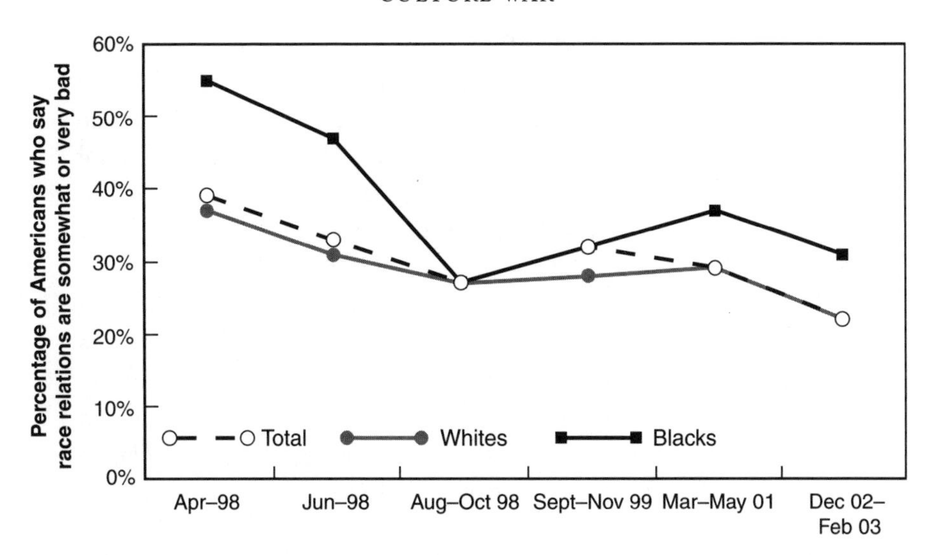

Figure 3.14. Percentage of Americans who say that race relations in the United States today are "somewhat bad" or "very bad," by race.
Source: www.gallup.com.

what good" or "very good."[117] More whites (56 percent) feel this way than blacks (48 percent), but the difference is not large. The percentages of whites and blacks who say that race relations are "somewhat bad" or "very bad" are the lowest for both groups since Gallup first asked this question in April 1998 (see fig. 3.14).

Is there a culture war? The evidence does not lend much support to the culture war thesis, especially its strong form. Could there be a culture war? Based on the evidence, it seems unlikely that the abortion issue, antigovernment movements, or racial conflict will erupt into sustained violence and widespread political disruption. Thus, it is unlikely that there could be an American culture war in the foreseeable future.

Conclusion

This chapter examined the third major explanation of the American crisis of values—the distribution hypothesis. According to this hypothesis, Americans are divided into two opposed groups, based on incompatible views of moral authority. These groups are fighting a culture war to decide the future of the American way of life. One group is the moral absolutists, who believe that morals and moral judgment exist outside the self in God or society. The other group is the moral relativists, who believe that morals and moral judgment exist only in the self. The strong form of the culture war thesis assumes that polarization runs deep: the two groups have opposed moral visions, opposed religious beliefs, and opposed social attitudes. The strong version assumes that moral visions and social attitudes are tightly coupled, so that knowing a person's moral vision—absolutism or relativism—means knowing the person's attitudes about social issues and policies. The weak form of the culture war thesis, in contrast, argues that moral visions and social attitudes are loosely coupled.

The first part of the analysis considered the culture war thesis on its own terms—a crisis indicated by a bipolar distribution of Americans' social attitudes, cultural-religious values, and moral visions. Generally, the evidence does not indicate a bipolar distribution. The social attitudes, cultural values, and religious beliefs of Americans are not polarized; Americans have a lot in common and tend to share the same attitudes, cultural values, and religious beliefs. Moreover, social attitudes are converging over time, with the main exception attitudes about abortion. There is some evidence of the polarization of moral visions, but this is only a tendency. Moral visions are significantly related to social attitudes, but the effects are moderate to weak. At most, the evidence supports the weak form of the culture war thesis—loose linkage of moral visions and social attitudes.

The second part of the analysis went beyond the definition of a culture war as a bipolar distribution of social attitudes, cultural-religious values, and moral visions, investigating the link between moral visions and social capital. This analysis put together Putnam's focus on America's social capital as social bonds with my focus on values, norms, and meanings. Absolutists and relativists have similar feelings of interpersonal trust and similar levels of confidence in the nation's institutions. They have similar levels of involvement in voluntary organizations. Compared to relativists, absolutists have more confidence in the church, tend to be members of religious organizations and to participate frequently in religious services, and support closer church-state ties. While absolutism leads to more involvement in and support of religion, relativism leads to more involvement in political acts. Even if Americans are losing their social bonds, as Putnam argues, the findings in this chapter suggest that the loss cannot be attributed to differences in the moral visions of Americans. Therefore, even if there is a decline in America's social capital as Putnam defines it, the community has not lost its traditional values, and it is not split into two irreconcilably opposed moral camps. The moral culture of the imagined community of America still stands.

The data in this chapter provide the most comprehensive test of the culture war thesis yet available. Based on this evidence, I conclude that the culture war is largely a fiction. My conclusion supports the conclusions of others who have put the culture war thesis to the test. For example, Rys Williams, editor of *Cultural Wars in American Politics*, rejects the culture war thesis, based on his interpretation of the volume's empirical studies: "There is not a 'culture war' in the United States—and asserting it only serves to mask the many important ways in which culture in fact shapes our collective political life."[118]

We are left with a puzzle. The evidence in chapters 2 and 3 does not support any of the three explanations of America's crisis of values. Chapter 2 showed that America has not lost its traditional values, and that it does not compare unfavorably with other societies (the trend and comparative hypotheses). Chapter 3 does not support the culture war thesis (the distribution hypothesis). And yet the perception of a crisis of values persists. Why? That is the question we take up in the next chapter.

✱ CHAPTER FOUR ✱

Dynamics of Crisis

WE HAVE ARRIVED at a puzzling discrepancy between fact and perception. The evidence presented in the previous two chapters shows that America has not lost its traditional values, that the nation compares favorably with most other societies, and that it is not polarized into two opposed moral camps. Americans today continue to have a lot in common and share many values, beliefs, and attitudes. Yet most Americans do not feel this way; most perceive a crisis of values. Does this fact-perception gap indicate mass ignorance of the facts, as some argue?[1] Or is it nothing more than another instance of moral panic, an overblown and disproportionate response to social problems and perceived threats?[2]

The perception of crisis should not be dismissed as ignorance or panic, warns Seymour Martin Lipset: "The critics [of America] have exaggerated many of the problems in the quest to demonstrate decay. There is, however, no denying that the impression of a change in basic values exists, and to dismiss public perception [of crisis] as somehow wrong or misinformed is to deny the reality of individual experience."[3] Lipset's warning echoes the wisdom of Thomas Carlyle's "condition of England question" a century and a half ago.[4] Carlyle's contemporaries were engaged in a similar debate about the meaning of the facts—in this case, whether industrialization had improved or worsened the quality of life of the English working classes. He argued that the question could not be resolved with "figures of arithmetic" about wages, expenditures, and the like. Rather, the "condition" and "disposition" of the English people—their values, norms, experiences, and meanings—had to be considered to answer the question of the effects of industrialization on the working classes.

This chapter addresses what may be called the "condition of America question." This condition is the seeming contradiction of fact and perception: the coexistence of stable traditional values and general agreement about values and social attitudes, along with the widespread impression of a deep division or loss of values. The condition of America question suggests that *both* the facts about values and the perception of a crisis of values are valid. Mass ignorance of the facts about shared values is not the source of the perception of crisis, nor is it an acute case of moral panic. The perception of crisis is more about *meaning* than the facts; it is more about *interpreting* the personal experience of crisis than it is about auditing the cultural "books."

The answer I offer to the condition of America question is an interpretation that resolves the seeming contradiction between the facts and perceptions about values. Unlike the previous chapters, where I marshaled a mass of quantitative data to test hypotheses, this chapter is necessarily more speculative in nature. The twenty-year span covered by the World Values Surveys is too brief to test this interpretation, and no opinion poll extends back far enough in time to do so. I believe this interpretation is reasonable because it is consistent with the empirical findings of previous chapters, consistent with five propositions I derive from my review of theories of political and religious change, and consistent with the writings of additional historians, sociologists, and psychologists. Further, it is consistent with new analyses of the survey data I conduct in this chapter to explore key points. The overall result explains why Americans perceive a widespread crisis of values even when the nation has not lost its traditional values, it compares favorably with other nations, and American society is not divided into polarized moral camps.

In the first section, I review some of the main theories used to explain alternations in American political history, such as theories of political cycles, critical elections, and critical realignments. I also examine theories used to explain patterns in American religious history, such as the so-called Great Awakenings, and "supply-side" explanations of religious change. Both sets of theories contribute to an understanding of the dynamics of crisis. Like most theories of social change, these theories differ in terms of what actually changes, the level at which change takes place, the rate of change, the duration of change, the magnitude of change, the causes of change, and the consequences of change.[5] Nonetheless, from my review I induce five propositions that may be used as guides for understanding the dynamics of crisis. With these propositions in hand, I proceed in the second section of the chapter to develop an interpretation of the dynamics of crisis that answers the condition of America question.

Tides of American History

In 1841 Ralph Waldo Emerson remarked on a pattern of alternation in the politics of the nation since its founding: "The two parties of which divide the state, the party of Conservatism and that of Innovation, are very old, and have disputed the possession of the world ever since it was made. . . . Now one, now the other gets the day, and still the fight renews itself as if for the first time, under new names and hot personalities."[6] In 1919 Henry Adams echoed Emerson's remark but added a measurement of the period of alternation: "A period of about twelve years measured the beat of the pendulum. After the Declaration of Independence, twelve years had been needed to create an efficient Constitution; another twelve years of energy brought a reaction against the government then created; a third period of twelve years was ending in a sweep toward still greater energy; and already a child could calculate the result of a few more such returns."[7]

These observations of American politics are examples of a ubiquitous (and ubiquitously debated) theme in the social sciences—the concept of cycles. The concept refers to the repetition of something over time. Described variously as alternation, fluctuation, oscillation, recurrence, and recrudescence, or with hydraulic metaphors such as ebb and flow, tides, and waves, or with mechanical metaphors such as pendulum or geometric shapes such as circle and spiral, the concept of cycles is used to explain the temporal dynamics of a wide range of phenomena: politics, prices, trade, population, religion, ideology, culture, philosophy, war, and so on.[8] In this section, I describe some key cycle theories of political, cultural, and religious change in America that pertain to an understanding of the dynamics of crisis, especially theories of political cycles, critical realignments, and Great Awakenings of religious enthusiasm. In the process, I shall also describe rival theories, such as "supply-side" explanations of religious change, which argue for a linear trend in the phenomena under study. The most strident proponents of these rival theories declare cycles to be fictions wrought by excessive interpretive license. This judgment, as I explain below, is too harsh, and a version of cycle theory aids an explanation of the dynamics of crisis. Moreover, cyclical and linear models of social change are not by definition mutually exclusive; each captures a different aspect of the same phenomena.

Political Cycles, Critical Elections, and Critical Realignments

The historian Arthur Schlesinger proposed a cycle theory of American politics, defining it as the alternation between conservativism and liberalism.[9] The aim of a conservative phase is to contain democracy; that of a liberal phase, to expand it. Since the nation's founding, he argued, American politics has exhibited recurring swings from conservatism to liberalism and back again with enough regularity to yield accurate predictions of coming political shifts.

Arthur Schlesinger, Jr., summarizes the eleven swings set forth in his father's 1949 *Paths to Present:* "His first three alternations correspond more or less to the three beats of Henry Adams's pendulum [see Adams's quote above]. There follow the period of Jeffersonian retreat after the War of 1812; the democratizing age of Jackson, 1829–1841; increasing domination of the national government by slaveholders, 1841–1861; abolition of slavery, 1861–1869; conservative rule, 1869–1901; the Progressive era, 1901–1919; the Republican restoration, 1919–1931; the New Deal era, 1931–1947."[10] The average length of these periods is sixteen and one-half years, with the adjacent periods of the abolition of slavery (1861–1869) and conservative rule (1869–1901) as the major exceptions. These exceptions occurred "because the Civil War and Reconstruction speeded up the tempo and widened the sweep of reform, achieving in a short time deep and exhausting changes that would otherwise have taken far longer."[11] The long period of conservative rule compensated for the short and intense preceding period.

Schlesinger first presented his cycle theory in a 1924 lecture, when he predicted that the prevailing conservative period would last until 1932. His thesis was published in the December 1939 issue of *Yale Review* under the title "Tides of American Politics." There, he predicted that the then-current liberal period would last until about 1947. In *Paths to Present,* he extended his predictions: "The recession from liberalism which began in 1947 was due to end in 1962, with a possible margin of a year or two in either direction. On this basis the next conservative epoch will commence around 1978."[12] All of Schlesinger's predictions were borne out.

Taking up where his father left off, Schlesinger, Jr., pondered the dynamics that animate the political cycle. He found the engine of change in the polarity between "private interests" and "public action" formulated by Albert O. Hirschman in *Shifting Involvements.*[13] According to Hirschman, American society cycles between periods of withdrawal into private affairs (and concomitant emphases on self-interest, pecuniary gain, and free markets) and expansion into public activity (with emphases on reform, idealism, and regulation). The younger Schlesinger argues that the alternation of "private interest" and "public purpose" drives the political cycles observed by the elder Schlesinger. This dynamic is complete unto itself (as we shall see shortly), but it is enacted through generational change.[14] The political life of a generation is about thirty years, the first half challenging those in power, the second half exercising power, "after which its policies pall and the generation coming up behind claims the succession."[15] One generation holds power and enacts private interests for about fifteen years; the next holds power and enacts public purpose for about fifteen years. These "fifteen-year oscillations roughly match Henry Adam's twelve years in the early republic (when life expectancy was shorter) and [the elder Schlesinger's] sixteen and a half years."[16]

Samuel P. Huntington proposes a reform theory with much longer cycles, arguing that American history oscillates in sixty-year intervals.[17] What he calls "the ideals-versus-institutions gap" animates these long cycles. Americans believe that an important role of government is to promote, express, and realize universal human rights, especially those that make up the American Creed, such as liberty, egalitarianism, individualism, populism, and laissez-faire.[18] Inevitably, human-made institutions fail to do so. Americans react when the gap between ideals and institutions grows too wide, engaging in collective action, social movements, and reform politics to realign American institutions with the American Creed. These are times of "creedal passion," says Huntington. Such times, he argues, occurred in the 1770s, 1830s, 1900s, and 1960s.[19]

Research on specific features of the political system supports the picture of swings between private interest and reform. These studies focus on short cycles, though they are not incompatible with Huntington's long cycles. Stephen Skowronek proposes a cycle theory of presidential succession and leadership style that corresponds to the Schlesingers' alternations.[20] His cycle theory contrasts with the dominant linear model of "increasing presidential power" over the U.S. Congress in particular and society in general.[21] Similarly, Andrew McFarland develops a cycle theory of interest-group participation in the political process, observed in alternations of "business control" (private interests) and "reform" (public action) phases.[22] What McFarland calls "economic producer groups" are always involved in pertinent issue-areas, due to their permanent economic interests, but interest groups become involved only periodically—after unchecked business groups have committed more and more "excesses" such as corporate crime, corruption, scandal, and "violations of widely shared values."[23] When excesses occur, interest-group reformers step into the political process to regulate and reign in business. McFarland observes that hundreds of issue areas "proceed in phase" during the reform cycle to abate business power across the board. Eventually, however, reformers lose interest and exit the political arena, leaving economic producer groups to build up power once again and start the next cycle. Like Skowronek's cycle theory of presidential power, McFarland's cycle theory stands in contrast to a linear model, in this case, the increasing proliferation of the number and types of interest groups that accompanies modernization and economic development.[24]

What accounts for the shift from one type of involvement to the other—from private interests to public purpose and back again? Schlesinger, Jr., argues that the cause is *internal* to the dynamics of cycles: "If it is a genuine cycle, the explanation must be primarily internal. Each new phase must flow out of the conditions—and contradictions—of the phase before and then itself prepare the way for the next recurrence. A true cycle, in other words, is self-generating. It cannot be determined, short of catastrophe, by external events. War, depression, inflations may heighten or complicate moods, but the cycle rolls on, self-contained, self-sufficient and autonomous."[25]

The reason cycles are self-generating, Schlesinger, Jr., contends, is that each period "breeds its own contradictions."[26] Public action demands time, effort, commitment, and sacrifice; it amasses a lot of change; and it inevitably produces disillusionment when results fail to meet expectations. Ultimately, a period of public action exceeds the capacities and will of the nation—"Worn out by the constant summons to battle, weary of ceaseless national activity, disillusioned by the results, [people] seek a new dispensation, an interlude of rest and recuperation."[27] This condition ushers in a period of withdrawal into the private sphere, leaving public problems in the hands of the free market. But this period, too, produces its own problems, such as increasing inequality, corruption, scandal and a host of neglected and growing social problems calling out for treatment. "People grow bored with selfish motives and vistas," says Schlesinger, Jr., "weary of materialism as the ultimate goal. The vacation from public responsibility replenishes the national energies and recharges the national batteries. People begin to seek meaning in life beyond themselves."[28] All that is needed is a catalyst, or what he calls a "detonating" issue (corporate crime, recession, racial strife), to bring in the new era. And so the cycle continues.

The notion of self-generating cycles is as much a subject of debate as the actual existence of cycles. Schlesinger, Jr., argues that the political cycle is independent of external factors, save for a catalytic agent. And so it is uncorrelated with, for instance, the business cycle—some depressions catalyze political shifts, but others do not. Similarly, McFarland argues for internal or endogenous causes of the cyclical pattern of interest-group involvement; as noted above, economic producer groups are continuously involved, and it is the accumulation of and reactions to their excesses that cause the cycle. Pitirim Sorokin, who attempted to chart fluctuations over centuries in a broad array of political, social, and cultural systems, would agree with the concept of self-generating cycles. Sorokin argued that *any* system must change simply because *every* system is inherently imperfect and inadequate, and these imperfections and inadequacies become more and more apparent as the system runs its course.[29] Change is cyclical rather than linear because the number of possibilities is limited and bounded. "Having run through all of them, [a system] either ends its existence, or, if it continues to live, it has to repeat again one or more of the turns and forms through which it has already passed."[30]

In contrast, other explanations of political dynamics locate the cause of change outside the political system, such as theories of "critical realignments." A critical realignment is "an aggregate level concept that refers to an abrupt, large and enduring form of change in prevailing electoral patterns, one that is initiated by a critical election and results in a significantly different partisan balance in the electorate."[31] For example, 1928, 1932, and 1936 are critical elections that caused a seismic shift of power from Republicans to Democrats. The most dramatic was 1932, which included the presidential election of Franklin D. Roosevelt, but the pro-Democratic shift began in 1928 when many regions outside the Deep South started to elect Democrats by wide margins of victory.[32] Regions continued to realign with Democrats in the 1936 elections. In total, the "New Deal" critical realignment spans the years 1928–1936.[33] V. O. Key documented this type of electoral shift in his seminal article on critical elections,[34] and the concept of critical realignments has enchanted political scientists since.

The causes of critical realignments in American history are diverse, each one generated by "a different mix of political, moral, cultural, and economic forces."[35] The *location* of the cause, however, is unambiguous: external or exogenous to the political system. For example, Walter Dean Burnham argues in his classic *Critical Elections and the Mainsprings of American Politics* that "abnormal stress in the socioeconomic system" causes realignment in the political system.[36] Others refer to it similarly as "severe stresses to the political system resulting from some cataclysmic event such as the Civil War or the Great Depression" or generally as "some exogenous 'shock' to the electoral system."[37] In this view of electoral cycles, events such as war, depression, and inflation do not merely "heighten or complicate moods," as Schlesinger, Jr., said, but directly cause political realignment. Presumably, these abrupt and lasting shifts in the electorate would not occur without external causes.

The critical realignment perspective has had enormous appeal, Peter Nardulli argues, because it makes voters, not elites, the drivers of political change, and because it offers an attractive alternative to the linear model of "pluralist-incrementalist" change.[38] Theories of critical realignment assert that rapid and massive responses to major crises are possible, despite a system of government structured through a complex system of checks and balances to prevent hasty action and limit the rate of change to gradual improvements over time. This appeal, observes Nardulli, encouraged scholars to quickly convert the concept of critical realignments into a "broad, encompassing theory of political change" and place the concept "at the center of the study of American political change."[39] This premature ascension meant that the concept never received proper scrutiny and refinement, thereby producing "a weak foundation for a theory of change, [and] causing a great deal of confusion, dissatisfaction, and frustration."[40] Accordingly, the concept of critical alignments has fallen into disfavor, with some critics calling to curtail or even abandon it.

The concept of critical realignments is still useful, Nardulli maintains, as long as one is "sensitive to issues of time and space."[41] He measures the temporal and spatial dynamics of critical realignments, using interrupted time-series techniques to analyze voting patterns in every county and most major cities for every presidential election from 1828 to 1984. (This amounts to over 3,000 counties and cities and over 100,000 unit elections.) While the unrefined concept of critical realignments assumed that the whole U.S. electorate would shift across the entire country at the same time, Nardulli's analysis shows that critical realignments vary in magnitude, duration, spatial diffusion, and impact. His analyses "reveal broadly based electoral eruptions of 40 to 50 points that endure for decades," but realignments have never been "the majestic national movements some believed them to be."[42] Indeed, they are regional phenomena. Only 1932 realigned as much as half of the country in a single election; all other critical elections were smaller in geographic scope.

This review of political cycles, critical elections, and critical realignments outlines the features of key cycle theories used to explain the alternations of American political history. Next, I consider theories of religious change, including the cycle theory of America's Great Awakenings. As we shall see, theories of political cycles and religious cycles have a lot in common. Indeed, we end this section by considering Robert Fogel's attempt to integrate political realignment theory and the theory of religious awakenings. From this review of both political and religious theories, I induce five propositions to the dynamics of crisis, which I use in the second main section of this chapter to develop my answer to the condition of America question.

Great Awakenings, Revivals, and "Supply Side" Religion

Many historians of religion invoke cycle theories to explain the periodic upsurges of religious enthusiasm, revivals, and reform in America. Looking backward, these historians generally recognize three major periods in American religious history—the three Great Awakenings.[43] Examining America today, some claim that the nation is in the middle of its fourth Great Awakening.[44] What are Great Awakenings? The leading voice on the subject, William McLoughlin, defines them as "periods of cultural revitalization that begin in a general crisis of beliefs and values and extend over a period of a generation or so, during which time a profound reorientation in beliefs and values takes place. Revivals alter the lives of individuals; awakenings alter the worldview of a whole people or culture."[45]

Awakenings, McLoughlin avers, are revitalizations of culture. They arise when religion and theology fail to give "meaning and order to the lives of a people," due to significant "social, ecological, psychological, and economic changes."[46] In these times people "begin to doubt their sense and their sanity and to search about for new gods, new ways to perceive and comprehend the power that guides the universe."[47] This condition is a crisis of legitimacy—a time when society has "deviated too far from the moral and religious understandings that legitimized authority in church and state."[48] The end result, after much travail and turmoil, is the emergence of a new worldview that gives meaning and order to personal experience, the confirmation of core values that provide continuity to the nation, the restructuring of old institutions, and renewed confidence and energy as a people.

Drawing on Anthony F. C. Wallace's work on revitalization movements, McLoughlin argues that each awakening moves through five stages.[49] The first stage is a "period of individual stress" in which more and more people lose their way, become emotionally unsettled or even physically ill, and withdraw from or act out against family, friends, community, and those in authority. The next stage is a "period of cultural distortion." Here, people discern the underlying cause of their private troubles to be "institutional malfunction"—the combined failures of churches, schools, police, courts, hospitals, and government to deal with the social problems and crisis of meaning wrought by economic, ecological, demographic, or political changes. This shift in perspective ignites social unrest, political protest, and "schismatic behavior" in the churches, but the populace is "at odds with itself" and cannot unite in common cause. Church and state authorities react to unrest and protest by clamping down and meting out sanctions and punishments. A traditionalist movement almost always arises among the older generations with a lot at stake in the existing order, who argue that the people's failure to follow the old ways is the real cause of social problems and the crises of meaning and legitimacy. "In the ecclesiastical system they point out that God is displeased because the old rituals have not been adhered to; in the civil system, they point to the rise of crime and insist that disrespect for law and order lies at the root of the problem."[50] At this point, a society has reached its nadir in the cycle of revitalization.

The third stage begins the process of cultural reorientation. Wallace says that a prophet now appears, who, after undergoing a traumatic religious rebirth experience, offers a new vision attuned to the needs of the people and starts to lead them out of the crisis. Revivals serve this function in the American context, argues McLoughlin, but he notes that these movements are beyond Wallace's theory. Instead of a prophet, a diverse set of revivalists emerges, operating in at most a loosely coordinated, decentralized manner. "Because [Americans] have had a voluntaristic religion and political structure, together with fundamental religious freedom, leadership in our awakenings has been widely dispersed, differing in emphasis or tone in different regions or groups."[51] McLoughlin's strategy, therefore, is to search for "common elements" among the diverse leaders in these awakenings, and focus on "key spokespeople" who "articulate and consolidate the new worldview for the mainstream majority."[52] (This strategy prompted McLoughlin's critics to attack his theory by questioning the role of specific individuals.[53]) The fourth stage occurs when the leaders of the new worldview begin to attract followers, usually the younger members of a society. This is not a period of harmony, as the "new lights" clash with the "old lights," and some leaders bring followers down false paths into destructive behavior. This stage is complete when the message of the new leaders has spread beyond them in time and space and their charisma has been routinized in organizations. The revitalization process ends in the fifth stage, when the large undecided majority of the population, plus some of the old traditionalists, are won over to the new worldview. "From the thesis to the antithesis of the revival generation a new synthesis emerges. But the old light never quite dies, and the process is never finished."[54]

Awakenings occur in all cultures, McLoughlin and Wallace argue. The great Puritan Awakening in England is the first directly related to the American experience. In it, the Puritans formed the basic values and beliefs that became the original core of American culture.[55] (I discussed some aspects of Puritan values and Protestant culture in chapter 2.) Since then, McLoughlin argues, America has experienced four awakenings on its soil. The First Great Awakening, 1730–60, united the thirteen colonies into a cohesive whole with a unique national self-identity, and it led directly to the American Revolution. The Second Great Awakening, 1800–1830, occurred after the Constitution "launched the American republic" and "created the definitions of what it meant to be 'an American' and what the manifest destiny of the new nation was." The Third Great Awakening, 1890–1920, helped Americans to interpret and adapt to the ethical challenges of evolutionary science and the disruptive effects of industrialization, and it "led us into the crusades 'to make the world safe for democracy' in 1917 and 1941."[56] Since 1960 Americans have been in the midst of the Fourth Great Awakening and are still awaiting its resolution in a revitalized culture.

A few paragraphs can convey only a sketch of McLoughlin's theory. He devotes a chapter to each awakening, including the Puritan one in England, and yet concludes that all his book can provide is a "suggestive model of social change" with a "hope to stimulate a more coherent approach to the history of religion."[57] McLoughlin's book stimulated criticism and debate (described below). It also stimulated economic historian Robert Fogel's attempt "to integrate Great Awakening constructs with 'political realignment theory,' quantitative analysis of congressional and popular voting behavior, the history of technological change (including its effect on economic growth, institutional change, and cultural change), and the evolving insights of biodemography."[58] This effort at synthesis culminated in *The Fourth Great Awakening and The Future of Egalitarianism*.

For Fogel, religious awakenings and political realignments are not separate cycles but overlapping phases of the *same* long cycle. "In my view," Fogel says, "there is not only more dynamic interaction between political and religious developments than McLoughlin allowed but also critically important synergism. Hence, the phases of religious intensification and of political ascendancy cannot be defined independently of each other, only in the light of each other."[59] "Contingent factors" also play large roles in shaping the interaction of political and religious dynamics. Table 4.1 presents Fogel's summary of his model. As shown, Fogel divides each awakening into three phases, each one lasting about a generation or so—a phase of "religious revival," a "rising political effect," and a phase of "increasing challenges to the dominance of the political program." Cycles overlap, so that the declining phase of the old cycle, the third phase, overlaps with the first phase of the new cycle. All told, each cycle runs about one hundred years.[60]

In the main, Fogel's theory is a "cultural lag" explanation of social change. Cultural lag refers to the delay between technological and economic transformations and the ability of human cultures and institutions to cope with and adjust to them.[61] A cycle begins and continues when these transformations disrupt the preexisting social order, destabilize culture, and create crises of meaning and legitimacy. For example, the disruptive technologies in the Second Great Awakening, says Fogel, included new industrial methods that began the process of urbanization, such as the factory system in agricultural milling, iron works, and textile production, and new transportation technologies that dramatically cut the costs of transportation, facilitated waves of mass immigration, and spread the growing population across the continent.[62] These technologies produced a host of social problems, among them class conflicts, poverty, and urban squalor and unrest. Such troubling conditions initiated a phase of religious revival and enthusiasm as a response, followed by a political phase in which the ethics and policies of the revivalists were institutionalized through social movements and new political programs. In the third phase, the programs, policies, and ethics of the now-dominant political coalition were increasingly challenged and it started to decline.

Each cycle exhibits elements of American exceptionalism. For example, the First Great Awakening strengthened the distinctive distrust of religious and political authority that the first immigrants to America had brought with them (see my discussion in chapter 2). For example, revivalists "called on people to trust their own experience and not depend on the authority of church officials."[63] The political phase of this cycle focused on the perceived moral corruption of the British and "provided much of the popular ideological foundation for the Revolution by questioning the legitimacy of established authority, eroding colonial boundaries, and promoting popular discontent."[64] This was a time of tension and discord in the colonies, as well as organized mobilization against the British. Colonial America was deeply split over its relations with England. Loyalists and sympathizers outnumbered patriots, and many fled north to become the ancestors of America's present-day Canadian neighbors. At the time, John Adams estimated that the colonial population was divided into thirds: one-third against the revolution, one-third neutral, and one-third in favor. At least 20 percent were "actively treasonous."[65]

The Second Great Awakening strengthened the values of individualism and egalitarianism. For example, the doctrine of predestination, already under attack in the First Great Awakening, was severely weakened in the Second. Hence, "anyone was capable of achieving saving grace through a determined inner and outer struggle against sin."[66] Revivalists preached that social perfection—building God's Kingdom on earth—was the nation's goal. Pursuit of this goal was institutionalized in the political phase of the cycle as the temperance movement, the nativist movement to protect the country's Protestant heritage from the waves of Catholic immigrants, the women's suffrage movement, and the abolitionist movement (culminating in the Civil War).

Industrialization sparked the Third Great Awakening near the turn of the twentieth century. This period experienced a wealth of disruptive technologies: automobiles, motion pictures, telephones, recorded sound, electric lights, X-rays, and many others. "I don't think you can exaggerate how much change was in the air," says historian John Milton Cooper, Jr. "Things that had been around, conditions that had been taken for granted since time immemorial, had changed. The scientific-technological-industrial revolution of that time was absolutely . . . unprecedented in human history."[67] We like to think of the late twentieth century as the time of great change (and the time of great moral crisis), but it pales in comparison to the technological change experienced in a single lifetime just a century ago. For example, as Judy Critchton writes in *America 1900: The Turning Point:*

> In Philadelphia, Elizabeth Cooper McIntyre, who had recently celebrated her ninety-ninth birthday, had been born the year Philadelphians lined the streets to watch President Adams, his wife Abigail, and congressional leaders leave the city for the new unfinished Capitol on the marshy banks of the Potomac.

> She could remember when there were no fireboxes or friction matches, no postage stamps or envelopes, when communication was as slow as it was uncertain and signaling was done from town to town by means of fires on mountaintops or waving flags. In her youth it had taken six weeks to get news from Europe; now it took six seconds. Mrs. McIntyre had seen the coming of the cable, the telegraph and telephone, trolleys and high-speed trains.[68]

The technological marvels of this time produced unprecedented social problems. For example, cities "were growing at an alarming rate and were viewed as centers of corruption, crime, drunkenness, prostitution, and graft that threatened to infect the entire society."[69] Labor strife reached unprecedented scale and scope, bringing with it the threat of unionism and socialism. Darwin's theory of evolution was an affront to the biblical story of creation, and it undermined the revivalist goal of the Second Great Awakening to build God's Kingdom on earth (because the theory implied that evolution was not guided toward the fulfillment of an ultimate goal of perfection). The disruptive effect of Darwin's theory was nearly as great as the disruptive effect of Copernicus's theory of a Sun-centered universe. As Thomas Kuhn notes, Copernican theory was more than a technical improvement in celestial mathematics—it threatened "the drama of Christian life and the morality that had been made dependent upon it."[70] Darwin's theory of evolution similarly shook the Christian conceptualization of the world. (Years later, Einstein's "theory of relativity" was perceived as a threat to Christian beliefs. One of the most famous reactions was Cardinal O'Connell's, who in 1929 argued that the theory of relativity is "a cloak beneath which lies the ghastly apparition of atheism."[71])

The evangelical churches were divided on how to address these issues and problems. The winning group (now called the modernists or the liberals) married science and religion to resolve the moral dilemmas and challenges posed by Darwinism and the problems of industrialization. For example, they applied scientific principles to the Bible, arguing that "it was an historical document written by men who were trying to understand God's will within the context of their own times and civilizations."[72] They argued that evolutionary theory and the bible are consistent: the laws of evolution are God's laws, and the natural process of evolution is moving us toward the ultimate goal of human perfection. (Similarly, some clerics believed Einstein's theory of relativity supported the existence of God and worked to demonstrate the consistency between Christian doctrines and the new scientific theories.[73]) Science was now seen as a guide to perfecting American society, re-establishing the goal of building God's Kingdom on earth. Views of sin also changed during this Awakening. Poverty was no longer seen as punishment for the sinful. Rather, sins of society, not personal sins, created poverty and other social problems. These revivalist responses laid the ideological groundwork for the reforms of the New Deal in the political stage, the rise of the welfare state, and what we now call Big Government. Indeed, the legacy of this period is the omnipresence of government in everyday life, one of the most notable features of American society that Richard Reeves observed when, on the 150th anniversary of Alexis de Toqueville's 1830's journey, he retraced the French aristocrat's steps.[74]

Many social scientists argue that America at the turn of the millennium is caught in the throes of another disruptive technological revolution. Manuel Castells emphasizes the revolution in information technologies.[75] "We are living through one of the most fundamental technological and social changes in history," he argues. "The revolution in information technologies that took shape in the early 1970s, and diffused throughout the economy, society, and culture in the last quarter of the twentieth century, has profoundly transformed the way we live, work, produce, consume, communicate, travel, think, enjoy, make war and peace, give birth, and die. It has also transformed, as have all major technological revolutions, the material foundations of human life, time, and space."[76] For Fogel, the list of disruptive technologies is longer:

> The ethical crises, religious upsurge, and programmatic demands that heralded the opening decades of the Fourth Great Awakening were precipitated by a series of major technological breakthroughs that destabilized prevailing culture. Some of these unsettling advances were

> in energy production (particularly nuclear energy), information retrieval, and communications. The unprecedented extension of control of human biology, particularly in the fields of reproductive technology and organ transplantation, also provoked widespread concern. The new technological breakthroughs raised profoundly difficult ethical and practical issues, including many that had never been considered previously, such as how to dispose of large quantities of radioactive waste. Among those who worried about these issues, some became alarmed that humanity was heading toward disaster, led by corrupt or mindless scientists and business leaders.[77]

This revolution, Fogel argues, is fundamentally different from earlier revolutions because it is the acceleration of the *technophysio evolution* of human life.[78] More than previous disruptive technological revolutions, this one is creating unprecedented challenges to and demands on preexisting ethical and social systems. The Fourth Great Awakening is a response to the destabilized preexisting cultural order, but it is still unfolding.

Are the Great Awakenings real? Has America experienced periodic upsurges of religious enthusiasm, driven by disruptive technologies, which result in political realignments and a revitalized culture? McLoughlin's and Fogel's accounts of American history have received both criticism and support.[79] For example, John Butler claims the First Great Awakening never really happened and that the awakening concept is little more than an "interpretive fiction."[80] In contrast, Bernard Bailyn calls this Great Awakening "the central event in the history of religion in America in the eighteenth century," one that stimulated democracy and human rights, while Richard Bushman claims that it turned Puritans into Yankees, unified New England, and prepared its inhabitants for a large role in the Revolution.[81] There are, similarly, any number of critics and supporters of the awakening thesis and its constructs.[82] The criticisms, Fogel outlines, include concerns about the actual existence of discontinuities in religious enthusiasm and revivals, ambiguous or arbitrary dating of discrete periods, the cause or causes of revivals, the causal link between religious upsurges and political reforms, the links between the awakenings themselves, and the cyclical (versus linear) pattern of religious change.[83] Fogel contends that his theory of religious-political cycles takes these criticisms into account.[84]

Instead of debating the pros and cons of each criticism, I focus here on the last one—cyclical versus linear models of change—since it pertains closely to the consideration of the dynamics of crisis. The cyclical view of awakenings lacks credibility, argues Timothy Smith, because revivals have been a steady and persistent—that is, linear—feature of American religious experience.[85] Fogel agrees that revivals have been continuous since the late seventeenth century but argues "not every stretch of years in which there were revivals had the same long-term effect on ideology or politics."[86] Some periods of revivals led to political realignments and reforms, he argues, but others did not. While most attacks on the cyclical view of awakenings rely on qualitative data and historical case studies (as do the proponents of the cyclical view, with the partial exception of Fogel[87]), advocates of the so-called supply-side explanations of religious change employ detailed quantitative data on church membership. With these data, Roger Finke and Rodney Stark document a steady increase in the "churching" of America.[88] For example, the percentage of Americans who were church members increased from only 17 percent in 1776 to over 60 percent in 1980 and beyond. Even with a drop in religious adherence after the Civil War, the data exhibit a significant and strong linear trend.[89]

The real pattern of religion of America is not the ebb and flow of religious enthusiasm, contend Finke and Stark, but "a long, slow, and consistent increase in religious participation."[90] This "master trend" is due to the steady deregulation of the religious marketplace, which allowed religious entrepreneurs greater and greater access to consumers of religion. More access, more competition, and more marketing increase the supply of religion and cause the percentage of church adherents to grow. This supply-side explanation contrasts with the traditional demand-side explanation that attributes religious change to the "shifting desires and needs of religious consumers."[91] Demand is considered to be stable and the "most significant changes in American religion derive from shifting supply."[92]

The dynamic of religion is not cultural lag produced by disruptive technologies, supply-siders argue, but what they call the "sect-church process."[93] Sects are religious organizations with a vivid otherworldly view; they demand a lot from their adherents in exchange for salvation. Sects are "high tension" organizations because their beliefs and practices put their followers at odds with outsiders. Churches are religious organizations with more of a this-worldly orientation; they neither demand nor promise much. These are "low-tension" organizations because their beliefs and practices do not put their adherents at odds with others. New religious bodies begin as sects and become churchlike as they add followers, shifting from an otherworldly to a this-worldly view and from a high-tension to low-tension organization. As this happens, "a religious body will become increasingly less able to satisfy members who desire a higher-tension version of faith."[94] Discontent and discord grow. Members with a taste for high-tension religion complain that the original beliefs and practices have been compromised. Escalating conflict encourages a split, and "the faction desiring a return to higher tension will leave to found a new sect."[95] This new sect will, eventually, become churchlike and the pattern will be repeated. "The result is an endless cycle of sect formation, transformation, and rebirth," say Finke and Stark. "The many workings of this cycle account for the countless varieties of each of the major faiths."[96]

The sect-church process accounts for the fall of mainline churches and the rise of upstart sects, according to Finke and Stark. This is why, for example, the fortunes of the dominant religious bodies in the colonial era (Congregationalists, Episcopalians, and Presbyterians) fell while those of the upstarts (Baptists, Methodists) rose so dramatically. For example, the percentage of Congregationalists fell from 20 percent in 1776 to only 4 percent in 1850, while the percentage of Methodists rose from 3 percent to 34 percent during the same time.[97] Finke and Stark describe similar patterns of rise and fall throughout American history, arguing that the net effect is a steady linear churching of America.

The supply-side approach may be a needed corrective to the awakenings perspective. The grand theory of Great Awakenings appears to suffer the same ailment that befell the unrefined critical realignment perspective. As noted above, the realignment idea was so appealing that scholars eagerly transmuted a useful concept into a broad, all-encompassing, majestic theory of political change. Placing the concept in the pantheon of political science protected it from close scrutiny but led to confusion, dissatisfaction, and ultimately pleas to jettison the concept altogether. Similarly, the idea of Great Awakenings is so appealing that it may have been placed prematurely at the center of the study of American religious change, thereby escaping close attention and refinement. For example, Butler says that the First Great Awakening "has received surprisingly little systematic study and lacks even one comprehensive history."[98] This premature ascension may account for the confusion, dissatisfaction, and frustration with the awakenings concept, and the calls to severely curtail or even abandon it. However, by rejecting the awakenings perspective, we risk losing a valuable concept—the concept of religious cycles. Awakenings may not be the all-encompassing, majestic, near-mystical national movements McLoughlin claims they are. Nonetheless, the concept of cyclical awakenings may still be useful if we are sensitive to time and space. Indeed, the evidence marshaled by critics of the awakenings perspective is consistent with the conclusion that, like critical realignments, religious revivals and enthusiasm vary in magnitude, duration, spatial diffusion, and impact.

Five Propositions for the Dynamics of Crisis

What can we glean from these theories of political and religious change that pertains to the dynamics of crisis? Based on my review, I induce five propositions to use as guides.

Proposition 1

A tension between opposites animates the dynamics of crisis. In the political field, these dualities include conservatism versus innovation (Emerson), conservatism versus liberalism (Schlesinger), private interest versus public action (Hirschman, Schlesinger, Jr.), economic producer groups versus public interest groups (McFarland), and Republicans versus Democrats (Key, Burnham, Nardulli, et al.). In the religious field, these dualities include sects versus churches (Finke and Stark) and "old lights" versus "new lights" (McLoughlin, Fogel). Our candidate for a tension between opposites in the moral field is absolutism versus relativism, the twin moral visions described and analyzed in previous chapters.

Proposition 2

Each side of a duality requires the other; neither side intends to demolish the other. Conservatives and liberals need one another (Schlesinger). Republicans and Democrats need one another (Burnham, Nardulli, et al.). As Schlesinger, Jr., puts it for the polar opposites of private interest versus public purpose: "The two jostling strains in American thought agree more than they disagree. Both are committed to individual liberty, the constitutional state and the rule of law. Both have their reciprocal functions in preserving the body politic. Both have their indispensable roles in the dialectic of public policy. They are indissoluble partners in the great adventure of democracy."[99] Similarly, sects and churches depend on one another to generate the "endless cycle of sect formation, transformation, and rebirth" (Finke and Stark). And the "new lights" are not bent on destroying the "old lights" (McLoughlin, Fogel). Revivalists "have never repudiated the older worldviews entirely; instead," says McLoughlin, "they have claimed merely to shed new light on them, that is, to look upon old truths from a new perspective."[100] If neither side of a duality intends to demolish the other, perhaps the same is true for the dual moral visions of absolutism versus relativism—both may have indispensable roles in the dialectic of morality.

Proposition 3

The causes of the dynamics of crisis may be endogenous, exogenous, or both. The inherent limitations of each side of a political duality induce a shift from one to the other (Emerson, Schlesinger, Hirschman, Schlesinger, Jr.). Similarly, the inherent tendency for sects to become churchlike induces schisms and splitting off (Finke and Stark). If each moral vision breeds its own contradictions, it may prompt a shift from one to the other and periodically create the impression of polarized moral visions. Exogenous causes of political and religious change include abnormal stress in the socioeconomic system (Burnham), a cataclysmic event such as the Civil War or the Great Depression (various political scientists), disruptive technologies (Castells, Fogel), deregulation of the religious marketplace (Finke and Stark), or some diverse mix of economic, ecological, political, and demographic forces (Nardulli, McLoughlin). Any of these external factors could induce a perception of crisis. Of course, both internal and external factors may come into play.

Proposition 4

Traditional values can remain stable over a long time even as crises come and go. McFarland implies the continuation of a stable core of "widely shared values" around which violations fluctuate. Similarly, Huntington's theory of long cycles assumes stable beliefs in the American Creed. (In support of his assumption, recall from chapter 2 that the 1996 Survey of American Political Culture reported very high levels of support for the American Creed.) Schlesinger, Jr., quoted in the paragraph above, maintains that the proponents of private interest and public purpose agree more than disagree; both are committed to the same core values. Supply-siders argue that demand for religion is stable (Finke and Stark), and religion is a major component of the traditional/secular-rational values dimension (chapters 2 and 3). (Consistent with the claim of stable demand, Gallup reports that the importance of religion and belief in God have remained high in America for over fifty years.[101]) And awakenings revolve around a constant cultural core that is reaffirmed in each one (McLoughlin).

Proposition 5

Linear models and cycle models are alternatives, but they are not necessarily incompatible. In politics, the linear model of "pluralist-incrementalist" change is an alternative to the cycle model of critical realignments, while the linear model of "increasing presidential power" is an alternative to Skowronek's cycle theory of presidential elections and leadership styles. Neither linear model is incompatible with its cycle model alternative because a process over time can exhibit both linear trend and periodic fluctuation.[102] Therefore, the long-term trend of political change may be incremental (linear) and critical realignments fluctuate around this trend. Likewise, presidential power may be increasing steadily over time *and* exhibit alternations. Even Schlesinger, Jr., remarks on a linear trend produced by his model of political cycles: "National swings back toward uncontrolled private interest are generally holding actions; swings in the democratic direction tend to produce enduring change. The spiral effect registers the continuing accretion of democratic reform."[103] Similarly, each rival theory of religious change—linear churching versus cycles of awakenings—exhibits both linear and cyclical processes. That religion and politics in America are cyclical "does not mean that cycles have been the dominant characteristic of life over the past three centuries," says Fogel. Rather, the trend is linear (or exponential): "relatively steady and rapid growth in the economy based on an accelerating pace of technological change."[104] The cyclical fluctuations around this trend are the repetitive cultural lags caused by "the tendency of these technological advances to outpace the development both of ethical guidelines for their utilization and of human institutions to control them."[105] The linear growth in the churching of America depends on the "endless cycle" of sects described above (Finke and Stark). The cycles in the churching process occur in repeated patterns of church schisms, splitting off of sects, their transformation into churches, and their fall as specific denominations. Perhaps, as John Wilson put it, linear and cyclical explanations are just different "frameworks of interpretation" used to study the same phenomena.[106]

The final point is a reminder rather than a proposition. Real people, not Olympian forces, enact change. Linear trends and cycles of change emerge from the concrete struggles and interactions of real social actors. It is all too easy to reify the concept of cycles, as William Strauss and Neil Howe do in *The Fourth Turning: An American Prophecy*, which purports to divine "what the cycles of history tell us about America's next rendezvous with destiny."[107] The presentation of cycles as grandiose, majestic, inexorable forces determining human fates is a reason why critics react so vehemently against cycle theories. Cycles (and linear trends) arise from the collective actions and interactions of voters and politicians, reformers and violators, high-tension and low-tension religious consumers, religious entrepreneurs and traditionalists, "old lights" and "new lights," members of older and younger generations, interest groups and economic producers, Republicans and Democrats, and so on. As Schlesinger, Jr., puts it, "It takes people to make the cycle work."[108]

An Interpretation of the Dynamics of Crisis

My objective in this section is to develop a reasonable interpretation of the dynamics of crisis. Given that opinion poll data do not exist to test this interpretation, I judge reasonableness as consistency with the empirical findings of previous chapters, consistency with the five propositions above, consistency with the writings of additional historians, sociologists, and psychologists, and consistency with findings from new analyses of the survey data. The overall result answers the condition of America question: the seeming contradiction between the facts about values and the widespread perception of a crisis of values.

The Dynamic Attraction of Opposed Moral Visions

In chapter 3, I defined the dual moral visions of absolutism and relativism, described them as radial categories (central tendencies with systematic variations), and analyzed shifts in the distribution of moral visions over time (the polarization claim) and the links among moral visions, religious-cultural values, and social attitudes (the linkage claim). Here, I further develop these ideas by exploring the origin of the two moral visions and their inherent tension, as well as their underlying social and psychological dynamics. By doing so, I hope to demonstrate why the attraction of opposed moral visions is central to an interpretation of the dynamics of crisis.

The origin of dual moral visions and their inherent tension, argues Karl Jaspers, is the "axis of history" over 2,500 years ago. "It is there," says Jaspers, "that we meet with the most deepcut dividing line in history" and the creation of "the fundamental categories within which we still think today."[109] Some psychologists argue that a basic change in human consciousness took place in this period.[110] During this time, says S. N. Eisenstadt, "a revolution took place in the realm of ideas and their institutional base which had irreversible effects on several major civilizations and on human history in general. The revolution or series of revolutions . . . have to do with the emergence, conceptualization and institutionalization of a basic tension between the transcendental and mundane orders."[111] Prior to the axial break, societies contained primitive concepts of the transcendental and mundane spheres, but "the higher world [was] symbolically structured according to principles very similar to those of the mundane or lower one."[112] The axial revolution increased the distance between the two spheres and created an inherent tension between them. "Breaking down their mutual interpenetration," summarizes Adam Seligman, "the Axial Age posited a new conception of the social order, autonomous from, but in tension with, the cosmic (henceforth conceived as transcendent) sphere."[113]

The axial revolution created the dual conceptual system of absolutism and relativism, but the concrete struggles of real social actors gave rise and form to it. "Truths do not arise in isolated brains or disembodied minds," argues Randall Collins. They arise in the real world of social networks, cooperation, and competition.[114] For example, new types of elites competed with one another to construct (and reconstruct) conceptions of the mundane and transcendental orders, to gain official recognition (or protection) from the state, to enlarge their memberships and constituencies, and to preserve and extend their autonomy and material base.[115] As Mark Chaves puts it, "The social significance of religion depends on the social and political conflicts of those who would gain or lose by supporting it."[116]

"The dichotomization of reality into sacred and profane spheres, however related," says Peter Berger, "is intrinsic to the religious enterprise."[117] Indeed, the promise of the salvational religions, according to Max Weber, is to overcome the finite, imperfect, and corrupted world by bridging the gap to the "perfection of the transcendent order."[118] The "chasm between the mundane and transcendental orders" and "the search to overcome this chasm" became institutionalized in the so-called Great Civilizations and Historical Religions.[119] Similarly, utopianism and millennialism are attempts to erect a bridge across the chasm.[120]

The absolutism-relativism duality is an example of a universal human phenomenon documented by anthropologists, historians, and sociologists, posed here by anthropologist David Maybury-Lewis as a question: "Why do societies all over the world organize their social thought and their social institutions in patterns of opposites? This is reported from so many different parts of the world that it is clearly a kind of system that human beings keep inventing and living by, independently of each other."[121] Or, as Daniel Bell asks, "How did man come to think of two radically different, heterogeneous realms, the sacred and the profane? Nature itself is a unified continuum in a great chain of being, from the microcosm to the macrocosm. Only man has created dualities: of spirit and matter, nature and history, the sacred and the profane."[122]

Binary or dualistic thinking appears to be based on the polarities that are perceived to exist in nature or as part of the essential conditions of human experience. "All cultures," says Maybury-Lewis, "note and deal with such oppositions as night-day (or darkness-light), male-female, sky-earth, life-death, and a host of others."[123] The perception of natural polarities is elaborated into dual cultural ideas (and sometimes into dual social organization) in which each part of the duality, such as absolutism or relativism, requires the other for definition and meaning. Indeed, it is impossible to conceive of one without the other. Absolutism and relativism, as Marco Orrù puts it, "are dialectically related as parts of a common discourse."[124] Absolutism and relativism are not *different* ways of thinking as much as they are parts of "a *single* way of thinking which is subject to an internal tension regarding the location of reality."[125]

Maybury-Lewis, among others, argues that dualistic thinking offers a solution to the problem of an ordered relationship between contradictions; it permits the "harmonious interaction of contradictory principles."[126] For example, social conflict and the need to resolve or manage it are unavoidable in human experience. Dualistic theories "offer a solution to the problem of social order by holding out the promise of balancing contending forces in perpetual equilibrium." Contradictions "do not tear the world apart, and humankind with it, because they are part of a cosmic scheme in which they are harmonized." Maybury-Lewis calls this dynamic "the attraction of opposites" in binary models of thinking and seeing the world. This attraction of opposites is the heart of what Stephen Barley and Gideon Kunda call the "bipolar ideational structure" of Western culture, in which societies "revolve around core ideas that are oppositional or dualistic in structure."[127] The attraction of opposites in its most human form, says Lloyd Sandelands, is the "living dialectic" of male and female in social life.[128]

The "attraction of opposites" serves a psychological function as well as a social function, driven by the well-known splitting-projecting dynamic. Because the two moral visions are considered to be incompatible, having them both causes psychological disequilibrium. Splitting off and projecting the "undesirable" moral vision (due, for example, to conflict with religious upbringing or reference-group beliefs) onto another person, group, or category restores a sense of equilibrium. This splitting-projecting dynamic operates at all levels—individuals, families, groups, organizations, and nations.[129] This dynamic, Kenwyn Smith and David Berg observe, drives intergroup conflict and hostility: "each group sees itself as good and its adversary as bad and uses this justification for being oppositional, applying logic such as 'only when they are eliminated will badness disappear.' Since each group takes the same position, the conflict escalates to the point where both are behaving self-righteously, wholeheartedly denying that the accusations of the opponent have *any* validity."[130] This is consistent with Lipset's observation that Americans "tend to view social and political dramas as morality plays, as battles between God and the Devil, so that compromise is virtually unthinkable."[131] But one side cannot eliminate the other; each unconsciously needs the other. Mutual need is an intrinsic part of the splitting-projecting dynamic. As Smith and Berg put it, "when A gets B to carry and express its displaced parts, A will be invested in remaining in the vicinity of B to obtain vicarious gratification as the disowned parts of itself are enacted and to maintain the strength of the subgroup that carries these disowned parts."[132] Thus, the moral visions of absolutism and relativism are attracted to one another for psychological reasons (to reduce cognitive dissonance) and for social reasons (to harmonize contradictory principles).

The coexistence and attraction of these moral visions can be seen in the different interpretations of the same symptoms of crisis. Symptoms of crisis can be viewed through the lens of absolutism or the lens of relativism. The crisis "looks different" depending on the lens used.[133] For example, political and economic change in Greece during the fifth-century B.C. disrupted existing values and norms, creating a period of moral crisis or "anomie."[134] Signs of this breakdown included skepticism about the divine origin of laws and norms, the decline of religion, disregard of laws and lack of enforcement, depravity, civil strife, and so on.[135] There were two sides to the debate about the breakdown. On the one side, Plato developed the absolutist view that anomie was evil in its very essence; it was a corrupted condition of society that must be eradicated at all costs, even at the expense of the individual. Plato located moral authority outside the individual in the realm of pure, unchanging, infallible ideas (his Forms, such as the supreme Form of the Good). He judged the facts of anomie against a transcendental standard of fixed moral absolutes. On the other side, the sophists had developed a relativist view, arguing that values were the invention of people working out practical problems in society; these values could and should change as conditions change. Anomie indicated social problems to be dealt with in a practical manner. "The transcendental side criticized the cultural values of Athenian democracy because they allowed anarchic freedom and the breakdown of social norms; the [mundane] side celebrated Athenian democracy and focused, at all times, on the immediate consequences of social control and of *anomia* on individual freedom and conduct."[136] The sophists' philosophy of value relativity is quite similar to discussions of value relativity today.

The attraction of opposite moral visions appears throughout history. It is clear, for example, in the writings of two sociologists and social philosophers, Emile Durkheim and Jean Marie Guyau, in nineteenth-century France.[137] Both witnessed a period of crisis or "anomie" in French history—the humiliating defeat of France by Bismarckian Prussia, the Paris Commune, revolution, popular uprisings, urban insurrection, and so on.[138] But each reacted differently to this "anomie," just as Plato and the sophists reacted differently to the evidence of crisis in ancient Greece. Like Plato, Durkheim interpreted moral crisis to be an evil and pathological state—anomie is "the contradiction of all morality."[139] Like Plato, Durkheim was a transcendentalist, locating moral authority in an absolute and external source; Plato's source was the unchanging realm of pure ideas, and Durkheim's was society itself. Both Plato and Durkheim were, in the colloquial language of today, "law-and-order" types, preoccupied with social order and obedience to absolute, external standards of morality.

Durkheim's contemporary, Jean Marie Guyau, developed a different moral philosophy. He saw the history of ethics as the evolutionary development of an individualized morality, one that, as Orrù summarizes,

> shows a gradual shift from collective and external criteria for ethical conduct towards individual and internal criteria. For Guyau, anomie was not to be considered an evil or illness of modern times, but its distinguishing quality. While many social thinkers were concerned about how to restore the social order eroded by the industrial evolution and the advent of positivism, Guyau presented the intellectual task of moral anomie as the challenge of the new era. Modern people could no longer rely on religious faith or transcendental truth. Rather, they had to find a standard of conduct within themselves, in their impulse toward life.[140]

For Guyau, anomie represents freedom from the dictates and strictures of dogma, ideology, and doctrine. Guyau's moral philosophy is built on premises quite similar to those of the sophists' centuries earlier.

All moral debates exhibit the attraction of opposites; every moral debate is, as a "twofold argument."[141] Seen in this light, America's crisis of values is a contemporary expression of the dynamic attraction of moral opposites. The culture war thesis (chapter 3) is its most obvious manifestation. Much of the culture war debate is neither new nor novel. The lineage of the two moral visions—absolutists versus relativists—can be traced to their creation in the axial revolution. On one side, absolutists such as William J. Bennett (*The Book of Virtues; The Death of Outrage*) claim that America has fallen into a deplorable state of extreme relativism. The lineage of such absolutist thinking may be traced with an unbroken line back to Plato. On the other side, relativists such as Lawrence W. Levine (*The Opening of the American Mind*) and multiculturalists view relativism as the blossoming of human thought. This lineage may be traced to the sophists of ancient Greece. The commonplace assumption that the "Ancients" were "right-wing conservatives" and the "Moderns" are "left-wing liberals" is a serious error that can be sustained by only the most selective reading.[142] Some specific ethical issues debated by modern-day absolutists and relativists are unique (such as human cloning), but the philosophical basis of their arguments is not. Indeed, the debates about moral crisis in America at the turn of the millennium are reminiscent of the debates about moral crisis in fifth-century B.C. Greece.[143] The flag proclaiming "culture war" is new, but it has been hoisted over well-explored moral territory.

Absolutism and relativism are indissoluble partners in the dialectic of morality (proposition 1). The goal of each moral vision is not to demolish the other (proposition 2), despite the apocalyptic language used in culture war rhetoric (see chapter 3). The attraction of moral opposites serves psychological functions (to reduce cognitive dissonance) and social functions (to harmonize contradictory principles). Perhaps the dynamic attraction of opposed moral visions also plays a role in the revitalization of culture, as McLoughlin says awakenings do.

Stable Traditional Values, Shifting Moral Visions

America's traditional values have remained stable over the past twenty years, but moral visions have shifted during the same time (chapters 2 and 3). A reasonable interpretation of the dynamics of crisis must take both patterns into account. In chapter 2, I developed the argument that America's traditional values persist for two interrelated reasons. First, America's traditional values are path dependent, embodied in American institutions and reproduced across generations. For example, the birth cohort analysis demonstrated that Americans of different generations share similar traditional values, unlike the pattern that exists in most economically advanced democracies where older generations hold traditional values and younger generations hold secular-rational values. Second, the preservation of America's traditional values is paramount because they are part of the foundation of the nation's imagined community. Unlike "birthright" nations, American collective identity is ideological. America would not be America if its people lost their traditional values. A function of crisis rhetoric, as I discussed in chapter 2, is to preserve traditional values. Crisis rhetoric exhibits the splitting-projecting dynamic I described above.

Moral visions shift, in contrast to the stability of traditional values. This shift was demonstrated in chapter 3 for the twenty-year period covered by the World Values Surveys. It is possible that traditional values have been stable over a much longer period of time (proposition 4). What about shifting moral visions? Both Jaspers and Orrù observe a repeated alternation of absolutism and relativism through history from the ancient Greeks to modern times.[144] Claiming that this alternating pattern is true for the length of American history is speculation, but it would be consistent with the observations of several historians and sociologists.

What causes moral visions to shift? The causes of the dynamics of crisis may be endogenous, exogenous, or both (proposition 3). If, as Sorokin agued, *every* "system of truth and reality" is inherently imperfect and inadequate, then the limitations of one moral vision as a guide to thought and action become increasingly apparent over time.[145] Each of the two fundamental moral visions, what Sorokin called "truth of faith" and "truth of senses" (absolutism and relativism),[146] is a half of a whole and hence inherently inadequate. Indeed, says Sorokin, each system increasingly "leads its human bearers away from the reality, gives them pseudo knowledge instead of real knowledge, and hinders their adaptation and the satisfaction of their physiological, social, and cultural needs."[147] If so, then moral visions may shift—or at least have a propensity to shift—for endogenous reasons.

What about exogenous reasons? Since intergenerational replacement drives value change in most economically advanced democracies (except for America's traditional values), this demographic process might explain shifting moral visions. For this process to account for the observed increase in absolutism and decrease in relativism (chapter 3), America's younger generations would have to be more absolutist than the older generations. A birth cohort analysis reveals this is not so. Figure 4.1 portrays the percentage of absolutists by age group in 1981, for the 1981, 1990, and 2000 surveys. The differences across generations are small, with a modest tendency for the older cohorts to have a higher percentage of absolutists compared to the younger cohorts (this modest tendency disappears by 2000).[148] These findings do not support a hypothesis of intergenerational replacement as the basis of rising absolutism in America.

Comparing age groups across surveys shows that Americans of *all ages* became more absolutist from 1981 to 1990. The youngest cohort in the 1981 survey, ages 18–27, continued this trend, becoming even more absolutist from 1990 to 2000. In fact, the percentage of absolutists in this cohort almost doubled during the two decades, starting at 33 percent in 1981 and ending at 64 percent in 2000. A middle age cohort in 1981, the 38–47 age group, is the only one that became less absolutist between 1990 and 2000, but it still ended up more absolutist than it was in 1981 (38 percent in 1981 versus 46 percent in 2000). Overall, the results reveal a rising tide of absolutism that swept over all age cohorts.

The rising tide of absolutism also appears to have swept over all social classes, men and women, whites and nonwhites, married and not married. For example, the percentage of absolutists in every socioeconomic group—working/lower, lower middle, upper middle, and upper—increased significantly from 1981 survey to 1990 (fig. 4.2). For example, 59 percent of working/lower-class Americans were absolutists in 1990, up from 43 percent in 1981.[149] Similarly, 42 percent of upper-class Americans were absolutists in 1990, up

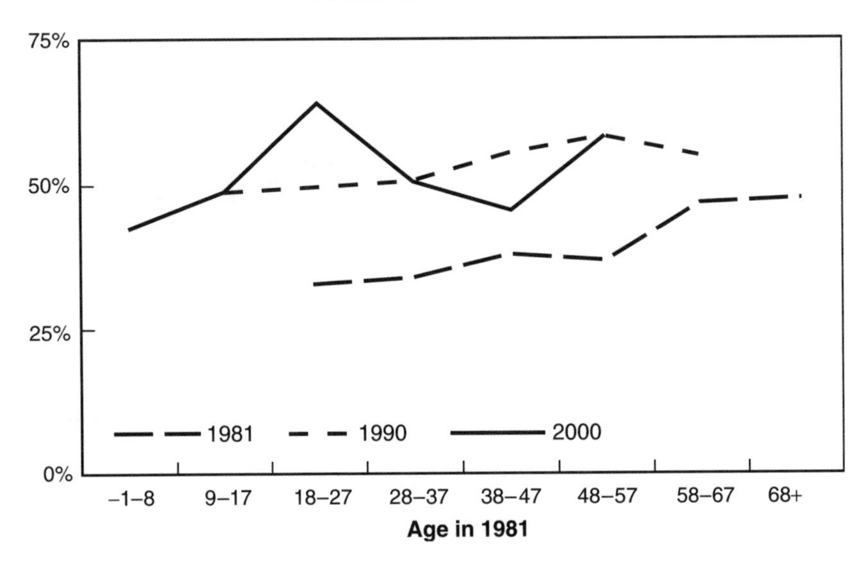

Figure 4.1. Percentage of absolutists by age group in 1981, United States.
Source: World Values Surveys, 1981, 1990, and 2000.

from 31 percent in 1981. The percentage of absolutists in every social class decreased slightly from 1990 to 2000, but these reversals are small and the proportion of absolutists for every social class in 2000 is higher than it was in 1981 (fig. 4.2). (The appearance of a negative correlation between percentage of absolutists and social class, suggested by the downward sloping lines, is not statistically significant; see findings in chapter 3.)

Absolutism rose during the decade of the 1980s among men, women, those who are married, those who are not, whites, and nonwhites (fig. 4.3). For example, 50 percent of American men were absolutists in 1990, up from 37 percent in 1981. Similarly, 55 percent of American women were absolutists in 1990, up from 39 percent in 1981. Levels for both men and women in 2000 are about the same as they were in 1990. The percentage of absolutists among the married increased from 38 percent in 1981 to 54 percent in 1990 and continued to rise by four percentage points ten years later. The pattern for the unmarried is similar to the married from 1981 to 1990, but, in contrast, the proportion of absolutists among the unmarried decreased slightly by 2000. The percentage of absolutists among whites in 1990

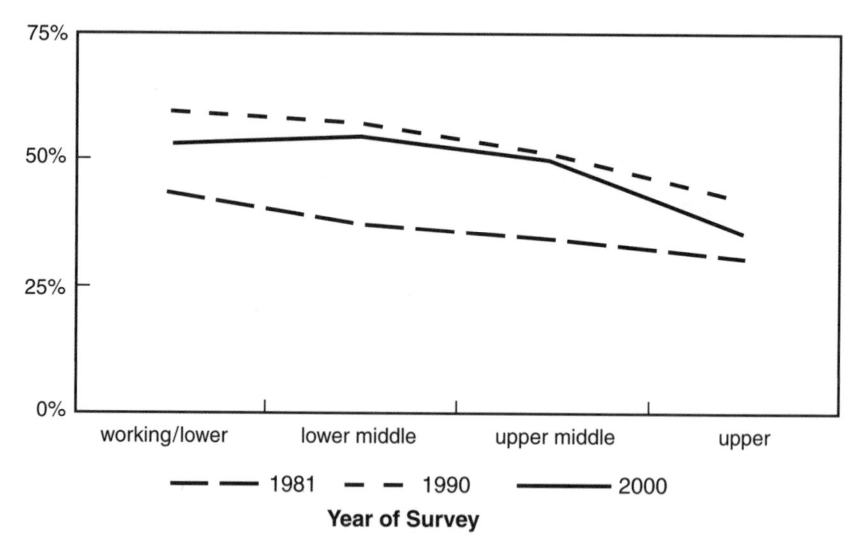

Figure 4.2. Percentage of absolutists by social class, United States.
Source: World Values Surveys, 1981, 1990, and 2000.

was 52 percent, up from 38 percent in 1981, while the proportions in 1990 and 2000 are the same. The percentage of absolutists among nonwhites in 1990 was 57 percent, up seven percentage points since 1981, but by 2000 the proportion returned to its 1981 level. The general pattern (except for nonwhites) is an increase in absolutism from 1981 to 1990, and small changes from 1990 to 2000.

Taken together, these patterns suggest that the decade of the 1980s was pivotal: The major shift in moral visions occurred from 1981 to 1990 for all age cohorts, for all social classes, for men and women, for married and unmarried, and for whites and nonwhites. From 1990 to 2000, moral visions exhibit stability or only small changes (except for nonwhites). We know that intergenerational replacement did not cause the shift, per the analysis above. What else could have caused moral visions to change in the 1980s? Jaspers, Orrù, and others observe that absolutism rises and relativism falls during times of economic and sociopolitical decline, and that absolutism falls and relativism rises during times of economic prosperity and sociopolitical growth.[150] As Orrù puts it, "periods of economic progress are accompanied by innovation in the cultural and moral spheres [rela-

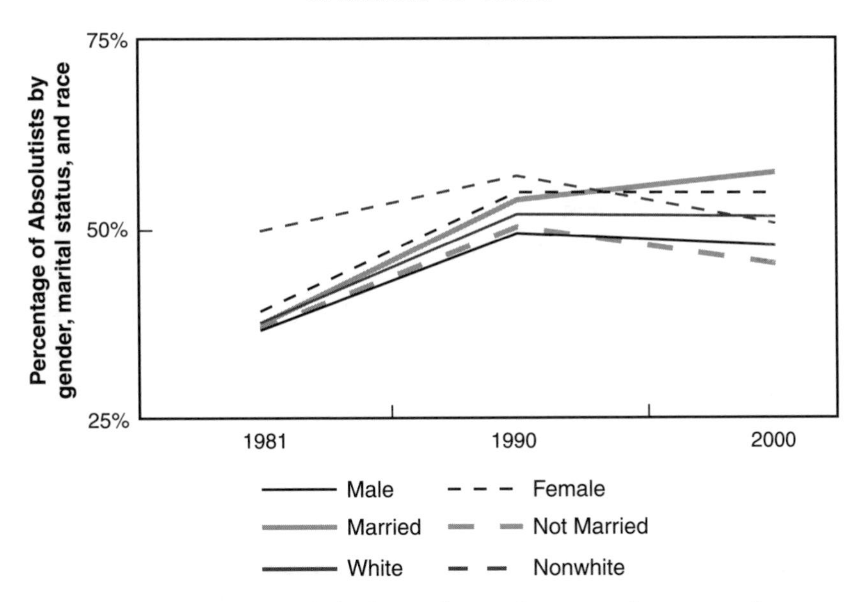

Figure 4.3. Percentage of absolutists by gender, marital status, and race, United States.

Source: World Values Surveys, 1981, 1990, and 2000.

tivism]. Likewise, situations of economic and political decline can be matched with the tendency to entertain idealistic and other-worldly views of the same social reality [absolutism]."[151] Similarly, Barley and Kunda show that managerial ideologies alternate between absolutism and relativism, driven by changes in economic conditions: "Rational rhetorics" (relativism) dominate during periods of economic expansion; "normative rhetorics" (absolutism) dominate during periods of economic contraction.[152] If these arguments are correct, then we should look to changes in socio-economic and political conditions for the cause of the shift in moral visions during the 1980s.

Many social indicators exhibit a large drop in America's "civic health" during the 1980s. One example is the Index of National Civic Health (INCH), a composite of twenty-two measures of political participation, trust, group memberships, personal security, and various family statistics.[153] As shown in figure 4.4, this index was fairly stable from 1974 to 1983, but then fell steeply thereafter.[154] Such statistics were alarming to many Americans. For example,

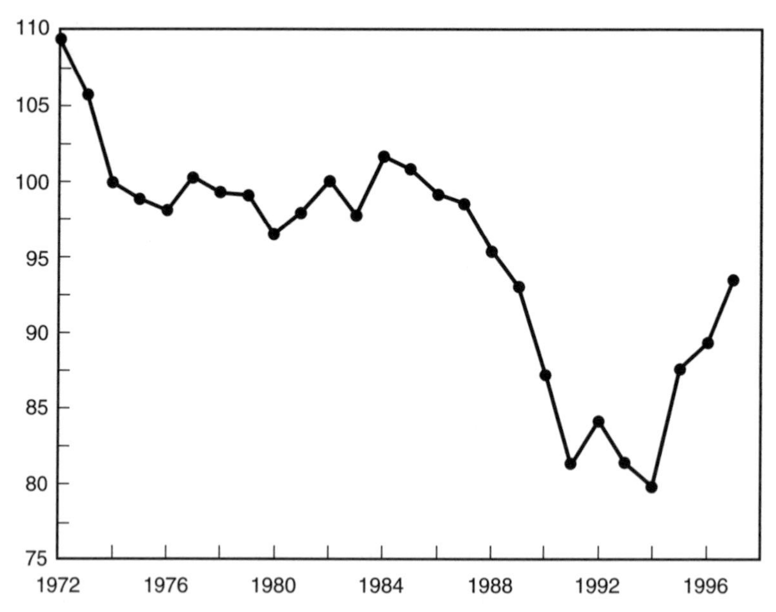

Figure 4.4. The Index of National Civic Health (INCH), 1972–1997.
Source: National Commission on Civic Renewal
Note: 1974 is baseline year, index set to 100.

Clem Brooks reports that public concern about "family decline" climbed steadily after 1980.[155]

Economic indicators tell a similar story of a tumultuous decade. According to data from the 1990 U.S. Census, the 1980s experienced modest economic growth. However, notes Reynolds Farley, this growth was not as favorable or as prosperous as growth in the several decades after World War II.[156] Moreover, the 1980s witnessed declining earnings, increasing poverty, increasing income inequality, increasing wealth inequality, and increasing racial inequality.[157] The gender gap in earnings narrowed, but the glass ceiling for women (and minorities) was not broken. Workers who were well educated and trained for specialized jobs thrived in the emerging information economy, but for the majority of Americans, who lacked the right education and skills, finding and holding onto good jobs became more tenuous and uncertain.[158] And, the 1980s saw the cutback or elimination of numerous social programs, removing the social safety net for many Americans. Thus, both social and economic indicators suggest that the decade of the 1980s was one of economic and social turmoil, if not decline, which may have caused the shift in moral visions between 1981 and 1990. Indeed, as Farley concludes from his analysis of the 1990 census data, "We do not seem to be on the road to becoming a more prosperous and equitable nation, and many people seem to be falling behind. This is the main reason for the persisting American Anxiety."[159]

It appears that moral visions shifted in the 1980s due to both endogenous and exogenous causes (proposition 3), but traditional values remained stable (chapter 2; proposition 4). The inherent limitations of moral visions supplied an endogenous propensity to change, while declining "civic health" and turbulent economic conditions provided an exogenous impetus to shift toward absolutism. Absolutism rose across American society. All age groups, social classes, men and women, married and unmarried, whites and nonwhites became more absolutist during the 1980s, and almost all of these groups and categories maintained their absolutist moral vision through the eve of the millennium.

An Answer to the Condition of America Question

The "condition of America question" is the seeming contradiction of fact and perception: Most Americans perceive a widespread crisis of values even though Americans have not lost their traditional values, the nation does not compare unfavorably with other nations, and American society is not split into two polarized moral camps (chapters 2 and 3). Americans have a lot in common and tend to share the most important values and beliefs. The answer to the fact-perception gap is linked to the shift during the 1980s from the dominance of relativism to an equal distribution of moral visions. When the two moral visions appear in equal measure, the inherent tension between them (proposition 1) reaches peak intensity. The splitting-projecting dynamic I defined above operates at its highest pitch at this time. Correspondingly, the "interaction of contradictory principles" that the attraction of opposites is supposed to manage appears to be at its most disharmonious, threatening "to tear the world apart, and humankind with it."[160] The intensity of the tension between moral visions creates the appearance of maximum disagreement about values and attitudes (even though religious beliefs, cultural values, and social attitudes are only loosely linked to moral visions), thereby producing a widespread perception of America's crisis of values.

The dynamics of crisis can be linear, cyclical, or both (proposition 5). The twenty-year coverage of the World Values Surveys is not long enough to adjudicate between linear and cyclical models. Based on my review of theories of political and religious change, I assume that the dynamics behind the condition of America question are both cyclical and linear. My interpretation of America's crisis of values emphasizes its cyclical features, while acknowledging that the dynamics of crisis also may have a linear component.

Consider the illustration of cyclical dynamics in figure 4.5. This figure is a highly stylized view of cyclical dynamics, but it captures the essence of the counterpoised fluctuations of moral visions over time observed by Orrù, Jaspers, and others. Each moral vision follows a transverse wave pattern, but each moves in a direction opposite to the other. The distribution of moral visions at a particular moment can be found by drawing a vertical line across the two waves. The points where the line intersects the waves indicate the distribution of absolutism and relativism at a given time. For example, a vertical line at Time 1 (T_1) intersects the crest of the absolutism wave (A_1) and the trough of the relativism wave (R_1), indicating that absolutism dominates relativism at that moment. Moving forward in time, absolutism falls to its trough (A_2) and relativism rises to its crest (R_2) by Time 2 (T_2). The notation "E" in figure 4.5 stands for a point in time when the two moral visions exist in equal measure. Points E_1 and E_2 indicate two times when the distribution of moral visions attains its maximum variation (50 percent absolutist and 50 percent relativist).

Assuming Fogel's estimates are accurate, the duration of a cycle—the wavelength of each transverse wave in figure 4.5—is about one hundred years (table 4.1). In 1981 one-third of Americans were absolutists; by 1990 half were absolutists (chapter 3). This pattern implies that America in 1981 was just to the left of point E_2 in figure

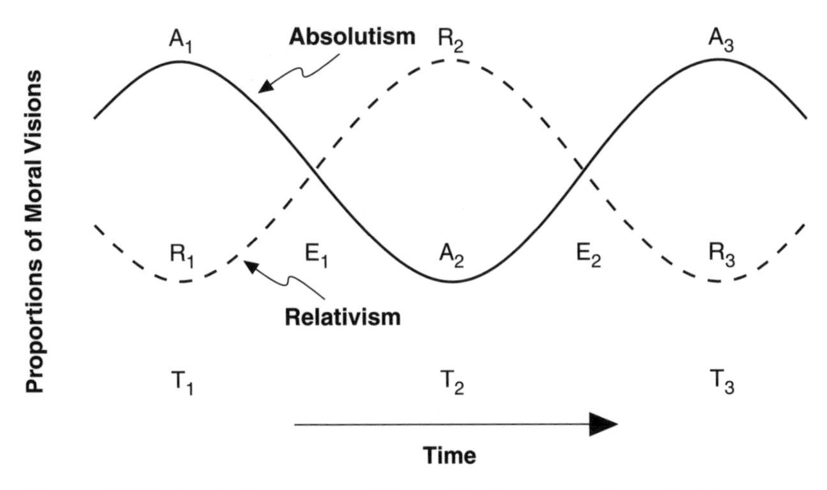

Figure 4.5. Stylized illustration of the cyclical pattern of moral visions.

4.5, arriving at E_2 in 1990. The inherent propensity to change, coupled with exogenous forces, may have produced the shift to E_2 (proposition 3).

Equal numbers of absolutists and relativists intensify a perception of a crisis of values because this distribution creates the appearance of maximum disagreement about the constellation of values surrounding these moral visions. These moral visions are significantly correlated with religious beliefs, cultural values, and social attitudes (chapter 3). For example, absolutists tend to have traditional and survival values; relativists tend to have secular-rational and self-expression values. The linkages of moral visions, cultural-religious values, and social attitudes are loose rather than tight; in the language of cognitive science, the radial categories of absolutism and relativism tend to "cohere," but there is enough variation for absolutists and relativists to share values and attitudes. In other words, Americans agree on important values and social issues yet disagree on the moral visions underlying their opinions. As mentioned in chapter 3, this loose linkage is consistent with attitude models in psychology that decompose attitudes into a set of beliefs, each having its own valuation; two people can share an attitude while having different underlying beliefs.

Figure 4.6 presents a stylized illustration of the patterns observed in

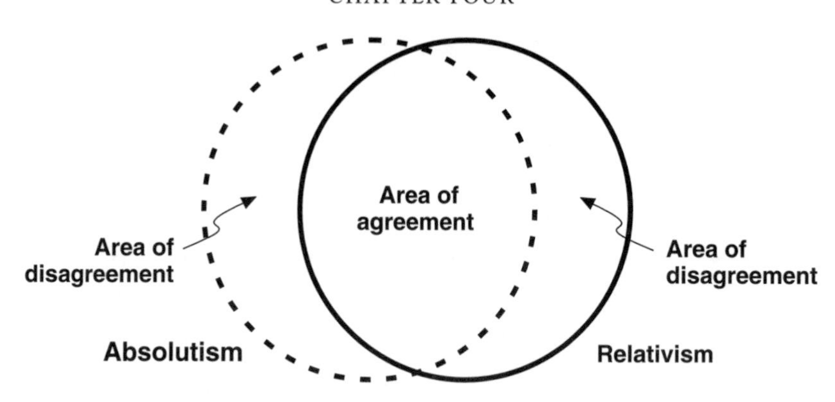

Figure 4.6. Stylized illustration of areas of agreement and disagreement associated with dual moral visions.

the various analyses of moral visions, values, and attitudes (chapters 2–3). This Venn diagram illustrates areas of agreement and disagreement between absolutists and relativists. Most Americans tend to share values and attitudes; despite differences in moral visions, most Americans are located in the intersection of the two circles. The minority of Americans, who take extreme positions based on moral visions, are located outside the area of intersection, to the left or to the right. The alternation of moral visions pulls the circles apart or pushes them together, expanding and contracting areas of agreement and disagreement. When the dual visions are held in equal measure (point E_2 in figure 4.5), the distance between the centroids of these circles is at its maximum, the area of agreement is at its minimum, and the areas of disagreement are at their maximums. This appears to be the condition of America at the end of the twentieth century. Even though the area of agreement is sizable, there is the appearance of maximum disagreement between the holders of the two moral visions. This appearance produces a widespread perception of a crisis of values.

Of course, the appearance of maximum disagreement would not be possible if absolutists and relativists were segregated. The perception of a crisis of values would not arise in a society composed of isolated groups, each with its own moral code. Opportunities for contact between holders of opposed worldviews are necessary for the opposition of views to become known and to contribute to the perception of crisis. For example, the moral crisis in ancient Athens was precipitated, in part, by new and unprecedented opportunities for contact: "At the social level," Orrù notes, "the democratic experience of Athens enhanced the free and open discussion of politics, while Athenian imperialism brought its citizens in touch with different cultures. Both factors prompted the scrutiny of cultural values which had been held, until then, to be fixed and unchanging."[161]

Usually, societies are segregated into more or less homogeneous social circles, based on age, class, geography, religion, occupation, and so forth. Interaction tends to occur inside these circles rather than between them.[162] For example, social interaction is often age-graded: the young tend to interact with the young, the old with the old. In the United States, the observed *lack* of significant associations between moral visions and most sociodemographic characteristics (chapter 3) indicates that absolutists and relativists are not segregated into separate social circles. Rather, they live in the same communities, work side-by-side, go the same schools, and socialize in the same places. Similarly, Diana Eck observes that members of the diverse religious groups in America—Muslims, Buddhists, Sikhs, Catholics, Jews, Protestants, and all their varieties—live in the same neighborhoods and go to the same schools.[163]

This intermixing contributes to the sense of a crisis of values because absolutists and relativists confront their incompatibilities on a regular basis. Moreover, rising absolutism is not confined to particular groups or categories of Americans: It swept over all age groups, classes, races, gender, and marital statuses. Intermixing equal numbers of absolutists and relativists produces the appearance of maximum disagreement about values, even though traditional values have not been lost, the nation compares favorably to other societies, and it is not divided into a dual social organization based on irreconcilably opposed moral visions.

The perception of a crisis may erupt irregularly and without warning, reflecting any number of external stimuli (natural disaster, epidemic, terrorist attack, stock market crash, and so on). Cycle theories suggest, however, that the perception of a crisis of values appears with some regularity. Recall that the basic structure of Fogel's model involves overlapping political and religious cycles, with each long awakening cycle divided into three overlapping phases. A sense of crisis and conflict is the most intense when the third phase of the old awakening cycle overlaps the first phase of the new awakening cycle, that is, when the phase of escalating challenge to the dominance of a political program overlaps the phase of religious revival. Using Fogel's dating, the latest occurrence of this overlap started circa 1970 and continued through the 1990s (see table 4.1). If these dates are correct, then the shift in moral visions captured by the World Values Surveys occurred in a time of cycle overlap—the third phase of the Third Great Awakening and the first phase of the Fourth Great Awakening. During this time, the counterpoised waves of absolutism and relativism fluctuated to the point when the distribution of moral visions obtained its maximum variation (50 percent absolutist and 50 percent relativist). And when the dual moral visions are held in equal measure, the appearance of disagreement about values obtains its maximum—hence, a perception of a crisis of values. Of course, this perception did not appear suddenly and all at once. It had to have started years earlier, prior to the first World Values Survey, when the overlap of the two cycles began (circa 1970). As the overlap increased, the perception of a crisis of values climbed over time to a high point in the 1990s.

Another way to say this is that America at the turn of the millennium was in the midst of a transition, marked by a shift in the distribution of moral visions. When the nation is in the midst of a period of transition, the subjective experience is a crisis of values, even though traditional values have not been lost, the nation compares favorably to other nations, and it is not divided into opposed moral camps. This transition period creates the appearance of maximum disagreement about moral values, thereby producing a widespread perception of America's crisis of values.

Consistent with this interpretation, reports of everyday experiences during times of cycle overlap in the past reveal recurrent bouts of acute uncertainty and anxiety. Consider, for example, Alexis de Tocqueville's observations of "American character" during his 1830s' sojourn in America—the end of the First Great Awakening and the start of the Second. He reported a "strange melancholy," the "serious and almost sad" demeanor of Americans, and the sense that "minds are anxious and on edge." He devoted a chapter of *Democracy in America* to the issue of "Why the Americans are often so restless in the midst of their prosperity."[164] In 1881 George Beard published *American Nervousness*, based on his observations of the overlap of the Second and Third Great Awakenings, and coined "neurasthenia" to describe the personal experience of social change, a term that enjoyed wide circulation in American society at the time.[165] Beard's book was a best-seller in its day.

America's so-called Gilded Age (also called the "incorporation of America"[166]), 1870–1920, was the declining phase of the Second Great Awakening and the rising phase of the Third. During this period, the nation experienced unprecedented technological change, economic growth, and social upheaval. The industrial transformation of the American economy had produced new levels of prosperity, great wealth (for a few), but also dire social problems, existential anxiety, and fear that the moral order of the nation was eroding. As Judy Hilkey describes,

> [V]isible extremes of wealth and poverty raised the specter of a two-class society in which opportunity for the average man might be curtailed. Along with these forebodings came the fear of corruption and vice, focusing especially on the city—the suspected refuge of foreigners, Catholics, political "bossism," gambling, liquor, prostitution, socialism, and all forms of ungodliness. For the middling sort of native-born, Protestant, small-town American, such fears may have been a displacement of other anxieties closer to home, where everything from the decline of self-employment to the rise of the New Woman and the advent of Darwinism threatened to change the way people worked, lived, and believed. Whatever the specific focus, some Americans, even those who enjoyed the gains in prosperity and life-improving advances brought by industrialization, were apprehensive about what they saw or experienced as social consequences of the industrial age, changes that might jeopardize the American tradition of individual opportunity, undermine the moral order of the nation, or threaten the legitimacy of the social order.[167]

The world had been made small, as Jack London wrote in January 1900: "What a playball has this planet of ours become! Steam had made its parts accessible and drawn them closer together. The telegraph annihilates space and time. Each morning every part knows what every other part is thinking, contemplating, or doing. A discovery in a German laboratory is being demonstrated in San Francisco within twenty-four hours. The death of an obscure missionary in China, or of a whiskey smuggler in the South Seas, is served up with the morning toast."[168] And "smallness" was the personal experience of these times, says John M. Staudenmaier—"the feeling of being 'made small' as an adult in the face of systems that transcend your intelligence."[169] Before the Gilded Age, ordinary people could understand the workings of everyday technologies. Starting in the Gilded Age, ordinary people could no longer understand the miraculous technologies that were part of daily experience.

Anxiety, doubt, uncertainty, and a sense of crisis ensued, the widespread experience of which created a demand for a new literary genre, the "success manual." These self-help manuals, as Hilkey defines in her definitive treatment, "were didactic, book-length works of nonfiction literature that promised to show men how to find success in life."[170] Aimed at the large market of alienated, confused, and disenchanted young men, these manuals offered hope, reassurance, and guidance in a time in which most Americans "lacked the conceptual tools and experience needed to grasp the degree to which the power to affect one's destiny had been removed from the individual, the family, and the local community and concentrated in a complex maze of interdependent, impersonal forces."[171] Over 144 different book-length success manuals were published in the Gilded Age. Many become best-sellers even by today's standards. For example, the 600-page *The Royal Path of Life* (first edition 1876) sold over 800,000 copies; four books by Samuel Smiles, *Self-Help* (1860), *Character* (1871), *Thrift* (1875), and *Duty* (1880), together sold more than a million copies.[172]

Any number of popular books could be cited as evidence of the personal experiences of the Third and Fourth Great Awakenings (see examples cited in chapter 1). For example, in the first phase of the

Third Great Awakening, a time that saw a shift to a more secular interpretation of the Bible, Walter Lippman described in his best selling *A Preface to Morals* our "modern uneasiness" and "anarchy in [our] souls" wrought by unbelief in religion and kings.[173] In the overlap of the Third and Fourth Great Awakenings, Robert Bellah, Richard Madson, Ann Swidler, and Steven Tipton in *Habits of the Heart* told about "the internal incoherence of our own society" caused by the moral dilemma of extreme individualism versus community.[174] Their book was a best seller. And, Richard Sennett in *Corrosion of Character* chronicles the personal consequences of work in the "new capitalism" of the 1980s and beyond.

My interpretation of America's crisis of values emphasizes cyclical patterns, but the dynamics of crisis also may have a linear component (proposition 5) such as a long-term steady baseline or a slowly rising trend. For example, the role that crisis rhetoric plays in the preservation of the nation's imagined community could produce a long-term steady (or slowly rising) perception of a crisis of values. As discussed in chapter 2, crisis rhetoric serves to maintain a sense of mutuality among people by focusing attention on the values that constitute the "collective conscience" of a nation.[175] A function of crisis rhetoric, therefore, is to preserve the ideological core America's imagined community. Since the need for preservation is always present, there may be a steady base level of demand for crisis rhetoric. If the supply of warnings of a "crisis of values" meets this steady demand, together they would produce a constant level of perceived crisis of values. Cyclical variations would rise above and fall back to this baseline, but the perception of crisis would not drop below this base level.

The argument of a base or constant level of perceived crisis of values (with cyclical variations) is a hypothesis, one that would require a new study to investigate. Within the boundaries of the current study, there is a different linear component to examine. The analysis in chapter 2 demonstrated a clear linear trend along the second cultural dimension—survival versus self-expression values. Since 1981 Americans have moved continuously away from survival values to self-expression values. This linear trend, coupled with the stability of traditional values, means that the *gap* between America's locations on these two dimensions has been growing over time. This widening gap itself is a linear trend. As I discuss in the next chapter, it may indicate growing cultural contradictions in American society because traditional values and self-expression values are contrary guides to conduct. Traditional values promote obedience to an absolute, external, transcendental moral authority, but self-expression values promote obedience to a relative, internal, mundane authority—oneself. This conflict of principles sends mixed messages about goals, guides to action, and standards for judging behavior, thereby contributing to a perception of a crisis of values. Moreover, to the extent Americans internalized these cultural contradictions, they experience cognitive dissonance—a personal sense of crisis. As I show in the next chapter, Americans who have internalized these contradictions use the cognitive dissonance it creates to spur the search for meaning.

Conclusion

This chapter addresses the "condition of America question." This condition is an apparent contradiction of fact and perception. On the one hand, the evidence in chapters 2 and 3 demonstrates that America has not lost its traditional values, that the nation compares favorably with other societies, and that it is not divided into two opposing moral camps based on incompatible moral visions. On the other hand, there is a widespread and persisting perception of a crisis of values. Most Americans believe that traditional values are in decline, that Americans no longer have much in common or share many values, and that the nation is divided when it comes to the most important values. Thus, the facts about values in America clash with beliefs about values. The condition of American question suggests that both the facts about values and the perception of a crisis of values are valid. The goal of this chapter was to develop an interpretation of the dynamics of crisis that accounts for the fact-perception discrepancy.

My review of theories of political and religious change suggests five propositions that a reasonable interpretation of a crisis of values must take into account: (1) A tension between opposites animates the dynamics of crisis; (2) Each side of a duality requires the other; neither side intends to demolish the other; (3) The causes of the dynamics of crisis may be endogenous, exogenous, or both; (4) Traditional values can remain stable over a long time even as crises come and go; and (5) Linear models and cycle models are alternatives, but they are not necessarily incompatible. The interpretation I develop in this chapter is consistent with these five propositions, consistent with the empirical findings of previous chapters, and consistent the writings of additional historians, sociologists, and psychologists. It is supported by new analyses of the survey data I conducted to explore key points. The overall result is an interpretation that provides a reasonable answer to the condition of America question.

The dynamics of crisis are animated by the tension between the dual moral visions of absolutism versus relativism. Absolutism and relativism are indissoluble partners in the dialectic of morality. The inherent limitations of each moral vision as guides to thought and action side provide a propensity to change from one to the other. Declining civic health and turbulent economic conditions induced the shift away from relativism toward absolutism. Absolutism rose across American society: All age groups, social classes, men and women, married and unmarried, whites and nonwhites became more absolutist during the 1980s.

The answer to the condition of America question is linked to the shift from the dominance of relativism to an equal distribution of moral visions. The inherent tension between absolutism and relativism reaches peak intensity at a time when the two moral visions appear in equal measure. The intensity of this tension produces the appearance of maximum disagreement about values and attitudes and thereby generates a widespread perception of America's crisis of values. This appearance of maximum disagreement and its attendant perception of a crisis of values are possible because absolutists and relativists have ample opportunities for contact. Because absolutism rose in all groups and categories, absolutists and relativists are intermixed and forced to confront their incompatibilities on a regular basis.

A sense of crisis may erupt irregularly and without warning, due to cataclysmic events, but my interpretation of the dynamics of crisis emphasizes that the perception of a crisis of values recurs with some regularity. This recurrence is based on the cyclical alternations of dual moral visions. It assumes that one or the other moral vision dominates most of the time (though both are always present). From time to time, however, absolutism and relativism appear in equal measure and produce the appearance of maximum disagreement about values and attitudes. These periods of apparent disagreement and discord occur in the overlap of long cycles, as when the third and last phase of an old awakening cycle overlaps the first phase of the new awakening cycle. It seems that America at the turn of the millennium is in the middle of a period of transition. The subjective experience is a crisis of values, even though traditional values have not been lost, the nation compares favorably to other societies, and it is not divided into a dual social organization based on irreconcilably opposed moral visions.

My interpretation emphasizes the cyclical component of a crisis of values, while acknowledging that the dynamics of crisis also may have a linear component. In the last chapter, I explore one such linear component of the dynamics of crisis, the trend toward self-expression values and the growing gap between America's locations on the two cultural dimensions. This gap indicates growing cultural contradictions in American society. As I show, Americans who have internalized these contradictions experience cognitive dissonance and use this dissonance to stimulate the search for meaning. Thus, we now turn to explore the "reality of individual experience" in a period of transition, seeing how the broad sociological and historical processes analyzed in the current chapter translate into personal experience.

✶ CHAPTER FIVE ✶

The Search for Meaning

THE GOAL OF THIS BOOK, set forth in the opening paragraph of chapter 1, is to clarify the widespread perception at the turn of the millennium of an American crisis of values. As such, this book is an attempt to regard old questions about moral values from a new angle. These questions are old because concerns and debates about moral values recur throughout American history and world history. The present-day crisis of values in America is the latest expression of cycles of crisis that can be traced back in history and, I believe, will continue in the future.

The questions about moral values are old in part because the same binary conceptual system—the dual moral visions of absolutism and relativism—has been used throughout history to think, conceptualize, and talk about moral questions. This dual conceptual system comes in many varieties, forms, and expressions, but the twin concepts of absolutism and relativism represent the central tendencies used in moral discourse. Of course, some of the *specifics* about America's contemporary crisis of values are new, such as the questions raised about human genetic engineering. Yet the moral debates about human genetic engineering reveal the same attraction of dual worldviews—the dynamic interplay of absolutism and relativism.[1] One of the main points of this book is that, regardless of the specifics of particular moral issues, the same conceptual system is used to think and talk about moral questions.

The new angle on old questions about moral values is a massive amount of data: comparative and longitudinal data on the value systems of a large number of societies, including the United States. The analysis in this book is based on data from multiple waves of the World Values Surveys, supplemented with findings from other surveys, archival sources, and other studies. The World Values Surveys are the largest systematic attempt ever made to document attitudes, values, and beliefs around the world (see appendix A for details). The United States has been included in every wave, providing four snapshots of America's value system from 1981 to 2000. These data provide an unprecedented opportunity to evaluate the American crisis of values from multiple angles. For example, the few comparative studies of America's values include, explicitly or implicitly, only a handful of other societies.[2] Data from the World Values Surveys, however, permit a comparison of America's values on a global scale. These data permit two examinations of value change: one comparing America to itself, tracing changes in its trajectory over time, and the other comparing the nation to others, examining America's trajectory over time in relation to the trajectories of others. Finally, the World Values Surveys data permit analysis of the internal variation of America's value system at a single point in time, as well as over multiple points in time. Together, these analyses make this book the most comprehensive study to date of America's crisis of values.

In this concluding chapter, I explore the search for meaning—the attempt to make sense of the personal experience of a crisis of values. This subject could be a book in itself. Here, I confine my remarks to three key areas directly related to the analysis in the preceding chapters. I begin by considering what America's mixed system of traditional and self-expression values means for the personal experience of crisis. This mixed system, as I argue below, provides contrary guides to conduct, sending mixed messages about goals, guides to action, and standards for judging behavior. Americans who have internalized these cultural contradictions experience cognitive dissonance and use this tension to stimulate thinking about the meaning and purpose of life. Next, I discuss the phenomena of rising spirituality and the interest in the amalgamation of cultural elements known as the "New Age" movement as additional expressions of the search for meaning. I then focus on the theme of absolutism in America, describing how this moral vision plays a special role in the preservation of the nation's imagined community. Without this role, it would appear as if the moral core of what it means to be American had been lost—metaphorically, it would seem as if the nation had lost its guiding light. Finally, I assess the possibility of and obstacles to a synthesis of the cultural contradictions contained in the nation's mixed value system—an integration of opposites that would resolve the widespread perception of a crisis of values. The chapter ends with a summary of fifteen key findings from the empirical analyses in chapters 2, 3, 4, and 5.

Mixed Systems, Cultural Contradictions, and Cognitive Dissonance

America has a mixed system of traditional values and self-expression values (chapter 2). This mixed system deviates from the general global pattern. The general tendency is the *congruence* of values on the two cultural dimensions, indicated by an imaginary line drawn at a 45-degree angle in figure 2.1a or 2.1b in chapter 2. For example, Denmark and Sweden are "high" on both dimensions (secular-rational and self-expression values). Zimbabwe and Morocco are "low" on both (traditional and survival values). Spain and Israel are in between, "intermediate" on both dimensions. Distance from the imaginary line indicates the extent of value *in*congruence in a society. Societies far from this line include the United States (lower right) and the ex-Communist countries (upper left).

A mixed system contains "cultural contradictions" when its prevailing principles provide contrary guides to conduct. For example, Daniel Bell argues that the "cultural contradictions of capitalism" arise from the conflict of principles in economy and culture: efficiency versus self-expression. The "character structure" demanded in the economy is "self-control and delayed gratification, of purposeful behavior in the pursuit of well-defined goals."[3] This conflicts with the "character structure" dictated by culture—"self-expression and self-gratification." Thus, the principles of efficiency and self-expression "now lead people in contrary directions."[4]

America's mixed system—traditional values and self-expression values—contains cultural contradictions because its prevailing principles provide contrary guides to conduct. The principle underlying traditional values is obedience to an absolute, external, transcendental authority—God, country, and the authoritarian father figure (see chapter 3). But the principle underlying self-expression values is obedience to a mundane authority—oneself—in the pursuit of "a particularized creative process of individual growth."[5] Thus, the two central tendencies in American culture lead people in contrary directions: obedience to an absolute, external, transcendental authority *and* obedience to a relative, internal, mundane authority.

These contradictions are consistent with America's core ideology. On the one hand, America is one of the most religious, moralistic, and patriotic societies anywhere. Preservation of traditional values is paramount because the loss of traditional values would be a direct assault on the ideological foundation of the imagined community of America. On the other hand, the postmodern quest for self-realization is also consistent with the American ideology; this individualistic quest is an expression of American core values as well. America is exceptional, and this exceptionalism, Lipset argues, is a "double-edged sword."[6] America's value system has built-in paradoxes and contradictions.

The cultural contradictions associated with traditional values and self-expression values create tensions in American society at large by prescribing contrary guides to conduct. But these cultural contradictions would create *cognitive dissonance* only if an individual internalizes them. Cognitive dissonance is an unpleasant feeling of psychological distress caused by a discrepancy between behavior and belief, or between two beliefs—such as belief in an absolute, external, transcendental moral authority and belief in a relative, internal, mundane moral authority. As I discuss below, a person who internalizes both traditional values and self-expression values experiences cognitive dissonance and is motivated to reduce it.

The extent to which individual Americans actually hold consistent or contrary values is an empirical question. To answer, I calculated a measure of value congruence based on deviations between standardized scores on the two cultural dimensions. A deviation score of zero indicates perfect value congruence—a person's position on one dimension is the same as the person's position on the other dimension. This person would be located on a 45° imaginary line in figure 2.1a or 2.1b. Deviation scores greater than zero indicate that a respondent is above the imaginary line, that is, with a tendency to be closer to the secular-rational pole of the traditional/secular-rational dimension than to the self-expression pole of the survival/self-expression dimension. A large positive deviation would indicate, for example, that a person holds secular-rational values and survival values. Deviation scores less than zero indicate that a respondent is below the imaginary line, with a tendency to be closer to the traditional pole of the traditional/secular-rational dimension than to the survival pole of the survival/self-expression dimension. A large negative deviation score would indicate, for example, that a person holds traditional values and self-expression values.

Generally, individual Americans tend to internalize traditional and self-expression values more than they internalize secular-rational and survival values.[7] This tendency is consistent with the results of nation-level analyses, which show that America, as a whole, has a mixed system of traditional and self-expression values (chapter 2). But are particular groups or categories of Americans more likely to have one or the other type of incongruent values? To answer, I compare the sociodemographic characteristics of Americans with positive deviation scores to Americans with negative deviation scores, estimating the likelihood that Americans would be to the right or to the left of zero as a function of various sociodemographic characteristics. In addition, I compare extreme cases: those in the 25th and 75th percentiles. The right tail includes Americans with extreme positive deviation scores, indicating a strong tendency toward secular-rational values coupled with survival values. The left tail includes Americans with extreme negative deviation scores, indicating a strong tendency toward traditional values linked with self-expression values.

Overall, the results reveal significant differences (tables 5.1–5.4). Americans who are older, white, female, married, of lower social classes, and Catholic are more likely to have internalized traditional and self-expression values. Conversely, those who are younger, nonwhite, male, unmarried, of higher social classes, and religions other than Protestantism or Catholicism are more likely to have internalized the alternative form of value incongruence—secular-rational and survival values.

Cognitive dissonance theory says that a person who feels psychological distress caused by discrepant beliefs is motivated to reduce it. The strength of this motivation is proportional to the degree of discrepancy between beliefs. Cognitive dissonance may be reduced in different ways. One option is to change one belief to be consistent with the other. For example, an American who holds traditional values *and* self-expression values could reduce cognitive dissonance by abandoning traditional values (such as religion) and becoming more secular-rational. The observed stability of traditional values in American society (chapter 2) implies that this course, on average, has not been taken. Another way to reduce cognitive dissonance is to change behavior, such as attending religious services less frequently, or switching membership from a conservative to a liberal congregation. However, social sanctions and social networks can constrain the ability to change behaviors. For example, attempting to avoid services or switch membership may incur rebuke, punishment, or outright ostracism (which would thereby prevent this method of reducing cognitive dissonance). A third way to reduce cognitive dissonance is to alter the importance placed on a belief or behavior. For example, a person could weigh the importance of traditional values less heavily, or place less value on attending services, either of which would reduce inconsistency with self-expression values.

I explore another alternative: reflection about the meaning and purpose of life. Thinking about the meaning and purpose of life may be a way to reduce the cognitive dissonance created by value incongruence. Thus, cognitive tension may be a catalyst in the search for meaning—one of the primary motivations in life.[8] Thinking about the meaning and purpose of life would be, in effect, an integration of contradictions at the individual level, a personal synthesis of opposites that attempts to "rise above" the apparent conflicts caused by contrary guides to action.

To test this hypothesis, I estimate the likelihood that Americans who experience value incongruence often think about the meaning and purpose of life, controlling for various sociodemographics and moral visions. First I compare Americans to the left of zero (negative deviation scores) with those to the right of zero (positive deviation scores). Next I compare Americans in the left tail (25th percentile) with those in the right tail (75th percentile). The results of the four waves of the World Values Surveys are shown in tables 5.5–5.8. The results vary somewhat from year to year, but the overall patterns are consistent with expectations. Generally, Americans who are to the left of zero are significantly more likely to think about the meaning and purpose of life, compared with those to the right of zero, even after controlling for moral visions and sociodemographics. This tendency is even stronger when we consider the extremes. For example, in 2000 Americans in the left tail of the distribution were 1.5 times as likely to think about the meaning and purpose of life, compared with those in the right tail, controlling for moral visions and sociodemographics. Moral visions themselves have predictable effects: Absolutists are more likely than relativists to think about the meaning and purpose of life, controlling for the other variables.

In other words, Americans who have traditional values and self-expression values are much more likely to think about the meaning and purpose of life, compared with those who have secular-rational and survival values. Perhaps the struggle to reconcile conflicting beliefs about sources of moral authority stimulates thinking about the meaning and purpose of life, while a survival orientation coupled with belief in a secular-rational moral authority encourages a focus on the here-and-now of everyday life in the mundane world. Thinking about the meaning and purpose of life may be an attempt at a personal integration of contradictions, an individual-level synthesis of the conflicting principles of a mixed system. If so, then it is an expression of what Thomas Luckmann calls the "little transcendences" experienced by the individual in everyday life.[9] Luckmann argues that, in modern life, such "little transcendences" are replacing the "great transcendences" of the salvational religions.

Since America retains its traditional values but continues to shift toward self-expression values, the gap between American's position on one dimension and its position on the other is widening over time. If this linear trend continues in the future, fewer Americans will have a mix of secular-rational and survival values, and more will have a mix of traditional and self-expression values. If so, then the proportion of Americans who often think about the meaning and purpose of life will rise over time as well.

Rising Spirituality and the "New Age"

America's crisis of values stimulates a search for transcendence—a rising above and integration of contradictions into a larger conceptual structure. Among Americans, the synthesis of contradictions occurs in an individual way, what Robert Wuthnow calls a "spirituality of seeking"—the exploration of new spiritual avenues and a personal quest for sacred moments.[10] This spirituality of seeking is replacing the "spirituality of dwelling"—transcendence experienced in sacred places—provided by traditional religion:

> A spirituality of dwelling emphasizes habitation: God occupies a definite place in the universe and creates a sacred place in which humans too can dwell. To inhabit sacred space—a church, synagogue, or mosque, for example—is to know its territory and to feel secure. By contrast, a spirituality of seeking emphasizes searching for sacred moments that reinforce their conviction that the divine exists. But these moments are fleeting; rather than knowing the territory, people explore new spiritual vistas, and they may have to negotiate among complex and confusing meanings of spirituality.[11]

Religious experience, argues Phillip Gorski, is becoming "a matter of personal preference. Individual 'consumers' fashion their personal worldviews out of the spiritual raw materials available in the contemporary religious marketplace."[12] These raw materials are the "spiritual capital" that Fogel says is required for the journey of self-realization.[13] The general trend, observes Luckmann, is one of "shrinking transcendence"—a process wherein the "little transcendences" experienced by seekers of spirituality replace the "great transcendences" of the salvational religions and the promise to bridge the chasm between the mundane and transcendental spheres.[14]

Accordingly, the World Values Surveys shows that church attendance is falling around the world, and at the same time spiritual concerns are rising (see chapter 2; table 5.9).[15] For example, the proportion of people who "often think about the meaning and purpose of life" has increased in 70 percent of the thirty-seven societies for which time-series data are available (table 5.9). The proportion of Americans who say they often think about the meaning and purpose of life has been higher than the global average in every year of the World Values Surveys, and higher than the proportions in virtually all other economically advanced democracies.[16] From 1995 to 2000, the proportion of Americans who often think about the meaning and purpose of life rose from 46 to 59 percent—a twenty-year high.[17] Gallup reports even higher numbers.[18] And, in my 2003 Detroit Area Study, 64 percent said that they often think about the meaning and purpose of life.

Similarly, the proportion of Americans who rate the "importance of God in their lives" as a "10" on a 10-point scale increased from 50 percent in 1995 to 58 percent in 2000. This figure, too, is a twenty-year high.[19] As mentioned before, 63 percent of respondents to the 2003 Detroit Area Study rated the importance of God in their lives as a "10." Nationwide, attendance at religious services increased from 1995 to 2000. The percentage of Americans attending at least once a month reached 60 percent in 2000, up five percentage points from the 1995 survey. This returned attendance at religious services to about the same levels observed in 1990 and 1981 (59 percent and 60 percent, respectively).[20] These statistics for the United States support the arguments Luckmann, Gorksi, and Wuthnow make about the trend of a rising spirituality of seeking. The persistent high levels of attendance at religious services, however, demonstrate that the spirituality of dwelling remains strong. Both forms of spirituality coexist in the American context.

Neither a spirituality of dwelling nor a spirituality of seeking is entirely new, according to Wuthnow.[21] Both types of spirituality are modes of thought and experience that have always existed in one form or another. The two types of spirituality appear to exhibit a cyclical pattern, rising and falling over time, driven by historical and material conditions. "In settled times," says Wuthnow, "people have been able to create a sacred habitat and to practice habitual forms of spirituality; in unsettled times, they have been forced to negotiate with themselves and with each other to find the sacred."[22]

Unsettled times, in general, open the possibility of "new or reorganized strategies of action."[23] These strategies are not built from scratch but draw on established cultural models to create new avenues of action.[24] The New Age movement is good example of a novel combination of beliefs, constructed from established cultural models during a time of a perceived crisis of values.[25] Observers such as Harold Bloom (*Omens of the Millennium*) view the New Age movement as little more than a "debased" version of Gnosticism, but the movement has roots everywhere, including nineteenth-century spiritualism and the 1960s' counterculture.[26] It is an amalgam of old traditions, myths, established religions, Eastern and occult mysticism, modern physics, astrology, high technology, alchemy, holistic medicine, feminism, ecology, music, psychology, parapsychology, spiritualism, millennialism, martial arts, shamanism, yoga, and other cultural elements.[27] The New Age belief system is so diverse and draws on so many cultural elements that it is as if the entire cultural tool kit were emptied and every tool put to some use. As a movement, it is organized as the type sociologists call "polycephalous" or many-headed—a loosely federated collection or network of individuals, groups, businesses, and organizations, operating without a single leader or centralized leadership structure and without a single authoritative source or formal doctrine. *The Celestine Prophecy*, James Redfield's best-selling adventure-parable, is a well-known and representative New Age work (which I interpret below as an exemplar of New Age value orientations).[28]

Few Americans may subscribe to the entire panoply of New Age beliefs, but the majority professes at least some of these beliefs, making it difficult to dismiss the New Age movement as a minor curiosity. For example, over 90 percent of Americans report believing in one or more of eighteen types of paranormal experiences.[29] Two of three Americans have experienced extrasensory perception (ESP).[30] Almost two-thirds report they have felt as though they were in touch with someone when they were far away from them.[31] Over 40 percent of Americans say they have felt as though they were really in touch with someone who had died.[32] One of three Americans believes in ghosts, and one of five believes in witches.[33] And almost one of two Americans believes that astrology has some scientific truth.[34] These New Age believers are not marginal members of society; according to Susannah Feher, they "tend to be wealthier and more educated than society as a whole."[35]

Part of the appeal of the New Age vision is all-inclusiveness: There is something for everyone, and no one is left out. Part of the appeal is hope—the promise of unity, of the integration of diverse and competing visions into a coherent whole, and perhaps, finally, the construction of a true bridge across the gulf separating the transcendental and mundane spheres. Part of the appeal is consistency with dominant American value orientations while extending them in compatible directions.[36] For example, human nature is considered to be essentially good and only in need of evolution. Human nature is perfectible; through reincarnation, each person has more than one chance to attain true spiritual awareness. This view of human nature continues a trend that started with the Puritanical concept of human nature as evil but perfectible, turning by the 1950s toward the concept of human nature as a mixture of good and evil, and arriving at the turn of the millennium with the New Age belief in the basic goodness of human nature.[37]

The millennial prediction of a spiritual transformation of society continues the dominant temporal emphasis on the future (though the New Age notion of "progress" is less materialistic than the dominant value orientation). In addition, the New Age movement extends the temporal focus of life into the past, restoring religions and spiritual traditions, and integrating them into a temporal whole of past-present-future. *The Celestine Prophecy*, for example, describes an ancient manuscript found in the rain forests of Peru that provides nine key insights into life and spiritual development and predicts the spiritual transformation of society to occur in the new millennium. The New Age emphasis on spiritual development shifts the focus of human activity from doing to being-in-becoming, a value orientation that "has as its goal the development of all aspects of the self as an integrated whole."[38] The value of doing is not lost, however, because New Age spiritual development requires deliberate action and produces results measurable by external standards.

New Age values retain the dominant emphasis on individualism but add greater concern for other people, past and present. In a sense, it closes the gap between individualism and collectivism. For example, the "interpersonal ethic" insight described in *The Celestine Prophecy* emphasizes relationships with family, friends, and others, while reincarnation emphasizes the lineal relationship of past lives.[39] New Age values are often assumed to express relativism, but the emphasis on reincarnation shows that New Age values are a mixture of absolutism and relativism. The absolutist tendencies of the New Age movement are often overlooked or ignored. However, the New Age system of belief posits the existence of an eternal transcendental domain, a realm of pure spirituality, to which each person travels upon death only to be returned to the mundane world for future spiritual development. A high level of spiritual enlightenment in the mundane world permits one to "cross over" to the transcendental world without dying. The process of continual reincarnation and spiritual development cannot be avoided; every person (and every society) continues on the path of inevitable spiritual evolution.

New Age beliefs depart somewhat from mainstream American value orientations in regard to the human relationship to nature and the cosmos. The New Age belief system rejects mastery over nature and embraces harmony with nature. The millennial image of *The Celestine Prophecy*, for example, depicts a culture that reveres nature, safeguards the environment, lives in small sustainable communities, and has decreased population size voluntarily to live within the limits of the ecosystem.[40] High technology is not banished from this ideal society, as long as it harmonizes with nature. According to *The Celestine Prophecy*, the coming ideal society will include the complete automation of production and farming, along with the use of fusion, superconductivity, and artificial intelligence, to provide the means of sustenance to all while allowing each person to pursue individual spiritual development.[41]

Whether or not New Age beliefs are "true," we can appreciate the New Age movement as a contemporary search for transcendence, an attempt to find purpose and meaning in life. In part, the movement represents the clamor and proliferation of ideas that come forth during times of social and cultural unrest. The movement also represents the millennial impulse that becomes active during turbulent times. "Periods of history characterized by anxiety and disruption," observes Michael St. Clair, "when the world seems out of joint to many people, seem specially fertile in generating millennial enthusiasm."[42] Although some of the claims of the New Age belief system seem far-fetched, it is important to recognize that New Age beliefs resonate with the prevailing climate of thought and experience. For example, the New Age belief system embraces, subsumes, and makes sense of the cultural contradictions described above—the mixed system of traditional values and self-realization values. The New Age prediction of sustainable communities is only a futuristic extension of rising concerns worldwide about the environment and increasing national efforts to protect the natural environment.[43] And the New Age de-emphasis of materialism in favor of spiritual development is consistent with the analysis of trends in the World Values Surveys data. Economic affluence is associated with a shift from materialistic values to postmaterialistic values, suggesting "that in an increasingly affluent world the relative marginal demand for material goods and services might decline in favor of a demand for nonmaterial items that tend to place less strain on the ecosystem. It is entirely possible," argues Glenn Firebaugh, "that a decreasing relative demand for resource-intensive material goods will emerge as a defining issue of the twenty-first century."[44]

Unsettled times create competition among cultural frameworks, as Ann Swidler points out, so that any social movement is "in active competition with other cultural frameworks—at least in competition with common sense and usually with alternative traditions and ideologies as well."[45] The New Age movement is not an exception. Many Christian groups, for example, take umbrage with New Age tenets. A scan of Christian publications and Web sites demonstrates tremendous effort spent combating New Age beliefs, such as monism, pantheism, and religious syncretism (all is one; everything is God and God is everything; all religions are true), and offering advice on how to debate these issues with New Age Christians.

Some dismiss the New Age movement as an unfortunate popular delusion. One interpretation finds the source of New Age beliefs in a human tendency to revert to superstition and irrationality during troubled times. For example, European writer Ignacio Ramonet observes the "ascent of the irrational" in modern life, as he describes in *A Directionless World*.[46] Active competition can be seen clearly in the debunking movement that has risen to counter many of the claims of the New Age Movement. Three popular examples—James Randi, Victor Stenger, and John Allen Paulos—use the cultural tools of logic, science, and mathematics to debunk New Age beliefs, pseudoscience, charlatanism, con games, fraud, and plain poor reasoning.[47] James Randi, a well-known magician and recipient of a MacArthur Foundation "genius award," writes and lectures extensively about his investigations and exposés of parapsychology, the paranormal, faith healers, occultism, shamanism, superstition, and so on. Victor Stenger, a physicist, attacks New Age beliefs that claim a scientific basis in modern physics. For example, he explains the lack of a scientific basis for "quantum consciousness," the belief that all human minds are connected to each other, allowing instantaneous communication, or that the cosmic field is connected to the universal mind of all humanity. Paulos, a mathematician and author of several debunking books, argues that mathematical illiteracy (or "innumeracy") turns many people into easy prey. He makes his case by attacking parapsychology, predictive dreams, astrology, UFOs, fraudulent medical treatments, numerology, stock market forecasts, conspiracy theories, and so forth. For example, he uses probability theory to debunk the New Age principle of "synchronicity" by revealing the frequency of unlikely events and chance encounters.[48]

Debunking is an admirable effort, an important corrective to ignorance, innocence, and naiveté; it serves to reduce fraud, abuse, and exploitation. Whether New Age beliefs fit the scientific facts, however, is beside the point. To dismiss New Age beliefs as an "eclipse of reason" (as Ramonet calls it) would be the same as indicting the Hopi ceremonial rain dance because it fails to produce rainfall. This dismissal misses the latent function beneath the manifest function. For many, New Age beliefs are a workable synthesis of cultural contradictions, providing guidance in unsettled times. Workable syntheses may not (and often do not) satisfy the requirements of science or logic. But workability cannot be judged only on these grounds. "Like bees who fly despite theories of aeronautics which deny them the right to do so," says Geertz, "probably the overwhelming majority of mankind are continually drawing normative conclusions from factual premises (and factual conclusions from normative premises . . .), despite refined, and in their own terms impeccable, reflections by professional philosophers on the 'naturalistic fallacy'."[49] The efforts to debunk New Age beliefs may not matter much to those seeking transcendence in a time of crisis.

The search for transcendence during unsettled times favors absolutism. This "absolutist impulse" stems, in part, from psychological forces. "People seem to need the idea that there is a world with pregiven features or ready-made information," says Karl Weick, "because to give up this idea of the world as a fixed and stable reference point is to fall into idealism, nihilism, or subjectivism, all of which are unseemly."[50] Myths, for example, are based on the assumption of a transcendental world that exists as a factual, fixed, and objective reality.[51] William James felt that we are absolutists by instinct.[52] Other psychologists believe absolutist thinking is a vestige of the preconscious mind,[53] or the outcome of an innate will to meaning. Absolutist thinking may stem from natural human credulity. According to Daniel Gilbert, human mental systems utilize a "Spinozan" belief procedure (comprehension and acceptance of an idea occur together and automatically) rather than a "Cartesian" belief procedure (explicit acceptance or rejection of an idea follows the act of comprehension and evaluation).[54] Thus, it is easier to accept New Age claims (or claims of an American culture war) without critical evaluation than it is to first subject such claims to close scrutiny.[55]

The Special Role of Absolutism in America

Thinking about the purpose and meaning of life and experimenting with New Age ideas may be some of the "little transcendences" of everyday life, but America was founded on the idea of the nation as a "great transcendence." A dominant theme in the early republic, notes Arthur Schlesinger, Jr., was "the idea of America as an experiment, undertaken in defiance of history, fraught with risk, problematic in outcome."[56] But alongside this theme emerged and grew "the mystical idea of an American national destiny."[57] Americans, wrote Reinhold Niebuhr, had "a religious version of our national destiny which interpreted the meaning of our nationhood as God's effort to make a new beginning in the history of mankind."[58] The conflict between these two themes—"realism and messianism, between experiment and destiny"—continues to this day.[59]

The mystical idea of an American national destiny is an expression of the special role of absolutism. The strength of absolutism in America is exceptional, qualitatively different from other economically advanced democracies (chapters 2 and 3). The reason absolutism thrives in America may be summarized by combining four arguments made in earlier chapters. As I elaborate below, these four taken together help to explain America's unusually high level of absolutism and the vital role absolutism plays in sustaining the imagined community of America.

1. The modern concept of national identity is the cultural basis for the constitutional state. As discussed in chapter 1, national identity helps to solve the twin problems of legitimation and social integration. In almost all cases, national identity—the popular self-consciousness of belonging to "the same" people—is based on common ancestry, religion, history, language, customs, traditions, and territory. In America, however, the self-consciousness of belonging to the "American people" is based on common ideas. Americans imagine themselves to be citizens of the same national community—to feel emotionally connected to one another—in part because they imagine that Americans share the same ideals, values, and aspirations. This ideational foundation of America is a chief feature of American exceptionalism. As Chesterton observed, America is "the only nation in the world that is founded on a creed."[60]

The American case supports Durkheim's argument that society itself is a source of absolute moral authority. The American ideology, as Emerson and Lincoln recognized, is the nation's "political religion," or, as Habermas puts it, the country's "civil religion." Similarly, Samuel Huntington says that Americans ascribe to their nation and its ideology "many of the attributes and functions of a church."[61] In contrast to other nations, America's imagined community is based on a set of ideas, and these ideas have as much legitimating and integrating force as religion.

2. The radial category of absolutism links the moral vision of absolutism to a constellation of traditional values. The analysis in this book demonstrates that absolutism is significantly related to God, religion, patriotism, authoritarian family values, conservative politics, and other traditional values. Other surveys provide supporting evidence. For example, a majority of Americans report, "God is the moral guiding force of American democracy."[62] Americans are the world's most patriotic people.[63] And Americans strongly support the American creed.[64] Thus, multiple transcendental sources of moral authority are interconnected in a mutually reinforcing system. In particular, America's civil religion and religion per se are interwoven, linking society as an absolute source of moral authority with religion as an absolute source of moral authority. Thus, the vitality of absolutism in America stems, in part, from its connection to more than one transcendental source.

3. America's traditional values are path dependent, incorporated in the nation's institutions and reproduced over time through intergenerational transmission. The set of values associated with overlapping sources of transcendental moral authority can be traced to the country's roots, where the initial conditions of the American value system were set down. Since then, the system has gone down a path of development that is not easily reversed. In other words, the complete radial category of absolutism is incorporated in the nation's institutions and reproduced over time as it is passed down from generation to generation. This path dependence is another reason for the vitality of absolutism in America.

4. Finally, the moral visions of absolutism and relativism are dialectically related, two parts of a single moral discourse expressed in a dynamic "attraction of opposites." Here, psychology joins sociology to

provide a multilevel explanation of the vitality of absolutism in America. As elaborated below, absolutists and relativists in America *need one another* for psychological reasons (to reduce cognitive dissonance) and for social reasons (to harmonize contradictory principles).

An individual person has both absolutist and relativist tendencies. This proposition is basic human psychology. It is expressed in various ways, such as the American belief in the perfectibility of human nature—human nature contains elements of the divine. Tocqueville observed, for example, that Americans hold fast to "the idea of the indefinite perfectibility of man." The American, he said, "is ever striving toward that immense grandeur glimpsed indistinctly at the end of the long track humanity must follow."[65] Having both absolutist and relativist tendencies, however, creates cognitive dissonance. This internal dissonance is aggravated by the contradiction of principles created by the cultural incongruence of traditional values and self-expression values. Cognitive dissonance is reduced through the splitting-projecting dynamic, casting the moral vision considered to be undesirable onto another person, group, or category. This process restores psychological equilibrium, but each side still needs the other. One side is "invested in remaining in the vicinity" of the other "to obtain vicarious gratification as the disowned parts of itself are enacted and to maintain the strength of the subgroup that carries these disowned parts."[66] Thus, psychological dynamics sustain both absolutism and relativism in America.

The attraction of opposites at the societal level, says David Maybury-Lewis, "offers a solution to the problem of social order by holding out the promise of balancing contending forces in perpetual equilibrium."[67] Many (primitive) societies achieve this balance by matching dual conceptual models with dual social organization, literally dividing a society into halves and forcing members to belong to one half or the other.[68] But this institutional expression of dualistic thinking is "exotic" and rare; it seldom occurs in modern societies.[69] Nonetheless, in America there are some forms of social organization that resemble dual social organization. For example, the attraction of opposites is often enacted in the two-party political system, where the splitting-projecting dynamic escalates conflict along party lines and leads to a hardening of political positions.[70] "The emphasis on Americanism as a political ideology," says Lipset," has led to a utopian and absolutist orientation among American liberals and conservatives. Both seek to impose their version of a good society."[71]

The evidence in previous chapters indicates that, by and large, the dual conceptual model of absolutism and relativism has not been enacted into dual social organization. Absolutists are more involved in religious organizations, while relativists are more involved in political action, but absolutists and relativists are not members of segregated social circles or groups. For the most part, absolutists and relativists are intermixed. The balance of contending moral visions appears to be achieved through the attraction of opposites in the realm of ideas, rhetoric, and discourse. For example, the culture war debate exhibits the splitting-projecting dynamic described above, where each side "sees itself as good and its adversary as bad" and "conflict escalates to the point where both are behaving self-righteously, wholeheartedly denying that the accusations of the opponent have *any* validity."[72] For instance, some years after Allan Bloom published his one-sided *The Closing of the American Mind* (1987), Lawrence Levine rebutted it with his one-sided *The Opening of the American Mind* (1996).[73] Instead of a true synthesis of twofold arguments, we see polarized intellectual debates among leading thinkers, where oppositional dynamics beget intellectual twins, such as the Bloom-Levine pair.[74]

The debate about the reality of a culture war is as much an expression of the attraction of opposites as the culture war is itself. Although the empirical evidence does not lend much support to the culture war thesis, the concept lives on in intellectual discourse, research, political debate, the media, and everyday life. The culture war debate illustrates that risks are *selected,* as Mary Douglas and Aaron Wildavsky argue, and that what gets defined as a danger to society is a clue to social and cultural organization.[75] Every community, notes Kai Erikson, has "its own characteristic style of deviant behavior."[76] Just as those that "emphasize political orthodoxy are apt to discover and punish much more sedition than their less touchy neighbors,"[77] those that emphasize absolutism, like America, are apt to see more moral transgression, moral poverty, moral confusion, and deficits of character and virtues than their more relativistic neighbors. "Men who fear witches," Erikson says, "soon find themselves surrounded by them."[78]

Crisis rhetoric, such as the culture war debate, defines a host of social issues as moral dangers—as risks to the American way of life. Accordingly, the concerns raised represent the components of the radial category of absolutism—concerns about the rule of law (society as a transcendental source of moral authority), concerns about the loss of family values (the authoritarian family model), concerns about multiculturalism, the decline of religion, and lack of moral education (traditional religious values), concerns about the status of American society in general (national pride), and so on. As discussed in earlier chapters, crisis rhetoric serves to sustain America's imagined community by reminding Americans of their common cultural identity.

The four points above show that the ideological foundation of the American imagined community is a durable *system of transcendental values*. The core of this system is America's civil religion, where society itself is viewed as an absolute source of moral authority. Other transcendental sources of moral authority, especially religion per se, reinforce this ideological core. This system of transcendental values is incorporated in the nation's institutions and reproduced over time through intergenerational transmission. In particular, the system perpetuates itself through its opposition to relativism in a dynamic attraction of opposites. The function of this system of transcendental values is to preserve the imagined community of America. Because America is not a birthright nation, the popular self-consciousness of being "American" depends on preservation of the absolutist foundation of the nation. Without its preservation, what it means to be American is undefined.

Absolutism plays a special role in the preservation of America's imagined community, but at the same time it contributes to the widespread perception of a crisis of values. Moral visions thrive in their mutual opposition, amplified by the splitting-projecting dynamic discussed above. To support their moral position, absolutists must fan the flames of crisis rhetoric, defining social problems as moral dangers. Even natural disasters and catastrophes can be interpreted as indicators of moral dangers. Consider, for example, that one out of every five Americans interpreted the 1993 midwestern floods as "admonishment by God for the sins of the people who live along the Mississippi."[79] Relativists, too, depend on crisis rhetoric to support their moral position, because each moral vision is defined in relation to the other. If the culture war concept had not existed, absolutists and relativists would have had to invent an alternative device for playing out their mutual opposition. The profound need to preserve America's imagined community demands repeated warnings of a "crisis of values," even when it is not split into two moral camps. Factual accuracy is "nice but not necessary," according to psychologists who study sensemaking.[80] Making sense of the realities of individual experience is more about *plausibility* than *accuracy*. A "crisis of values" is a plausible—if not factually accurate—explanation of the experience of the transitional phase of a cycle of change.

Defining social problems as moral dangers sustains America's imagined community, but it can also lead to the misinterpretation of social indicators. Consider, for example, the rising "illegitimacy rate" from 1960 to 1975, a statistic often cited as evidence of declining morals. By itself, this rate is misleading. It must be decomposed to be interpreted properly. Such factors as marital fertility (the rate at which married women have children), timing of marriage, and the proportion of women who are married influence the illegitimacy rate. A careful consideration of the statistics demonstrates that the increase in this rate from 1960 to 1975 was caused by "the decline in the fertility of married women and the delaying of marriage," not by increases in childbearing by single mothers.[81] Defining social problems as moral dangers can also lead to feckless, counterproductive, or pernicious remedies. For example, conflicting views of the morality of using methadone to break heroin addiction are "resolved" with the common practice of prescribing low doses of methadone known to be ineffective.[82] Other examples are the moral disputes about needle-exchange programs for intravenous drug users and effective sex education for adolescents.[83]

In addition to sustaining the pervasive sense of crisis, misinterpreting social indicators, and prescribing ineffective or dysfunctional remedies, the special role of absolutism includes hindering the integration of cultural contradictions and a true synthesis of moral opposites. As Kenneth Burke observed, "a way of seeing is also a way of not seeing."[84] For example, the pre-Copernican Earth-centered model of the universe prevented observation of new celestial phenomena because these did not fit the model of an immutable universe. Chinese cosmology, however, did not suffer the same blind spots, and so Chinese astronomers were able to observe new stars and sunspots centuries before Europeans "discovered" them.[85] America's imagined community is "a way of seeing" the world as bipolar moral opposites that is also "a way of not seeing" the possibilities beyond the duality of absolutism and relativism. "The problem of man's knowledge is not to oppose and to demolish opposing views," argues Ernest Becker, "but to include them in a larger theoretical structure."[86] Part of the special role of absolutism in America is to prevent the development of this larger theoretical structure, for this integration would threaten the integrity of the imagined community of America.

An Integration of Opposites

Is an integration of opposites possible? The actual contours and features of an integrated system cannot be foretold, in part because a genuine integration arises organically and the work behind it is a collective effort.[87] We do know, however, that building a larger theoretical structure requires a shift in *awareness context*.[88] An awareness context is "the total combination of what specific people, groups, organizations, communities or nations know about a specific issue."[89] An awareness context "structures" what is known and unknown, what is noticed and unnoticed, what is attended to and what is ignored. The ideological foundation of America's imagined community is an awareness context; it determines, for example, the risks that are selected and defined as moral dangers to society. A shift in awareness context would mean recognizing that the American system of truth and reality, like any system of truth and reality, is inherently imperfect, incomplete, and inadequate.[90] It would mean recognizing that the American system of values *is* an ideology—"a complex of ideas or notions which represents itself to the thinker as an absolute truth for the interpretation of the world and his situation within it." And an ideology "leads the thinker to accomplish an act of self-deception for the purpose of justification, obfuscation, evasion, and in some sense or other his own advantage."[91] In other words, it would mean recognizing that the American ideology is as much "a way of not seeing" as it is "a way of seeing."

Shifting awareness context would mean confronting the inherently paradoxical nature of dual moral visions. It would require finding "a common frame that gives meaning to the simultaneous coexistence of opposites," and acquiring the "ability to look through a paradoxical lens" and seek the "connections between the opposites, to explore and contain the contradictions, and to find a productive path."[92] The goal is to change the awareness context of crisis, looking through a "paradoxical lens" at social problems, conflict, issues, and solutions.[93]

How likely is a genuine integration? That is impossible to predict, but there are indications of certain favoring conditions that increase its likelihood:

1. Contradiction and crisis precede breakthroughs. Breakthroughs are not inevitable, but they are more likely during the transitional times in a cycle that produce contradictions and the perception of crisis. Randall Collins notes, for example, that creativity is fostered "at the *moment of transition* when the networks [of intellectuals] recombine cultural capital."[94] America's mixed value system today exhibits a wide incongruence between traditional values and self-realization values. Correspondingly, the moral visions of absolutism and relativism exhibit an even split, and it appears as if America's values are at a point of maximum disagreement. These conditions produce contradictory principles in the culture at large and cognitive dissonance in the individual. The drive to harmonize cultural contradictions and reduce cog-

nitive dissonance may create the impetus and energy for a genuine integration.

2. America is fertile ground for the emergence of an integration of opposites, compared to other nations, despite the primacy of sustaining the nation's imagined community. Paradoxically, the nation's base in transcendental values is also a favoring condition, because the integration of opposites is an exercise and experience of transcendence. While birthright nations are secularizing and losing their traditional values, Americans have had to integrate the forces of secularization with the preservation of their traditional values. One outcome is that Americans have created a unique mixed value system, one "that embraces both the transcendental order of the living group *and* the immanent order of the living self."[95] This history and experience favors the development of a new synthesis of opposites.

3. There is an intermixing of holders of different values and different worldviews, and there is sufficient overlap of the differences for common ground. Absolutists and relativists, for example, are not segregated into separate social circles or groups. Dual moral visions have not been enacted into dual social organization. If they had been—if the culture war thesis were true, for example—this dual social organization would be a barrier to a synthesis of opposites. Simply put, the need to harmonize contradictory principles and reduce cognitive dissonance would have been resolved effectively by the division of society into halves, and the impetus and energy for a synthesis would have been dissipated. Instead, absolutists and relativists tend to live, work, worship, recreate, and reside in the same places. This intermixing sets the "communicative context" for a shift of awareness context. People make sense of crisis through everyday social interaction, by developing shared meanings, and by jointly defining the situation.[96] The unity of a nation of citizens, argues Habermas, is "an intersubjectively shared context of possible mutual understanding."[97] The intermixing of people with different values and moral visions is necessary for the level and intensity of social interaction required for developing an intersubjectively shared synthesis of opposites.

Whether or not the American mixed system becomes integrated, the individual alone can make the transcendent journey of self-enlightenment. Indeed, Joseph Campbell thought that this was the challenge of the hero today.[98] Now that the great myths are known as lies, now that they have lost their legitimating, integrating, and vitalizing force, the hero-deed today is "that of rendering the modern world spiritually significant—or rather (phrasing the same principle the other way round) nothing if not that of making it possible for men and women to come to full human maturity through the conditions of contemporary life."[99] The modern hero's task is to guide and save society, a reversal of the roles and relationships of the individual and the community in the past.[100] Perhaps the hero's journey will remain a private affair, and its experience nothing grander than one of the "little transcendences" of everyday life. Or, perhaps, society can once again guide and save the individual by achieving a genuine synthesis of contradictions. For, as William James said, "This life *is* worth living, we can say, *since it is what we make it, from the moral point of view;* and we are determined to make it from that point of view, so far as we have anything to do with it, a success."[101]

Summary of Key Findings

Discourse about moral crisis in America reveals three ways of thinking about a crisis of values: crisis as loss of traditional values over time, crisis as unfavorable comparisons with the value systems of other nations, and crisis as the division of society into warring moral camps. These are the trend, comparative, and distribution hypotheses, respectively. The first key findings pertain to these hypotheses:

1. America has not lost its traditional values. The survey evidence on America's values does not support the widespread concern about the loss of traditional values, at least during the two decades covered by the World Values Surveys. America's values today are as traditional as they were in 1981, and in 1981 they were among the most traditional in the world, especially for an economically advanced democracy. Even when social and economic indicators over this twenty-year

period appear to support "decline of America" claims, America's traditional values have remained stable throughout the same period.

2. America's value system compares favorably to the value systems of other societies. Americans have much more traditional values than any advanced industrial or postindustrial democracy—indeed, much more traditional than the values of almost *any* society, regardless of level of economic development and type of political system. Over time, almost all affluent democracies have lost their traditional values, becoming secular-rational societies. In contrast, America's value system has *not* converged over time to join other societies with secular-rational values, and it has *not* diverged over time from the paths of societies with traditional values.

3. Americans are not divided into two opposed camps based on incompatible views of moral authority. Despite the heat of culture war rhetoric, America's social attitudes, cultural values, and religious beliefs are not polarized. In fact, Americans tend to share attitudes, values, and beliefs, and to be united when it comes to the most important values. The data indicate the polarization of moral visions over time: one of three Americans in 1981 was an absolutist, but by the 1990s, one of two was an absolutist. The increase in absolutism during the 1980s was not confined to certain groups or categories; the rising tide of absolutism swept over all age groups, classes, races, gender, and marital statuses. This equal division of moral worldviews contributes to the perception of a crisis of values (see 12 and 13 below) but it is only a tendency, not the basis of two morally opposed camps. In fact, absolutists and relativists tend to share similar social attitudes, feelings of interpersonal trust, and confidence in institutions. Their significant differences (see 9 below) are not big enough to conclude that absolutists and relativists are irreconcilably divided.

Other key findings, generated in the course of investigating the three main hypotheses, include the following:

4. America has shifted dramatically away from survival values to self-realization values. Thus, Americans have experienced both stability *and* change—stability on the traditional/secular-rational values dimension, and rapid change on the survival/self-expression values di-

mension. The reason for the nation's dramatic shift on the survival/self-expression dimension is the same reason the nation resists change on the traditional/secular-rational dimension: America's cultural heritage. This heritage is antithetical to the rise of secular-rational values, but favorable to the rise of self-expression values.

5. America's value system is a unique mixture of traditional values and self-expression values. This is a "mixed" system because many societies exhibit a congruence of values on each cultural dimension; usually, a nation's location on one dimension is consistent with its location on the other dimension. In contrast, America's location on the traditional/self-expression dimension makes it one of the most traditional societies in the world, while its location on the survival/self-expression dimensions makes it one of the most advanced in the pursuit of self-realization values.

6. The incongruence of America's value system is growing over time, due to the combination of stable traditional values and continuing movement toward the self-expression pole.

7. Individual Americans vary in their positions on the two cultural dimensions. The nation's unique mix of traditional values and self-expression values represents the central tendencies in American culture, but there is considerable individual variation. The personal value systems of individual Americans tend to be incongruent in a way that matches cultural patterns. Individuals internalize traditional and self-expression values more than they internalize secular-rational and survival values.

8. Americans who have internalized the cultural contradictions of traditional and self-expression values tend to be older, white, female, married, of lower socioeconomic classes, and Catholic. In contrast, Americans with the alternative form of value incongruence—secular-rational and survival values—tend to be younger, nonwhite, male, not married, of higher socioeconomic classes, and adherents of religions other than Protestantism or Catholicism.

9. Moral visions are loosely linked to social attitudes and social capital, exerting their influence directly and/or indirectly via the relationship of moral visions and the two cultural dimensions. The main significant differences between absolutists and relativists are attitudes

about family/life values, attitudes about the separation of church and state, and forms of civic engagement (religious participation for absolutists, political action for relativists).

The lack of empirical support for the three main hypotheses about America's crisis of values prompted the search for an alternative theory, one that could account for the "condition of America question"—the coexistence of stable traditional values and general agreement about values and social attitudes, along with the widespread impression of a crisis of values. This alternative theory takes as valid both the facts about values and the reality of individual experience, explaining why Americans see a crisis of values even when they have a lot in common, share many values, and are united when it comes to the most important values.

10. Unlike birthright nations, where collective identity is based on common ancestry, history, language, customs, religion, and so on, the basis of America's imagined community is a shared set of ideas. Since the foundation of national identity is ideological, there is a profound need to preserve the traditional values that compose and support it. Crisis rhetoric serves the valuable social function of keeping America's traditional values in mind, affirming and reinforcing the ideological core of America's imagined community—the values that define "who we are." At the same time, crisis rhetoric contributes to a continuing perception of a crisis of values.

11. Cyclical dynamics create inevitable periodic crises of values. Part of the answer to the condition of America question lies in the normal cycles of crisis caused by the recurring lag between technological and economic transformations and the ability of human cultures and institutions to cope with and adjust to them. The perception of crisis is acute at the midpoint in a cycle, even when traditional values are stable, the nation's value system compares favorably to others, and it is not divided into two opposed moral camps.

12. Equal numbers of absolutists and relativists appear at the midpoint of a cycle, intensifying the perception of crisis. The perception of crisis is acute at this point because the equal distribution of moral visions creates the appearance of maximum disagreement about val-

ues. America arrived at this equal distribution by the 1990s (see 3 above). Given this "condition of America," the constellations of attitudes, values, and beliefs surrounding these central models appear to be farther apart than they really are.

13. America's mixed system of traditional values and self-expression values (see 5–8 above) contains cultural contradictions because its prevailing principles provide contrary guides to conduct. American culture advocates obedience to an absolute, external, transcendental authority *and* obedience to a relative, internal, mundane authority (oneself). This conflict of principles sends mixed messages about goals, guides to action, and standards for judging behavior. This condition contributes to the perception of a crisis of values. The cultural contradictions will become even stronger—and the sense of crisis even greater—if America continues to retain its traditional values and moves farther along the path to self-expression values.

14. Americans who have internalized the cultural contradictions of traditional and self-expression values experience cognitive dissonance—personal experiences of crisis caused by conflicting principles—and use it to think about the purpose and meaning of life. This is an example of the "little transcendences" of everyday life. Other examples include rising spirituality and interests in New Age ideas. If America retains its traditional values and continues its progress toward self-realization values, the proportion of Americans who experience cognitive dissonance and use it to think about the purpose and meaning of life will also increase.

15. America has a durable system of transcendental values in which multiple sources of absolutism, such as society itself and religion per se, are mutually reinforcing. The function of this system is to preserve the imagined community of America. Nonetheless, an integration of the moral opposites of absolutism and relativism into a larger theoretical structure is possible.

✻ APPENDIX A ✻

World Values Surveys: Methods, Sampling, and Measures

THE PURPOSE OF THIS Appendix is to provide details about the design, samples, and methods of the World Values Surveys (WVS), and to provide precise definitions of the measures used in this study. This appendix is derived from information available from the WVS web site, from various publications, and from discussions with the WVS designers. For additional information about the WVS and copies of the questionnaires, visit http://wvs.isr.umich.edu/.

The National Science Foundation has supported the WVS through a series of grants starting twenty years ago, and most recently in October 2001. At the September 2001 meeting of American Political Science Association, the Comparative Politics Section awarded the WVS the title of "Most useful dataset in comparative politics." The WVS have given rise to more than four hundred publications, in twenty languages. According to the Inter-University Consortium for Political Research, the WVS are their second most frequently requested datasets.

DESIGNING THE WORLD VALUES SURVEYS

The WVS were designed by an international group of scholars with cross-cultural comparisons in mind: "building on extensive previous cross-national survey research and extensive pilot testing, with input from social scientists on five [now six] continents, it was developed to ask questions that *do* have a shared meaning across many cultures"[1] The current WVS's Executive, Strategy, and Methodology committees include scholars from Argentina, Australia, Bangladesh, Canada, China, France, Germany, Iran, Japan, Jordan, Korea, Nigeria, Peru, Philippines, Poland, Russia, Spain, Sweden, Turkey,

United States, and Ukraine. The WVS are coordinated by a U.S. political scientist (Ronald Inglehart), but the design of the surveys is interdisciplinary as well as international, including sociologists, political scientists, economists, psychologists, historians, and even theologians.

The WVS design committee intentionally selects and designs survey items that are meaningful across cultures. Experience with the WVS shows, for example, that a question about the importance of God in one's life is meaningful in virtually every society. The same is true for other survey items. Translation of the survey into different languages includes translation/back-translation techniques and extensive pilot testing.

The empirical evidence itself suggests that the WVS designers have been generally successful in framing cross-culturally meaningful questions. For example, the patterns observed in the WVS data are coherent and theoretically meaningful. The findings about specific countries are consistent with what is known about these countries from other surveys (when other surveys exist), as well as with other sources of data, such as area studies scholars, historians, and political scientists.

Sampling

Generally, the quality of WVS samples tends to be higher in advanced industrial societies that have been conducting representative national samples for several decades than in countries in which survey research is new. The logistical difficulties involved in interviewing a representative national sample of the population of such countries as China, Peru, or Nigeria are far greater than they are for countries such as Sweden, the United States, or Japan. In a number of the societies included in this project, survey research has only recently become possible, and in some cases (e.g., Vietnam) the WVS were the first representative national surveys ever carried out in those countries. In many developing countries, a significant part of the population is illiterate and/or lives in inaccessible areas. The cost of carrying out random probability samples in such cases may be prohibitive. Although illiterate rural respondents have been interviewed, they tend to be undersampled, and weighting the sample accordingly compensates imperfectly.

Even though the quality of the WVS samples tends to be higher in advanced societies, the quality of all the samples is substantially above the threshold of scientific acceptability. The WVS data have been analyzed extensively and, where possible, compared with the findings of other surveys, as well as with what is known about these societies from other social science sources. The results show that, even with the societies where survey techniques are new, the findings are generally reliable.

Virtually all of the samples are probability samples. In almost all nations, stratified multistage random sampling was used, with the samples selected in two stages. First, a random selection of sampling points was carried out, with a number of points drawn from all administrative regional units after stratification by region and degree of urbanization. Random selection of sampling locations was made, ensuring that all types of location were represented in proportion to their population. Next, a random selection of individuals was compiled. In some countries, individuals were selected from electoral rolls or from a central registry of citizens. All of these surveys were carried out through face-to-face interviews, with a sampling universe consisting of all adult citizens, ages 18 and older. All interviews were carried out at home, in the respective national languages.

The United States and Canada used stratified random samples, with three callbacks. In Norway, Denmark, and Sweden, stratified random samples were interviewed. The Japanese used a stratified multistage random sample, drawing names from records maintained by local government agencies. Most countries used multi-stage random sampling to select the household, with a respondent in a household selected using a Kish grid based on a listing of all eligible respondents in the household. In some countries, the final selection was made by quota sampling, with quotas assigned on the basis of sex, age, occupation, and region, using census data as a guide to the distribution of each group in the population. Note that the General Social Survey used the same sampling method (final selection made by quota sampling) in 1972, 1973, 1974, and in the "transition years" of 1975 and 1976 (in the transition, both block quota and full probability sampling were used).

Subnational surveys were carried out in Northern Ireland and the greater Moscow region (which was surveyed in 1990 in addition to the entire Russian republic). In 1981 when it was not possible to survey the entire Russian republic, a survey was carried out in Tambov oblast of the Russian republic. Tambov oblast was surveyed again in 1995, to permit time-series comparisons; a representative Russian national sample of 2,040 was interviewed in addition to the subsample of 500 persons in the Tambov region.

In Chile the sample covers the central portion of the country, which contains 63 percent of the total population; the income level of this region is about 40 percent higher than the national average. In Argentina, sampling was limited to the urbanized central portion of the country, where about 70 percent of the population is concentrated, and which also has above-average incomes. Within this region, two hundred sampling points were selected, with approximately five individuals being interviewed in each sampling point through multistage probability sampling moving through zones, sections, and dwellings to individuals.

In India in both 1990 and 1995, the sample was stratified to allocate 90 percent of the interviews to urban areas and 10 percent to rural areas, and to have 90 percent of the interviews with literate respondents (who are slightly less than 50 percent of the population). The interviews were distributed among sixteen states in proportion to their population. This sample was stratified to be representative of age, sex, and region but overrepresents urban and literate respondents: only 10 percent of these interviews were carried out in rural areas, as was the case with the 1990 survey. Weighting is necessary to approximate national population parameters.

In Nigeria in 1990 the fieldwork was limited to urban areas plus a sample of rural areas within 100 kilometers of an urban center. National samples of the adult population were interviewed, in all thirty states in proportion to their population. The interviews were carried out in the respective languages of the given region and were stratified to be 40 percent urban and 60 percent rural. In the 1995 Nigerian survey, in the South, rural areas were randomly selected from a list of rural settlements within a 10-kilometer radius of the selected urban towns; in the North they were selected from within a 50-kilometer radius of the selected towns. In China the sample is 90 percent urban and largely excludes the illiterate population.

The surveys from most other low-income countries undersample the illiterate portion of the public and oversample the urban areas and the more educated strata. The present dataset is weighted to correct for these and other features of sampling; but it would be unrealistic to view the samples from the low-income countries as fully comparable to those from advanced industrial societies.

The more educated and more urbanized oversampled groups within low-income countries tend to have orientations relatively similar to those found in the publics of industrial societies. Thus, the WVS data tend to *underestimate* the size of cross-national differences involving these countries; however, the WVS show sizable differences between the prevailing values of rich and poor societies.

Measures

Measures were selected on the basis of theoretical considerations. If it was theoretically justified, preference was given to measures that were included in all four waves of the WVS.

Absolutism/relativism—1 = absolutist, 0 = relativist (the few cases with "intermediate" values are excluded from analysis)

Traditional/secular-rational values—Factor scores constructed as described in chapter 2

Survival/self-expression values—Factor scores constructed as described in chapter 2. (In 1981, one item from the materialism/postmaterialism scale was not included in the survey. A constant was included for this item, based on data from the National Election Study. Using a constant tends to suppress variation, but it allows 1981 to be included in this analysis.)

Value incongruence—Deviation between standardized scores for traditional/secular-rational values and survival/self-expression values

Age—Six age cohorts, 1 = 18–24, 6 = 65+

Race—1 = White, 0 = otherwise

Gender—1 = male, 0 = female

Marital status—1 = married, 0 = otherwise

Subjective social class—Four categories, originally coded as 1 = upper, 2 = upper-middle, 3 = lower-middle; 4 = working class; 5 = lower. Working and lower are combined, due to data limitations. Codes reversed in analysis.

Education—Years of schooling, with over 21 years truncated to 21, due to data limitations

Protestant—1 = Protestant; 0 = otherwise

Other religion—1 = Jew, Muslim, Hindu, Buddhist, other, none; 0 = otherwise

Economic ethics scale—First factor from factor analysis (varimax rotation) of how often each of eight actions can be justified, each measured with ten categories, 1 = never, 10 = always; claiming government benefits not entitled to, avoiding fare on public transportation, cheating on tax, accepting bribe, prostitution, divorce, euthanasia, and suicide

Family/life values scale—Second factor from factor analysis (varimax rotation) of how often each of eight actions can be justified, each measured with ten categories, 1 = never, 10 = always; claiming government benefits not entitled to, avoiding fare on public transportation, cheating on tax, accepting bribe, prostitution, divorce, euthanasia, and suicide

Politicians who do not believe in God are unfit for public office—Four-point scale; 1 = agree strongly; 4 = disagree strongly (2000 survey only)

Religious leaders should not influence how people vote in elections—Four-point scale; 1 = agree strongly; 4 = disagree strongly (2000 survey only)

It would be better for America if more people with strong religious beliefs held public office—Four-point scale; 1 = agree strongly; 4 = disagree strongly (2000 survey only)

Religious leaders should not influence government—Four-point scale; 1 = agree strongly; 4 = disagree strongly (2000 survey only)

Confidence in institutions scale—Count of "a great deal" of confidence in seven institutions: the church, armed forces, press, labor unions, police, civil service, and major companies

Frequency of attendance at religious services—Seven categories, 1 = more than once a week; 8 = never, practically never. 1981 and 1990 surveys included eight categories; "Christmas/Easter day" and "Other specific holy days" were collapsed to conform with categories in 1995 and 2000 surveys (codes reversed in analysis)

Voluntary organizations scale—Count of "belong to" or "member" of six voluntary organizations: church or religious group, sport or recreation organization, art, music or educational organization, political party, environmental organization, professional association

Political acts scale—Count of "have done" or "might do" for signing a petition, joining in boycotts, attending lawful demonstrations, joining unofficial strikes, occupying buildings or factories (first item is excluded in scale used in regression analyses because it is an item in the survival/self-expression scale)

Think about meaning and purpose of life— 1 = often; 0 = sometimes, rarely, never.

APPENDIX B

Statistical Tables

TABLE 2.1

Two Dimensions of Cross-cultural Variation: Nation-level Analysis

	Factor Loadings
Traditional vs. Secular-Rational Values[a]	
Traditional values emphasize the following:	
God is very important in respondent's life.	0.91
It is more important for a child to learn obedience and religious faith than independence and determination [Autonomy index].	0.89
Abortion is never justifiable.	0.82
Respondent has strong sense of national pride.	0.82
Respondent favors more respect for authority.	0.72
(Secular-rational values emphasize the opposite.)	
Survival vs. Self-expression Values[b]	
Survival values emphasize the following:	
Respondent gives priority to economic and physical security over self-expression and quality of life [4-item Materialist/Postmaterialist Values index].	0.86
Respondent describes self as not very happy.	0.81
Homosexuality is never justifiable.	0.80
Respondent has not and would not sign a petition.	0.78
You have to be very careful about trusting people.	0.56
(Self-expression values emphasize the opposite.)	

Source: From 65 societies surveyed in the 1990–1991 and 1995–1998 World Values Surveys. This table is based on Inglehart and Baker, "Modernization," p. 24, table 1.

Note: The original polarities vary. The above statements show how each item relates to a given dimension, based on factor analysis with varimax rotation.

[a]Explains 44 percent of cross-national variation.

[b]Explains 26 percent of cross-national variation.

TABLE 2.2
Two Dimensions of Cross-cultural Variation: Individual-level Analysis

	Factor Loadings
Traditional vs. Secular-Rational Values[a]	
Traditional values emphasize the following:	
God is very important in respondent's life.	0.70
It is more important for a child to learn obedience and religious faith than independence and determination [Autonomy index].	0.61
Abortion is never justifiable.	0.61
Respondent has strong sense of national pride.	0.60
Respondent favors more respect for authority.	0.51
(Secular-Rational values emphasize the opposite.)	
Survival vs. Self-expression Values[b]	
Survival values emphasize the following:	
Respondent gives priority to economic and physical security over self expression and quality of life [4-item Materialist/Postmaterialist Values index].	0.59
Respondent has not and would not sign a petition.	0.58
Respondent describes self as not very happy.	0.59
Homosexuality is never justifiable.	0.54
You have to be very careful about trusting people.	0.44
(Self-expression values emphasize the opposite.)	

Source: From 65 societies surveyed in the 1990–1991 and 1995–1998 World Values Surveys. Based on Inglehart and Baker, "Modernization," p. 24, table 1.

Note: The original polarities vary. The above statements show how each item relates to a given dimension, based on factor analysis with varimax rotation. Total N for individual analysis is 165,594 (smallest N for any of the above items is 146,789).

[a]Explains 26 percent of individual-level variation.

[b]Explains 13 percent individual-level variation.

TABLE 2.3
Two Dimensions of Cross-cultural Variation: Individual-level Analysis with Twenty-four Variables

	Factor Loadings
Traditional vs. Secular-Rational Values	
Traditional values emphasize the following:	
God is very important in respondent's life.	0.75*
Religion is very important in respondent's life	0.73
Respondent believes in Heaven.	0.69
Abortion is never justifiable.	0.64*
Divorce is never justifiable.	0.57
It is more important for a child to learn obedience and religious faith than independence and determination [Autonomy index].	0.56*
Euthanasia is never justifiable.	0.52
One of main goals in life is to make parents proud.	0.46
Respondent has strong sense of national pride.	0.46*
Respondent favors more respect for authority.	0.42*
Respondent would never take part in a demonstration.	0.33
Respondent seldom or never discusses politics.	0.32
(Secular-rational values emphasize the opposite.)	
Survival vs. Self-expression Values:	
Survival values emphasize the following:	
Men make better political leaders than women.	0.55
Respondent would not like to have homosexuals as neighbors.	0.55
Homosexuality is never justifiable.	0.53*
A woman has to have children in order to be fulfilled.	0.51
Respondent describes self as not very happy.	0.50*
Respondent does not describe own health as very good.	0.50
Respondent is dissatisfied with financial situation of his/her household.	0.48

(*continued*)

TABLE 2.3 (*continued*)

	Factor Loadings
Respondent gives priority to economic and physical security over self-expression and quality of life [4-item Materialist/Postmaterialist Values Index].	0.47*
Respondent has not and would not sign a petition.	0.47*
A university education is more important for a boy than for a girl.	0.44
Respondent would not like to have people with a criminal record as neighbors.	0.54
You have to be very careful about trusting people.	0.29*
(Self-expression values emphasize the opposite.)	

Source: From 65 societies surveyed in the 1990–1991 and 1995–1998 World Values Surveys. Based on tables provided by Ronald Inglehart.

Note: The original polarities vary. The above statements show how each item relates to a given dimension, based on factor analysis with varimax rotation. Total N for individual analysis is 165,594.

*Indicates items used in the 10-item scales.

TABLE 2.4
Correlation of Additional Items with the Traditional/Secular-Rational Values Dimension

Item	Correlation
Traditional values emphasize the following:	
Religion is very important in respondent's life.	0.89
Respondent believes in Heaven.	0.88
One of respondent's main goals in life has been to make his/her parents proud.	0.81
Respondent believes in Hell.	0.76
Respondent attends church regularly.	0.75
Respondent has a great deal of confidence in the country's churches.	0.72

TABLE 2.4 (*continued*)

Item	Correlation
Respondent gets comfort and strength from religion.	0.72
Respondent describes self as "a religious person".	0.71
Euthanasia is never justifiable.	0.66
Work is very important in respondent's life.	0.65
There should be stricter limits on selling foreign goods here.	0.63
Suicide is never justifiable.	0.61
Parents' duty is to do their best for their children even at the expense of their own well-being.	0.60
Respondent seldom or never discusses politics.	0.57
Respondent places self on right side of a left-right scale	0.57
Divorce is never justifiable	0.57
There are absolutely clear guidelines about good and evil.	0.56
Expressing one's own preferences clearly is more important than understanding others' preferences	0.56
My country's environmental problems can be solved without any international agreements to handle them.	0.56
If a woman earns more money than her husband, it's almost certain to cause problems	0.53
One must always love and respect one's parents regardless of their behavior	0.49
Family is very important in respondent's life.	0 .45
Respondent is relatively favorable to having the army rule the country.	0.43
Respondent favors having a relatively large number of children.	0.41
(Secular-rational values emphasize the opposite.)	

Source: Nation-level data from 65 societies surveyed in the 1990–1991 and 1995–1998 World Values Surveys. Inglehart and Baker, "Modernization," p. 26, table 2.

Note: The original polarities vary; the above statements show how each item relates to the Traditional/Secular-Rational Values dimension, as measured by the items in table 2.1.

TABLE 2.5
Correlation of Additional Items with the Survival/Self-expression Values Dimension

Item	Correlation
Survival values emphasize the following:	
Men make better political leaders than women.	0.86
Respondent is dissatisfied with financial situation of his/her household.	0.83
A woman has to have children in order to be fulfilled.	0.83
Respondent rejects foreigners, homosexuals, and people with AIDS as neighbors [Outgroup index].	0.81
Respondent favors more emphasis on the development of technology.	0.78
Respondent has not recyled things to protect the environment.	0.76
A university education is more important for a boy than for a girl.	0.81
Respondent has not attended meeting or signed a petition to protect the environment.	0.75
When seeking a job, a good income and safe job are more important than a feeling of accomplishment and working with people you like [Job Motivation index].	0.74
Respondent is relatively favorable to state ownership of business and industry.	0.74
A child needs a home with both a father and mother to grow up happily.	0.73
Respondent does not describe own health as very good.	0.73
One must always love and respect one's parents regardless of their behavior.	0.71
When jobs are scarce, men have more right to a job than women.	0.69

Table 2.5 (*continued*)

Item	Correlation
Prostitution is never justifiable.	0.69
Government should take more responsibility to ensure that everyone is provided for.	0.68
Respondent does not have much free choice or control over his/her life.	0.67
A university education is more important for a boy than for a girl.	0.67
Respondent does not favor less emphasis on money and material possessions.	0.66
Respondent rejects people with criminal records as neighbors.	0.66
Respondent rejects heavy drinkers as neighbors.	0.64
Hard work is one of the most important things to teach a child.	0.65
Imagination is not one of the most important things to teach a child.	0.62
Tolerance and respect for others are not the most important things to teach a child.	0.62
Scientific discoveries will help, rather than harm, humanity.	0.60
Leisure is not very important in life.	0.60
Friends are not very important in life.	0.56
Having a strong leader who does not have to bother with parliament and elections may be a good form of government.	0.58
Respondent has not taken part and would not take part in a boycott.	0.56
Government ownership of business and industry should be increased.	0.55

(*continued*)

TABLE 2.5 (*continued*)

Item	Correlation
Democracy is not necessarily the best form of government.	0.45
Respondent opposes sending economic aid to poorer countries.	0.42
(Self-expression values emphasize the opposite.)	

Source: Nation-level data from 65 societies surveyed in the 1990–1991 and 1995–1998 World Values Surveys. Inglehart and Baker, "Modernization," p. 27, table 3.

Note: The original polarities vary. The above statements show how each item relates to the survival/self-expression values dimension, as measured by the items described in table 2.1.

TABLE 2.6
Standardized Coefficients from the Regression of Traditional/Secular-Rational Values and Survival/Self-expression Values on Economic Development and Cultural Heritage Zone

Independent Variable	Traditional/ Secular-Rational	Survival/ Self-expression
Ex-Communist zone (=1)	0.424**	−0.393***
Real GDP per capita, 1980	0.496***	.575***
Percentage employed in industrial sector, 1980	0.216	—
Percentage employed in service sector, 1980	—	0.098
Adjusted R^2	0.50	0.73
Protestant Europe zone (=1)	0.370**	0.232*
Real GDP per capita, 1980	0.025	0.362*
Percentage employed in industrial sector, 1980	0.553***	—
Percentage employed in service sector, 1980	—	0.331*

TABLE 2.6 (*continued*)

Independent Variable	Traditional/ Secular-Rational	Survival/ Self-expression
Adjusted R^2	0.50	0.63
English-speaking zone (=1)	−0.300**	0.146
Real GDP per capita, 1980	0.394**	0.434**
Percentage employed in industrial sector, 1980	0.468***	—
Percentage employed in service sector, 1980	—	0.319*
Adjusted R^2	0.47	0.61
Latin-American zone (=1)	−0.342**	0.108
Real GDP per capita, 1980	0.195	0.602**
Percentage employed in industrial sector, 1980	0.448***	—
Percentage employed in service sector, 1980	—	0.224
Adjusted R^2	0.51	0.60
African zone (=1)	−0.189	0.021
Real GDP per capita, 1980	0.211	0.502**
Percentage employed in industrial sector, 1980	0.468***	—
Percentage employed in service sector, 1980	—	0.320*
Adjusted R^2	0.43	0.59
South Asian zone (=1)	0.070	0.212*
Real GDP per capita, 1980	0.258*	0.469**
Percentage employed in industrial sector, 1980	0.542***	—
Percentage employed in service sector, 1980	—	0.455**

(*continued*)

TABLE 2.6 (*continued*)

Independent Variable	Traditional/ Secular-Rational	Survival/ Self-expression
Adjusted R^2	0.40	0.62
Orthodox zone (=1)	0.152	−0.457***
Real GDP per capita, 1980	0.304*	0.567***
Percentage employed in industrial sector, 1980	0.432**	—
Percentage employed in service sector, 1980	—	0.154
Adjusted R^2	0.42	0.80
Confucian zone (=1)	0.397***	−0.020
Real GDP per capita, 1980	0.304**	0.491**
Percentage employed in industrial sector, 1980	0.505***	—
Percentage employed in service sector, 1980	—	0.323*
Adjusted R^2	0.56	0.59
Number of countries	49	49

Source: Inglehart and Baker, "Modernization," p. 33, table 4.
Note: Reduced N reflects missing data on one or more independent variables.
*p<.05 **p<.01 ***p<.001 (two-tailed tests)

TABLE 2.7A

Unstandardized Coefficients from the Regression of Traditional/Secular-Rational Values on Independent Variables Measuring Modernization and Cultural Heritage

Independent Variable	Model 1	Model 2	Model 3	Model 4	Model 5	Model 6
Real GDP per capita, 1980	0.066*	0.086*	0.131**	0.042	0.08**	0.122***
(in $1,000s U.S.)	(0.031)	(0.043)	(0.036)	(0.029)	(0.027)	(0.030)
Percentage employed in	0.052***	0.051***	0.023	0.061***	0.052***	0.03*
industrial sector, 1980	(0.012)	(0.014)	0.015)	(0.011)	(0.011)	(0.012)
Percentage enrolled	—	−0.01				
in education	—	(0.01)	—	—	—	—
Ex-Communist (=1)	—		1.05**	—	—	0.952***
			(.351)			(0.282)
Historically Catholic (=1)	—	—	—	−0.767**		−0.409*
				(0.216)		(0.188)
Historically Confucian (=1)	—	—	—	—	1.57***	1.39***
					(0.370)	(0.329)
Adjusted R^2	0.42	0.37	0.50	0.53	0.57	0.70
Number of countries	49	46	49	49	49	49

TABLE 2.7B

Unstandardized Coefficients from the Regression of Survival/Self-expression Values on Independent Variables Measuring Modernization and Cultural Heritage

Independent Variable	Model 1	Model 2	Model 3	Model 4	Model 5	Model 6
Real GDP per capita, 1980 (in $1,000s U.S.)	0.090* (0.043)	0.095* (0.046)	0.056 (0.043)	0.120** (0.037)	0.098** (0.037)	0.144*** (0.017)
(Percentage employed in service sector, 1980)	−0.042** (.015)	0.011* (.000)	0.035* (.015)	0.019 (.014)	0.018 (.013)	—
Percentage employed in service sector, 1980	—	−0.054 (.039)	—	—	—	—
Percentage enrolled in education	—	−0.005 (.012)	—	—	—	—
Ex-communist (=1)	—	—	—	−0.920*** (0.204)	−0.883*** (0.197)	−0.411* (0.188)
Historically Protestant (=1)	—	—	0.672* (0.279)	—	0.509* (0.237)	0.415** (0.175)
Historically Orthodox (=1)	—	—	—	—	—	−1.182*** (.240)
Adjusted R^2	0.63	0.63	0.66	0.74	0.76	0.84
Number of countries	49	46	49	49	49	49

Source: Latest available survey from 1990–1991 or 1995–1998 World Values Surveys. Reproduced from Inglehart and Baker, "Modernization," p. 39, tables 5a, 5b.

Note: Number in parentheses is standard error.

$^*p<.05$ $^{**}p<.01$ $^{***}p<.001$

TABLE 2.8
Percentage Attending Religious Services at Least Once a Month, by Country and Year, 1981–1998

Country	1981	1990–1991	1995–1998	Net Change
Advanced industrial democracies[a]				
Australia	40	—	25	−15
Belgium	38	35	—	−3
Canada	45	40	—	−5
Finland	13	13	11	−2
France	17	17	—	0
East Germany	—	20	9	−11
West Germany	35	33	25	−10
Great Britain	23	25	—	+2
Iceland	10	9	—	−1
Ireland	88	88	—	0
Northern Ireland	67	69	—	+2
South Korea	29	60	27	−2
Italy	48	47	—	−1
Japan	12	14	11	−1
Netherlands	40	31	—	−9
Norway	14	13	13	−1
Spain	53	40	38	−15
Sweden	14	10	11	−3
Switzerland	—	43	25	−18
United States	60	59	55	−5
Ex-communist societies[b]				
Belarus	—	6	14	+8
Bulgaria	—	9	15	+6
Hungary	16	34	—	+18

(continued)

TABLE 2.8 (*continued*)

Country	1981	1990–1991	1995–1998	Net Change
Latvia	—	9	16	+7
Poland	—	85	74	−11
Russia	—	6	8	+2
Slovenia	—	35	33	−2
Developing and low-income societies[c]				
Argentina	56	55	41	−15
Brazil	—	50	54	+4
Chile	—	47	44	−3
India	—	71	54	−17
Mexico	74	63	65	−9
Nigeria	—	88	87	−1
South Africa	61	—	70	+9
Turkey	—	38	44	+6

Source: Reproduced from Inglehart and Baker, "Modernization," p. 46, table 6.
[a]Sixteen of 20 advanced industrial democracies declined; mean change = −5.
[b]Five of 7 ex-Communist societies increased; mean change = +4.
[c]Five of 8 developing and low-income societies declined; mean change = −4.

TABLE 2.9
Percentage Rating the Importance of God in Their Lives as "10" on a 10-Point Scale, by Country and Year, 1981–1998

Country	1981	1990–1991	1995–1998	Net Change
Advanced industrial democracies[a]				
Australia	25	—	21	−4
Belgium	9	13	—	+4
Canada	36	28	—	−8
Finland	14	12	—	−2
France	10	10	—	0
East Germany	—	13	6	−7
West Germany	16	14	16	0

TABLE 2.9 (*continued*)

Country	1981	1990–1991	1995–1998	Net Change
Great Britain	20	16	—	−4
Iceland	22	17	—	−5
Ireland	29	40	—	+11
Northern Ireland	38	41	—	+3
Italy	31	29	—	−2
Japan	6	6	5	−1
Netherlands	11	11	—	0
Norway	19	15	12	−7
Spain	18	18	26	+8
Sweden	9	8	8	−1
Switzerland	—	26	17	−9
United States	50	48	50	0
Ex-communist societies[b]				
Belarus	—	8	20	+12
Bulgaria	—	7	10	+3
Hungary	21	22	—	+1
Latvia	—	9	17	+8
Russia	—	10	19	+9
Slovenia	—	14	15	+1
Developing and low-income societies[c]				
Argentina	32	49	57	+25
Brazil	—	83	87	+4
Chile	—	61	58	−3
India	—	44	56	+12
Mexico	60	44	50	−10
Nigeria	—	87	87	0
South Africa	50	74	71	+21
Turkey	—	71	81	+10

Source: Reproduced from Inglehart and Baker, "Modernization," p. 47, table 7.

[a]Eleven of 19 advanced industrial democracies declined; mean change = −1.

[b]Six of 6 ex-Communist societies increased; mean change = +6.

[c]Five of 8 developing and low-income societies increased; mean change = +6.

TABLE 3.1

Moral Visions of Seventy-nine Societies, Ranked by Percentage of Absolutists

Society	Absolutists	Neither	Relativists	Society	Absolutists	Neither	Relativists
Morocco	78.0	3.3	18.7	Portugal	39.0	3.7	57.3
Ghana	69.6	6.5	23.9	Ireland	38.8	9.3	51.9
Tanzania	68.7	4.2	27.1	E. Germany	38.8	15.4	45.8
S. Africa	62.8	3.3	33.9	Russia	38.6	3.5	57.9
Uganda	58.9	3.9	37.2	Argentina	38.6	4.0	57.4
Georgia	58.9	3.2	37.9	Colombia	38.0	2.9	59.1
Vietnam	58.4	6.3	35.3	S. Korea	37.0	0.0	63.0
Zimbabwe	57.3	3.5	39.2	Slovakia	36.4	9.4	54.1
Azerbaijan	56.7	6.1	37.3	Italy	36.4	13.2	50.5
Philippines	55.2	0.9	43.9	China	36.2	9.1	54.4
Macedonia	55.1	6.7	38.2	Domn. Rep.	35.8	7.9	56.3
Bosnia	53.7	7.3	39.0	Lithuania	34.9	5.5	59.6
Chile	53.0	3.4	43.6	Uruguay	33.9	5.9	60.2
Peru	52.8	4.1	43.1	W. Germany	33.9	4.4	61.7
Tambov	51.5	3.8	44.7	Bulgaria	33.3	6.8	60.0
Poland	50.8	3.6	45.6	Croatia	32.2	4.5	63.4
Brazil	49.2	0.1	50.8	Belgium	30.7	6.2	63.1
U.S.	49.2	4.2	46.6	India	30.0	8.2	61.8
Albania	49.1	12.1	38.9	Estonia	29.9	8.2	61.9

Montenegro	48.9	10.9	40.1	Finland	29.3	4.7	66.0
El Salvador	48.8	6.2	45.0	Norway	29.1	3.6	67.3
Malta	48.7	3.1	48.3	Switzerland	28.4	8.6	63.0
Bangladesh	47.7	1.7	50.6	Taiwan	28.0	4.7	67.3
N. Ireland	46.9	5.1	48.1	Valencia	27.8	2.8	69.4
Serbia	46.5	8.5	45.0	Netherlands	26.9	4.1	69.0
Andalusia	45.2	4.3	50.5	Galicia	26.2	3.7	70.1
Singapore	45.2	1.4	53.4	France	24.9	7.5	67.6
Puerto Rico	44.9	3.0	52.2	Belarus	24.8	5.3	69.9
Spain	43.7	5.9	50.4	Czech Rep.	23.5	6.3	70.2
Ukraine	42.9	3.1	54.1	Luxembourg	23.3	7.7	69.0
Canada	42.4	2.4	55.2	Greece	22.6	7.0	70.5
New Zealand	42.4	12.1	45.5	Basque	22.4	7.0	70.6
Australia	41.7	2.5	55.7	Slovenia	21.9	13.0	65.1
Britain	41.5	4.8	53.8	Austria	20.3	6.4	73.3
Armenia	41.0	6.3	52.7	Japan	19.2	11.5	69.3
Latvia	41.0	4.9	54.1	Sweden	15.8	3.2	81.0
Mexico	40.9	5.7	53.4	Hungary	15.4	9.1	75.5
Venezuela	40.9	9.4	49.7	Denmark	10.4	4.3	85.3
Moldova	39.7	5.2	55.1	Iceland	9.0	2.8	88.2
Romania	39.5	5.7	54.8				

Source: World Value Surveys. This table is based on data from the latest survey for each nation.

TABLE 3.2
Religious Beliefs of Absolutists and Relativists in the United States, (Percent Who Believe), 1981–2000

	1981		1990		1995		2000	
Belief in…	*Absolutists*	*Relativists*	*Absolutists*	*Relativists*	*Absolutists*	*Relativists*	*Absolutists*	*Relativists*
God	99	97*	99	93***	98	94***	99	93***
Soul	96	91***	96	87***	98	91***	97	95*
Heaven	95	85***	94	79***	94	80***	95	80***
Life after death	85	78***	83	71***	88	74***	87	75***
Hell	84	64***	81	59***	85	66***	84	65***

Source: World Values Survey, 1981, 1990, 1995, 2000.
$*p < .05$, $**p < .01$, $***p < .001$

TABLE 3.3

Binary Logit Coefficients from Regression of Moral Visions on Two Dimensions of Cultural Variation, Controlling for Sociodemographic Variables, United States, 1981–2000

Independent Variables	1981		1990		1995		2000	
Cultural Indices								
Traditional/Secular-Rational Values	−0.876***	−0.820***	−0.904***	−0.879***	−0.771***	−0.802***	−0.992***	−1.057***
Survival/Self-expression Values	−0.625***	−0.575***	−0.394***	−0.352***	−0.340***	−0.288**	−0.387***	−0.439***
Sociodemographics								
Age		0.046		−0.010		−0.059		−0.073
Race		−0.307		−0.110		−0.101		0.323*
Gender		0.020		−0.150		0.020		−0.068
Marital status		−0.018		−0.161		−0.028		0.313*
Social class		−0.035		0.047		0.080		0.139
Education		−0.031		−0.019		0.086*		0.063

(continued)

Table 3.3 (*continued*)

Independent Variables	1981		1990		1995		2000	
Protestant		−0.448***		0.254		0.353		0.271
Other religion		−0.190		−0.219		−0.309		−0.164
Constant	−0.822***	0.118	−0.011	0.470	−0.066	−1.813	0.106	−1.809*
Nagelkerke pseudo R^2	0.14	0.15	0.18	0.20	0.14	0.16	0.20	0.23
N of observations	1,892	1,674	1,420	1,137	1,176	863	1,071	959

Source: World Values Surveys, 1981, 1990, 1995, 2000.

Notes: See appendix A for definitions of all variables. Coefficients reported are logistic regression estimates (dependent variable: absolutism = 1, relativism = 0). Omitted category is unmarried, nonwhite, female, and Catholic. Number of observations reported is unweighted.

$^*p < .05$, $^{**}p < .01$, $^{***}p < .001$

TABLE 3.4
Internal Consistency of Two Opinion Domains, by Moral Visions, United States, 1981–2000

Opinion Domain		1981	1990	1995	2000
Economic Ethics scale	Total	0.70	0.78	0.69	0.74
	Absolutists	0.72	0.79	0.70	0.73
	Relativists	0.68	0.78	0.67	0.73
Family/Life Values scale	Total	0.67	0.71	0.73	0.72
	Absolutists	0.64	0.64	0.69	0.66
	Relativists	0.65	0.72	0.72	0.71

Source: World Values Surveys, 1981, 1990, 1995, 2000.

Notes: See appendix A for definitions of all variables. Numbers reported are Cronbach's alpha measure.

TABLE 3.5

OLS Coefficients from Regression of Economic Ethics Scale and Family/Life Values Scale on Moral Visions and Two Dimensions of Cultural Variation, Controlling for Sociodemographic Variables, United States, 1981 and 1990

Independent Variables	Economic Ethics Scale 1981			Family/Life Values Scale 1981			Economic Ethics Scale 1990			Family/Life Values Scale 1990		
Moral visions												
Absolutism	−0.182***	−0.095*	−0.059	−0.464***	−0.085**	−0.076*	−0.094	−0.120*	−0.133*	−0.487***	−0.083*	−0.058
Cultural indices												
Traditional/Secular-Rational		0.233***	0.166**		0.691***	0.689***		0.083**	0.068		0.600***	0.599***
Survival/Self-expression		−0.051	−0.027		0.393***	0.396***		−0.129***	−0.072		0.310***	0.313***
Sociodemographics												
Age			−0.099***			0.004			−0.142***			0.035*
Race			−0.494***			0.103			−0.372***			−0.087
Gender			0.156**			−0.098*			0.154*			0.031

Marital status			−0.123*			−0.085			−0.183**			−0.027
Social class			0.009			0.007			−0.066			0.063*
Education			0.004			−0.005			−0.062***			0.019
Protestant			0.224***			−0.073			−0.115			0.070
Other religion			0.056			0.069			0.049			0.139
Constant	−0.008	0.107**	0.606	0.007	0.062*	0.142	0.125**	0.248***	2.266***	0.132***	−.044	−0.669*
Adjusted R^2	0.01	0.05	0.14	0.06	0.40	0.40	0.01	0.02	0.12	0.07	0.42	0.41
N of observations	1,297	1,177	1,099	1,297	1,177	1,099	1,267	1,117	892	1,267	1,117	892

Source: World Values Surveys, 1981, 1990.

Notes: See appendix A for definitions of all variables. Coefficients reported are unstandardized OLS regression estimates. Omitted category is unmarried, nonwhite, female, and Catholic.

$*p < .05$, $**p < .01$, $***p < .001$ (one-tailed test for moral visions)

TABLE 3.6

OLS Coefficients from Regression of Economic Ethics Scale and Family/Life Values Scale on Moral Visions and Two Dimensions of Cultural Variation, Controlling for Sociodemographic Variables, United States, 1995 and 2000

Independent Variables	Economic Ethics Scale 1981			Family/Life Values Scale 1981			Economic Ethics Scale 1990			Family/Life Values Scale 1990		
Moral visions												
Absolutism	−0.159***	−0.008	−0.060	−0.595***	−0.192**	−0.126**	−0.180**	−0.123*	−0.079	−0.642***	−0.153***	−0.156***
Cultural indices												
Traditional/Secular-Rational		0.111***	0.073*		0.643***	0.653***		0.110**	.070		0.672***	0.652***
Survival/Self-expression		−0.071**	−0.032		0.333***	0.334***		−0.209***	−0.131***		0.386***	0.371***
Sociodemographics												
Age			−0.091***			−0.006			−0.134***			0.040*
Race			−0.092			0.036			−0.377***			0.084

Gender			0.086			0.064			0.136*			0.072
Marital status			−0.117*			0.052			−0.149*			0.029
Social class			−0.039			−0.014			−0.094			−0.003
Education			−0.031*			−0.023			−0.081***			−0.006
Protestant			0.205**			0.028			−0.297***			−0.106
Other religion			−0.167**			0.073			−0.107			0.011
Constant	−0.064	−0.069	1.118**	0.334***	0.193*	0.529	0.277	0.457***	3.040***	0.567***	0.148***	0.069
Adjusted R^2	0.01	0.01	0.07	0.09	0.46	0.44	0.01	0.03	0.13	0.09	0.43	0.43
N of observations	1,234	1,100	817	1,234	1,100	817	1,386	1,319	1,189	1,386	1,319	1,189

Source: World Values Surveys, 1995, 2000.

Notes: See appendix A for definitions of all variables. Coefficients reported are unstandardized OLS regression estimates. Omitted category is unmarried, non-white, female, and Catholic.

*$p < .05$, **$p < .01$, ***$p < .001$ (one-tailed test for moral visions)

TABLE 3.7

OLS Coefficients from Regression of Attitudes about Church-State Separation on Moral Visions and Two Dimensions of Cultural Variation, Controlling for Sociodemographic Variables, United States, 2000

Independent Variables	Politicians who do not believe in God are unfit for public office	Religious leaders should not influence how people vote in elections	It would be better for America if more people with strong religious beliefs held public office	Religious leaders should not influence government decisions
Moral visions				
Absolutism	−0.220***	0.243***	−0.326***	0.238***
Cultural indices				
Traditional/Secular-Rational Values	0.465***	−0.310***	0.555***	−0.366***
Survival/Self-expression Values	0.321***	−0.007	0.287***	−0.199***
Sociodemographics				
Age	0.001	−0.007***	0.004*	−0.007**
Race	0.192**	0.266***	0.001	0.178*

Gender	0.237***	−0.004	0.122*	−0.136*
Marital status	0.002	.006	−0.002	−0.001
Social class	0.008*	−0.007	0.006	−0.005*
Education	0.001	0.007***	−0.001	0.008***
Protestant	−0.157	0.006	−0.255***	0.122
Other religion	−0.146	−0.006	−0.001	−0.008
Constant	2.375***	1.147**	2.652***	1.296**
Adjusted R sq.	0.21	0.10	0.32	0.14
N of observations	1,198	1,200	1,198	1,195

Source: World Values Surveys, 2000.

Notes: See appendix A for definitions of all variables. Coefficients reported are unstandardized OLS regression estimates. Omitted category is unmarried, nonwhite, female, and Catholic.

$*p < .05$, $**p < .01$, $***p < .001$ (one-tailed test for moral visions)

TABLE 3.8

OLS Coefficients from Regression of Social Capital on Moral Visions and Two Dimensions of Cultural Variation, Controlling for Sociodemographic Variables, United States, 1981

Independent Variables	Confidence in Institutions Scale			Frequency of Attendance at Religious Services			Voluntary Organizations Scale			Political Acts Scale		
Moral visions												
Absolutism	0.387***	0.100	0.053	0.923***	0.506***	0.528***	0.018	0.140*	0.135*	−0.275***	0.049	0.097
Cultural indices												
Traditional/Secular-Rational Values		−0.635***	−0.527***		−1.076***	−0.927***		−0.014	0.029		0.501***	0.354***
Survival/Self-expression Values		−0.154*	0.013		0.010	−0.053		0.409***	0.276***		0.411***	0.353***
Sociodemographics												
Age			0.129***			0.059			0.130***			−0.186***
Race			−0.639***			−0.364*			−0.083			−0.325**

Gender			−0.013			−0.289**			0.071			0.202**
Marital status			−0.269**			0.171			0.133*			−0.169**
Social class			0.062			−0.098*			−0.107***			−0.007
Education			−0.059**			0.099***			0.118***			0.054***
Protestant			0.115			0.471***			−0.082			0.193*
Other religion			−0.118			−1.484***			−0.674***			−0.053
Constant	1.395***	1.222***	2.442***	4.146***	3.755***	2.431***	1.316***	1.113***	-1.031**	1.393***	1.402***	1.181***
Adjusted R^2	0.01	0.08	0.14	0.05	0.21	0.27	0.00	0.06	0.15	0.01	0.14	0.25
N of observations	1,380	1,225	1,143	1,361	1,209	1,128	1,380	1,225	1,143	1,380	1,225	1,143

Source: World Values Surveys, 1981.

Notes: See appendix A for definitions of all variables. Coefficients reported are unstandardized OLS regression estimates. Omitted category is unmarried, non-white, female, and Catholic.

$*p < .05$, $**p < .01$, $***p < .001$ (one-tailed test for moral visions)

Table 3.9

OLS Coefficients from Regression of Social Capital on Moral Visions and Two Dimensions of Cultural Variation, Controlling for Sociodemographic Variables, United States, 1990

Independent Variables	Confidence in Institutions Scale			Frequency of Attendance at Religious Services			Voluntary Organizations Scale			Political Acts Scale		
Moral visions												
Absolutism	0.527***	0.106	0.145	1.190***	0.542***	0.516***	−0.037	−0.006	0.015	−0.385***	0.016	0.005
Cultural Indices												
Traditional/Secular-Rational Values		−0.588***	−0.522***		−1.112***	−1.045***		−0.105*	−0.128		0.454***	0.342***
Survival/Self-expression Values		−0.211***	0.151**		−0.134*	−0.254***		−0.358***	0.228***		0.391***	0.370***
Sociodemographics												
Age			0.041			0.013			0.049*			−0.235***

Race			−0.259*			−0.340*			0.122			−0.048
Gender			0.032			−0.123			−0.035			0.257***
Marital status			−0.120			0.058			0.157*			0.038
Social class			0.076			−0.349***			−0.280***			0.017
Education			−0.020			0.076***			0.120***			0.053*
Protestant			−0.156			−0.331***			0.150			0.095
Other religion			−0.277*			−1.465***			−0.124			0.019
Constant	1.058***	1.191***	1.675**	3.753***	3.695***	4.222***	1.278***	0.954***	−0.878**	1.957***	1.715***	1.265***
Adjusted R^2	0.03	0.14	0.15	0.08	0.26	0.38	0.00	0.06	0.18	0.02	0.14	0.24
N of observations	1,354	1,160	928	1,346	1,152	923	1,354	1,160	928	1,354	1,10	928

Notes: See appendix A for definitions of all variables. Coefficients reported are unstandardized OLS regression estimates. Omitted category is unmarried, non-white, female, and Catholic.

*$p < .05$, **$p < .01$, ***$p < .001$ (one-tailed test for moral visions)

Table 3.10

OLS Coefficients from Regression of Social Capital on Moral Visions and Two Dimensions of Cultural Variation, Controlling for Sociodemographic Variables, United States, 1995

Independent Variables	Confidence in Institutions Scale			Frequency of Attendance at Religious Services			Voluntary Organizations Scale			Political Acts Scale		
Moral visions												
Absolutism	0.075	−0.202**	−0.240**	1.009***	0.570***	0.598***	0.010	0.034	−0.009	−0.168**	0.198**	0.093
Cultural Indices												
Traditional/Secular-Rational Values		−0.509***	−0.503***		−1.101***	−0.970***		−0.167*	0.183*		0.433***	0.344***
Survival/Self-expression Values		−0.078	−0.044		0.064	−0.017		0.403***	0.258***		0.502***	0.432***
Sociodemographics												
Age			0.066*			0.061			−0.065			−0.142***

Race			−0.195			−0.561***			−0.562**			−0.335**
Gender			0.011			−0.527***			0.052			0.119
Marital status			−0.154			0.216			0.214			−0.023
Social class			−0.026			−0.150*			−0.435***			−0.015
Education			0.025			0.094**			0.160***			0.092***
Protestant			−0.003			−0.325			0.014			0.080
Other religion			−0.094			−0.990***			−0.119			0.223*
Constant	1.102***	1.070***	0.755	3.872***	3.494***	3.191***	2.917***	2.584***	1.315	1.687***	1.375***	0.269
Adjusted R^2	0.01	0.09	0.09	0.06	0.24	0.32	0.00	0.03	0.09	0.01	0.18	0.26
N of observations	1,357	1,157	855	1,348	1,150	849	1,357	1,157	885	1,357	1,160	855

Source: World Values Surveys, 1995.

Notes: See appendix A for definitions of all variables. Coefficients reported are unstandardized OLS regression estimates. Omitted category is unmarried, non-white, female, and Catholic.

$*p < .05$, $**p < .01$, $***p < .001$ (one-tailed test for moral visions)

TABLE 3.11

OLS Coefficients from Regression of Social Capital on Moral Visions and Two Dimensions of Cultural Variation, Controlling for Sociodemographic Variables, United States, 2000

Independent Variables	Confidence in Institutions Scale			Frequency of Attendance at Religious Services			Voluntary Organizations Scale			Political Acts Scale		
Moral visions												
Absolutism	0.049	−0.190*	−0.160*	1.105***	0.308***	0.272**	0.057	0.005	0.040	−0.217***	0.057	0.094
Cultural indices												
Traditional/Secular-Rational Values		−0.423***	−0.388***		−1.251***	−1.064***		−0.156***	−0.082		0.359****	0.257***
Survival/Self-expression Values		−0.150**	−0.096		0.138*	−0.195***		0.253***	0.150**		0.214***	0.231***
Sociodemographics												
Age			0.029			0.071*			0.105***			−0.157***

Race			−0.362***			−0.432***			0.032			−0.215**
Gender			0.081			−0.365***			0.077			0.185**
Marital status			−0.125			0.112			−0.002			−0.121
Social class			−0.025			−0.058			−0.109*			0.017
Education			−0.096***			0.131***			0.190***			0.064
Protestant			0.092			0.330**			0.275**			−0.054
Other religion			0.076			−0.482***			−0.148			0.014
Constant	1.253***	1.385***	3.444***	4.023***	4.194***	2.285***	1.832***	1.568***	−2.178***	2.319***	2.099***	1.307**
Adjusted R^2	0.01	0.06	0.07	0.07	0.32	0.37	0.00	0.03	0.11	0.01	0.08	0.15
N of observations	1,418	1,338	1,205	1,415	1,335	1,205	1,418	1,338	1,205	1,418	1,338	1,205

Source: World Values Surveys, 2000.

Notes: See appendix A for definitions of all variables. Coefficients reported are unstandardized OLS regression estimates. Omitted category is unmarried, non-white, female, and Catholic.

*$p < .05$, **$p < .01$, ***$p < .001$ (one-tailed test for moral visions)

Table 3.12
Summary of Effects of Moral Visions on Economic Ethics Scale, Family/Life Values Scale, and Social Capital, United States, 1981–2000

	Economic Ethics Scale				Family/Life Values Scale			
Effects of Moral Visions	*1981*	*1990*	*1995*	*2000*	*1981*	*1990*	*1995*	*2000*
Direct effect	−0.052	−0.058	−0.005	−0.054	−0.044	−0.045	−0.097	−0.073
Indirect effect via Traditional/Secular-Rational	−0.049	−0.023	−0.033	−0.031	−0.137	−0.185	−0.155	−0.202
Indirect effect via Survival/Self-expression	0.007	0.017	0.014	0.021	−0.051	−0.046	−0.051	−0.041
Total indirect effect	−0.041	−0.006	−0.020	−0.010	−0.188	−0.231	−0.206	−0.243
Total effect	−0.093	−0.064	−0.025	−0.064	−0.232	−0.276	−0.303	−0.316
	Confidence in Institutions				Frequency of Church Attendance			
	1981	*1990*	*1995*	*2000*	*1981*	*1990*	*1995*	*2000*
Direct effect	0.028	0.036	−0.076	−0.063	0.123	0.129	0.140	0.075

Indirect effect via Traditional/Secular-Rational	0.069	0.113	0.091	0.089	0.100	0.151	0.129	0.194
Indirect effect via Survival/Self-expression	0.011	0.019	0.009	0.011	−0.001	0.009	−0.005	0.008
Total indirect effect	0.080	0.132	0.100	0.100	0.100	0.159	0.124	0.202
Total effect	0.108	0.168	0.024	0.037	0.223	0.288	0.264	0.277

	Voluntary Organizations Scale				Political Acts Scale			
	1981	*1990*	*1995*	*2000*	*1981*	*1990*	*1995*	*2000*
Direct effect	0.056	−0.002	0.008	0.002	0.019	0.006	0.074	0.023
Indirect effect via Traditional/Secular-Rational	0.002	0.023	0.019	0.035	−0.076	−0.094	−0.077	−0.092
Indirect effect via Survival/Self-expression	−0.042	−0.038	−0.030	−0.021	−0.041	−0.039	−0.057	−0.020
Total indirect effect	−0.039	−0.015	−0.011	0.015	−0.117	−0.132	−0.134	−0.112
Total effect	0.017	−0.017	−0.003	0.017	−0.098	−0.126	−0.060	−0.089

Source: World Values Surveys, 1981, 1990, 1995, 2000.

Notes: See appendix A for definitions of all variables.

TABLE 3.13

Summary of Effects of Moral Visions on Attitudes about Church-State Separation, United States, 2000

Independent Variables	Politicians who do not believe in God are unfit for public office	Religious leaders should not influence how people vote in elections	It would be better for America if more people with strong religious beliefs held public office	Religious leaders should not influence government decisions
Direct effect	−0.100	0.111	−0.148	0.113
Indirect effect via Traditional/Secular-Rational	−0.130	0.075	−0.163	0.094
Indirect effect via Survival/Self-expression	−0.030	0.004	−0.030	0.015
Total indirect effect	−0.159	0.079	−0.193	0.108
Total effect	−0.259	0.190	−0.341	0.221

Source: World Values Surveys, 2000.

Notes: See appendix A for definitions of all variables.

TABLE 4.1

Phases of the Four Great Awakenings in the United States

	Phase of Religious Revival	Phase of Rising Political Effect	Phase of Increasing Challenge to Dominance of the Political Program
First Great Awakening, 1730–1830	1730–1760: Weakening of predestination doctrine; recognition that many sinners may be predestined for salvation; rise of ethic of benevolence	1760–1790: Attack on British corruption; American Revolution	1790–1820: Breakup of revolutionary coalition
Second Great Awakening, 1800–1920	1800–1840: Rise of belief that anyone can achieve saving grace through inner and outer struggle against sin; widespread adoption of ethic of benevolence; upsurge of millennialism	1840–1870: Rise of abolitionist, temperance, and nativist movements; attack on corruption of South; Civil War; women's suffrage	1870–1920: Replacement of prewar evangelical leaders; Darwinian crisis; urban crisis
Third Great Awakening,	1890–1930: Shift from emphasis on personal	1930–1970: Attack on corruption of big business	1970–?: Attack on liberal reforms; defeat of Equal

(*continued*)

TABLE 4.1 (*continued*)

	Phase of Religious Revival	Phase of Rising Political Effect	Phase of Increasing Challenge to Dominance of the Political Program
1890–?	to social sin; shift to more secular interpretation of Bible and creed	and the rich; labor reforms; civil rights and women's rights movements	Rights Amendment; rise of tax revolt; rise of Christian Coalition and other political groups of the religious Right
Fourth Great Awakening, 1960–?	1960–?: Return to sensuous religion and reassertion of experiential content of Bible; reassertion of concept of personal sin	1990–?: Attack on materialist corruption; rise of prolife, profamily, and media reform movements; campaign for more values-oriented school curriculum; expansion of tax revolt; attack on entitlements	?:

Source: Robert William Fogel, *The Fourth Great Awakening and the Future of Egalitarianism* (Chicago: University of Chicago Press, 2000), p. 28, table 1.1.

Table 5.1

Binary Logit Coefficients from Regression of Value Incongruence on Moral Visions and Sociodemographic Variables, United States, 1981

Independent Variables	Value Incongruence (left of zero vs. right of zero)	Value Incongruence (left tail vs. right tail)
Moral visions		
Absolutism	0.299**	0.441*
Sociodemographics		
Age	0.078*	0.210***
Race	0.652**	1.005**
Gender	−0.404***	−0.651***
Marital status	0.689***	1.199***
Social class	−0.104*	−0.257**
Education	0.061*	0.037
Protestant	0.080	−0.356
Other religion	−1.481***	−2.226***
Constant	−2.184**	−2.424*
Nagelkerke pseudo R^2	0.12	0.26
N of observations	1,674	799

Source: World Values Surveys, 1981.

Notes: See appendix A for definitions of all variables. Left tail is 25th percentile; right tail is 75th percentile. Omitted category is unmarried, nonwhite, female, and Catholic. Number of observations reported is unweighted.

*$p < .05$, **$p < .01$, ***$p < .001$

TABLE 5.2
Binary Logit Coefficients from Regression of Value Incongruence on Moral Visions and Sociodemographic Variables, United States, 1990

Independent Variables	Value Incongruence (left of zero vs. right of zero)	Value Incongruence (left tail vs. right tail)
Moral visions		
Absolutism	0.436***	0.735***
Sociodemographics		
Age	0.059	0.145**
Race	0.253	0.570*
Gender	0.002***	−0.265
Marital status	0.476***	0.487*
Social class	−0.366***	−0.384**
Education	−0.031	−0.020
Protestant	0.136	0.183
Other religion	−0.408*	−0.636**
Constant	0.755	−0.842
Nagelkerke pseudo R^2	0.10	0.18
N of observations	1,137	583

Source: World Values Surveys, 1990.

Notes: See appendix A for definitions of all variables. Left tail is 25th percentile; right tail is 75th percentile. Omitted category is unmarried, nonwhite, female, and Catholic. Number of observations reported for is unweighted.

$^*p < .05$, $^{**}p < .01$, $^{***}p < .001$

TABLE 5.3

Binary Logit Coefficients from Regression of Value Incongruence on Moral Visions and Sociodemographic Variables, United States, 1995

Independent Variables	Value Incongruence (left of zero vs. right of zero)	Value Incongruence (left tail vs. right tail)
Moral visions		
Absolutism	0.467***	0.975***
Sociodemographics		
Age	0.051	0.106
Race	0.016	0.372
Gender	0.024	−0.167
Marital status	0.808***	1.217***
Social class	−0.238**	−0.392**
Education	−0.025	0.015
Protestant	−0.217	−0.485
Other religion	−0.008	−0.663**
Constant	0.699	0.006
Nagelkerke pseudo R^2	0.09	0.23
N of observations	863	453

Source: World Values Surveys, 1995.

Notes: See appendix A for definitions of all variables. Left tail is 25th percentile; right tail is 75th percentile. Omitted category is unmarried, nonwhite, female, and Catholic. Number of observations reported for is unweighted.

$^{*}p < .05$, $^{**}p < .01$, $^{***}p < .001$

Table 5.4
Binary Logit Coefficients from Regression of Value Incongruence on Moral Visions and Sociodemographic Variables, United States, 2000

Independent Variables	Value Incongruence (left of zero vs. right of zero)	Value Incongruence (left tail vs. right tail)
Moral visions		
Absolutism	0.353**	0.901***
Sociodemographics		
Age	0.211***	0.257***
Race	−0.215	−0.237
Gender	−0.241*	−0.598**
Marital status	0.378**	0.504**
Social class	−0.244***	−0.352***
Education	−0.021	0.054
Protestant	−0.094	0.152
Other religion	−0.756***	−0.851***
Constant	1.042	−0.418
Nagelkerke pseudo R^2	0.13	0.27
N of observations	959	479

Source: World Values Surveys, 2000.

Notes: See appendix A for definitions of all variables. Left tail is 25th percentile; right tail is 75th percentile. Omitted category is unmarried, nonwhite, female, and Catholic. Number of observations reported for is unweighted.

$^{*}p < .05$, $^{**}p < .01$, $^{***}p < .001$

Table 5.5

Binary Logit Coefficients from Regression of Thinking Often about the Meaning and Purpose of Life on Value Incongruence, Controlling for Moral Visions and Sociodemographic Variables, United States, 1981

Independent Variables	Often think about meaning and purpose of life (excluding value incongruence)	Often think about meaning and purpose of life (for value incongruence, left of zero vs. right of zero)	Often think about meaning and purpose of life (for value incongruence, left tail vs. right tail)
Value incongruence			
Traditional and self-expression values†	—	0.652***	0.872***
Moral visions			
Absolutism	0.525***	0.464***	0.254
Sociodemographics			
Age	0.019	0.007	−0.014
Race	−0.656***	−0.780***	−0.639*
Gender	−0.404***	−0.313**	−0.182
Marital status	−0.001	−0.140	−0.292
Social class	−0.082	−0.068	−0.010

(*continued*)

TABLE 5.5 (*continued*)

Independent Variables	Often think about meaning and purpose of life (excluding value incongruence)	Often think about meaning and purpose of life (for value incongruence, left of zero vs. right of zero)	Often think about meaning and purpose of life (for value incongruence, left tail vs. right tail)
Education	0.026	0.011	0.017
Protestant	−0.246	−0.234	−0.195
Other religion	−0.420*	−0.186	−0.152
Constant	0.284	0.446	0.025
Nagelkerke pseudo R^2	0.06	0.08	0.08
N of observations	1,870	1,670	798

Source: World Values Survey, 1981.

Notes: See appendix A for definition of all variables. Omitted category is unmarried, nonwhite, female, and Catholic. Number of observations reported is unweighted.

†Value incongruence = 1 if a person tends to have traditional and self-expression values. For the second column, this is left of of 0 in the distribution of value incongruence scores. For the third column, this is the 25th percentile.

$*p < .05$, $**p < .01$, $***p < .001$

Table 5.6

Binary Logit Coefficients from Regression of Thinking Often about the Meaning and Purpose of Life on Value Incongruence, Controlling for Moral Visions and Sociodemographic Variables, United States, 1990

Independent Variables	Often think about meaning and purpose of life (excluding value incongruence)	Often think about meaning and purpose of life (for value incongruence, left of zero vs. right of zero)	Often think about meaning and purpose of life (for value incongruence, left tail vs. right tail)
Value incongruence			
Traditional and self-expression values†	—	0.495***	0.840***
Moral visions			
Absolutism	0.475***	0.381***	0.236
Sociodemographics			
Age	0.132***	0.122	0.065
Race	−0.434*	−0.510**	−0.507
Gender	0.083	0.083**	−0.041
Marital status	−0.371**	−0.536***	−0.435*

(*continued*)

Table 5.6 (*continued*)

Independent Variables	Often think about meaning and purpose of life (excluding value incongruence)	Often think about meaning and purpose of life (for value incongruence, left of zero vs. right of zero)	meaning and purpose of life (for value incongruence, left tail vs. right tail)
Social class	−0.020	0.006	−0.108
Education	−0.001	0.008	0.032
Protestant	−0.307*	0.207	0.205
Other religion	−0.080	0.032	0.201
Constant	−0.211	−0.396	−0.567
Nagelkerke pseudo R^2	0.06	0.07	0.09
N of observations	1,304	1,132	582

Source: World Values Survey, 1990.

Notes: See appendix A for definition of all variables. Omitted category is unmarried, nonwhite, female, and Catholic. Number of observations reported is unweighted.

†Value incongruence = 1 if a person tends to have traditional and self-expression values. For the first column, this is left of of 0 in the distribution of value incongruence scores. For the second column, this is the 25th percentile.

$^*p < .05$, $^{**}p < .01$, $^{***}p < .001$

TABLE 5.7

Binary Logit Coefficients from Regression of Thinking Often about the Meaning and Purpose of Life on Value Incongruence, Controlling for Moral Visions and Sociodemographic Variables, United States, 1995

Independent Variables	Often think about meaning and purpose of life (excluding value incongruence)	Often think about meaning and purpose of life (for value incongruence, left of zero vs. right of zero)	Often think about meaning and purpose of life (for value incongruence, left tail vs. right tail)
Value incongruence			
Traditional and self-expression values†	—	0.652***	0.306
Moral visions			
Absolutism	0.358**	0.187	0.576**
Sociodemographics			
Age	0.122**	0.088	0.119
Race	−0.487**	−0.554**	−0.555
Gender	−0.309*	−0.201	−0.398*
Marital status	0.105	0.030	0.182
Social class	−0.066	−0.053	−0.085

(*continued*)

TABLE 5.7 (*continued*)

Independent Variables	Often think about meaning and purpose of life (excluding value incongruence)	Often think about meaning and purpose of life (for value incongruence, left of zero vs. right of zero)	meaning and purpose of life (for value incongruence, left tail vs. right tail)
Education	0.063*	0.039	0.015
Protestant	0.301	0.329	0.325
Other religion	0.886***	0.950***	0.986***
Constant	−1.684	0.446	−0.903
Nagelkerke pseudo R^2	0.07	0.07	0.11
N of observations	1,002	856	450

Source: World Values Survey, 1995.

Notes: See appendix A for definition of all variables. Omitted category is unmarried, nonwhite, female, and Catholic. Number of observations reported is unweighted.

†Value incongruence = 1 if a person tends to have traditional and self-expression values. For the first column, this is left of of 0 in the distribution of value incongruence scores. For the second column, this is the 25th percentile.

$^*p < .05$, $^{**}p < .01$, $^{***}p < .001$

TABLE 5.8

Binary Logit Coefficients from Regression of Thinking Often about the Meaning and Purpose of Life on Value Incongruence, Controlling for Moral Visions and Sociodemographic Variables, United States, 2000

Independent Variables	Often think about meaning and purpose of life (excluding value incongruence)	Often think about meaning and purpose of life (for value incongruence, left of zero vs. right of zero)	Often think about meaning and purpose of life (for value incongruence, left tail vs. right tail)
Value incongruence			
Traditional and self-expression values†	—	0.224	0.437***
Moral visions			
Absolutism	0.585***	0.603***	0.335*
Sociodemographics			
Age	0.128**	0.109**	0.050
Race	−0.971***	−1.060***	−0.927***
Gender	−0.345**	−0.316**	−0.342*
Marital status	−0.257*	−0.324**	−0.192
Social class	−0.063	0.065	0.105

(*continued*)

TABLE 5.8 (*continued*)

Independent Variables	Often think about meaning and purpose of life (excluding value incongruence)	Often think about meaning and purpose of life (for value incongruence, left of zero vs. right of zero)	Often think about meaning and purpose of life (for value incongruence, left tail vs. right tail)
Education	0.072*	0.041	−0.025
Protestant	0.080	0.022	−0.179
Other religion	0.020	−0.038	−0.182
Constant	−0.943	0.446	1.004
Nagelkerke pseudo R^2	0.09	0.11	0.09
N of observations	1,011	958	478

Source: World Values Survey, 2000.

Notes: See appendix A for definition of all variables. Omitted category is unmarried, nonwhite, female, and Catholic. Number of observations reported is unweighted.

†Value incongruence = 1 if a person tends to have traditional and self-expression values. For the first column, this is left of of 0 in the distribution of value incongruence scores. For the second column, this is the 25th percentile.

*$p < .05$, **$p < .01$, ***$p < .001$

TABLE 5.9

Percentage Saying They "Often" Think about the Meaning and Purpose of Life, by Country and Year, 1981–1998

Country	1981	1990–1991	1995–1998	Net Change
Advanced industrial democracies[a]				
Australia	34	—	44	+10
Belgium	22	29	—	+7
Canada	38	43	—	+5
Finland	32	38	40	+8
France	36	39	—	+3
East Germany	—	40	47	+7
West Germany	29	30	41	+12
Great Britain	34	36	—	+2
Iceland	39	36	—	−3
Ireland	25	34	—	+9
Northern Ireland	29	33	—	+4
South Korea	29	39	—	+10
Italy	36	48	—	+12
Japan	21	21	26	+5
Netherlands	21	31	—	+10
Norway	26	31	32	+6
Spain	24	27	24	0
Sweden	20	24	28	+8
Switzerland	—	44	43	−1
United States	48	48	46	−2
Ex-Communist societies[b]				
Belarus	—	35	47	+12
Bulgaria	—	44	33	−11
China	—	30	26	−4

(*continued*)

Table 5.9 (*continued*)

Country	1981	1990–1991	1995–1998	Net Change
Estonia	—	35	39	+4
Hungary	44	45	—	+1
Latvia	—	36	43	+7
Lithuania	—	41	42	+1
Russia	—	41	45	+4
Slovenia	—	37	33	−4
Developing and low-income societies[c]				
Argentina	30	57	51	+21
Brazil	—	44	37	−7
Chile	—	54	50	−4
India	—	28	23	−5
Mexico	32	40	39	+7
Nigeria	—	60	50	−10
South Africa	38	57	46	+8
Turkey	—	38	50	+12

Source: Inglehart and Baker, "Modernization," p. 48, table 8.
[a]Sixteen of 20 advanced industrial democracies increased; mean change = +6.
[b]Six of 9 ex-Communists societies increased; mean change = +1.
[c]Four of 8 developing and low-income societies increased; mean change = +3.

✵ *Notes* ✵

Chapter One: A Question of Values

1. As described in Seymour Martin Lipset, *American Exceptionalism* (New York: W. W. Norton, 1996), p. 19.

2. Allan Bloom, *The Closing of the American Mind* (New York: Simon & Schuster, 1987); Robert Putnam, "Bowling Alone: American's Declining Social Capital," *Journal of Democracy* 6 (January 1995): 65–78; Putnam, *Bowling Alone: The Collapse and Revival of American Community* (New York: Simon & Schuster, 2000); Robert Hughes, *Culture of Complaint: The Fraying of America* (New York: Oxford University Press, 1993); Gertrude Himmelfarb, *The De-Moralization of Society* (New York: Vintage, 1994); Richard Sennett, *The Corrosion of Character* (New York: W. W. Norton, 1998); James Davison Hunter, *The Death of Character* (New York: Basic, 2000); Robert N. Bellah et al., *Habits of the Heart: Individualism and Commitment in American Life* (New York: Harper and Row, 1985); Francis Fukuyama, *The Great Disruption* (New York: Simon & Schuster, 1999); John Miller, *Egotopia: Narcissism and the New American Landscape* (Tuscallosa: University of Alabama Press, 1997); and William J. Bennett, ed., *The Book of Virtues* (New York: Simon & Schuster, 1993). See also William J. Bennett, John J. DiIulio, Jr., and John P. Walters, *Body Count: Moral Poverty . . . And How to Win America's War Against Crime and Drugs* (New York: Simon & Schuster, 1996); William J. Bennett, *The Death of Outrage: Bill Clinton and the Assault on American Ideals* (New York: The Free Press, 1998).

3. Lipset, *American Exceptionalism*, p. 17.

4. Urie Bronfenbrenner et al., *The State of Americans: This Generation and the Next* (New York: Free Press, 1996), p. x.

5. William J. Bennett, *The Index of Leading Cultural Indicators*, vol. 1 (Washington, DC: Heritage Foundation and Empower America, 1993). An updated version of this index is called The Index of National Civic Health or INCH, compiled by the National Commission on Civic Renewal. This updated version is reproduced in chapter 4 of this book.

6. Reynolds Farley, ed., *State of the Union, Volume Two: Social Trends* (New York: Russell Sage, 1995).

7. For example, as by Himmelfarb, *The De-Moralization of Society*, pp. 228–34. Fukuyama, in contrast, argues that these statistical improve-

ments indicate a "renorming" and possible reconstruction of American society (*The Great Disruption*, chap. 16).

8. Robin M. Williams, Jr., *American Society* (New York: Knopf, 1951), p. 375. Emphasis deleted from original.

9. In the broadest sense, "[m]orals are the rules by which a society exhorts (as laws are the rules by which it seeks to compel) its members and associations to behave consistent with its order, security, and growth." Will and Ariel Durant, *The Lessons of History* (New York: Simon & Schuster, 1968), p. 37.

10. Williams, *American Society*, p. 376.

11. Bronfenbrenner et al., *The State of Americans*, p. 260.

12. Bennett, DiIulio, and Walters, *Body Count*, p. 196.

13. William J. Bennett, "A Strategy for Transforming America's Culture," address to The Heritage Foundation's Annual Board Meeting and Public Policy Seminar, Amelia Island, FL, April 16, 1995. The text of his speech was obtained at http://www.townhall.com/empower/moral-strategy.html.

14. Bennett, *The Death of Outrage*.

15. William J. Bennett, *The Moral Compass* (New York: Simon & Schuster, 1995).

16. Stephen R. Covey, *The 7 Habits of Highly Effective Families* (New York: St. Martin's Griffen/Golden Books, 1997), p. 127.

17. According to the General Social Survey, 1993–1994 combined, question 457A. About 61 percent of men and 63 percent of women feel this way. This is not a statistically significant difference ($p > .05$). A higher percentage of blacks feel this way, compared to whites (60 percent vs. 69 percent). This is a statistically significant difference ($p < .001$), but it is not large.

18. From Princeton Survey Research Associates, Newsweek Poll, released June 28, 1995, cited in Paul DiMaggio, John Evans, and Bethany Bryson, "Have Americans' Social Attitudes Become More Polarized?" *American Journal of Sociology* 102 (1996): 63; see also Rys H. Williams, ed., *Cultural Wars in American Politics* (New York: Aldine de Gruyter, 1997), pp. 63–99.

19. James Davison Hunter and Carl Bowman, *The State of Disunion*, Executive Summary (Ivy, VA: In Medias Res Educational Foundation, 1996), p. 4. This is a summary of results from the 1996 Survey of American Public Culture, part of the Post-Modernity Project at the University of Virginia.

20. From Alan Wolfe's Middle Class Morality Project, an in-depth interview study of two hundred middle-class Americans, *One Nation, After All* (New York: Viking, 1998). Percentages reported are obtained by combining "strongly agree" and "agree" responses, tables 3.5 (p. 117) and 6.1 (p. 231).

21. Pew Research Center for the People & the Press and Pew Forum on Religion and Public Life, 2002 Religion and Public Life Survey, conducted by Princeton Survey Research Associates. Report available at the center's web site, http://www. people-press.org/.

22. From subscription to www.gallup.com.

23. James Davison Hunter, *Culture Wars: The Struggle to Define America* (New York: Basic, 1991). For another early statement, see, e.g., Os Guinness, *The American Hour: A Time of Reckoning and the Once and Future Role of Faith* (New York: Free Press, 1993).

24. Nancy J. Davis and Robert V. Robinson, "Are the Rumors of War Exaggerated? Religious Orthodoxy and Moral Progressivism in America," *American Journal of Sociology* 102 (1996): 756.

25. According to the *Washington Post*, February 23, 1997, final edition, p. C5. Reported in Ted Mouw and Michael W. Sobel, "Culture Wars and Opinion Polarization: The Case of Abortion," *American Journal of Sociology* 106 (2001): 914.

26. Bronfenbrenner et al., *The State of Americans*, p. 261.

27. Clifford Geertz, *The Interpretation of Cultures* (New York: Basic Books, 1973), p. 3.

28. Ronald Inglehart and Wayne E. Baker, "Modernization, Cultural Change, and the Persistence of Traditional Values," *American Sociological Review* 65 (2000): 23.

29. Ibid., pp. 23–25; Ronald Inglehart, *Modernization and Postmodernization: Cultural, Economic and Political Change in 43 Societies* (Princeton: Princeton University Press, 1997); Inglehart, *Culture Shift in Advanced Industrial Society* (Princeton: Princeton University Press, 1990).

30. Inglehart and Baker, "Modernization," p. 25; Inglehart, *Modernization and Postmodernization*; Inglehart, *Culture Shift*.

31. Inglehart, *Modernization and Postmodernization*, p. 5.

32. For example, see ibid., chap. 3.

33. The definition, concept, and measurement of "secularization" are contentious issues. See, for example, the debate between Gerald Marwell and N. J. Demerath III ("'Secularization' by Any Other Name") and Michael Hout and Claude S. Fischer ("O Be Some Other Name") in the

American Sociological Review 68 (2003): 314–18. As Phillip Gorski points out, "secularization theory is *not* a unified theory of religious decline. It is a family of theories about religious change, some of which posit religious decline, and some of which do not." Phillip S. Gorski, "Historicizing the Secularization Debate: Church, State, and Society in Late Medieval and Early Modern Europe, ca. 1300 to 1700," *American Sociological Review* 65 (2000): 141. Gorski describes four positions in the secularization paradigm: disappearance, decline, transformation, and privatization. The "decline of traditional values" hypothesis is consistent with the disappearance and decline positions.

34. Lipset, *American Exceptionalism*, p. 17.

35. George Ritzer, *The McDonaldization of Society*, 3rd ed. (Thousand Oaks, CA: Pine Forge Press, 2000).

36. Hunter, *Culture Wars*, p. 42. The first clear statement of the Culture War thesis is found in this book. Hunter's thesis is sometimes called the "strong form" of the Culture Wars thesis, a distinction I discuss in detail in chapter 3. See also James Davison Hunter, *Before the Shooting Begins: Searching for Democracy in America's Culture War* (New York: Free Press, 1994).

37. For example, see Marco Orrù, *Anomie: History and Meanings* (Boston: Allen & Unwin, 1987), pp. 3–7; S. N. Eisenstadt, "The Axial Age," *European Journal of Sociology* 23 (1982): 294–314; Karl Jaspers, *The Origin and Goal of History*, trans. Michael Bullock (London: Routledge & Kegan Paul, 1953).

38. Gertrude Himmelfarb, *One Nation, Two Cultures* (New York: Knopf, 2001), pp. 117–18.

39. Benedict Anderson, *Imagined Communities: Reflections on the Origin and Spread of Nationalism*, rev. ed. (London: Verso Books, 1991). Jürgen Habermas uses the concept and phrase in *The Inclusion of the Other*, ed. Ciaran Cronin and Pablo De Grieff (Cambridge: MIT Press, 1998), p. 111.

40. Habermas, *The Inclusion of the Other*, p. 111.

41. The core personal networks of Americans tend to be small, closed, and homogeneous. See, for example, Peter V. Marsden, "Core Discussion Networks of Americans," *American Sociological Review* 52 (1987): 122–31.

42. Habermas, *The Inclusion of the Other*, p. 113. Italics in original.

43. Ibid., pp. 111–12.

44. Ibid., p. 112.

45. Ibid., pp. 158–59, Habermas argues that it is possible for the Euro-

pean Union to overcome its cultural diversity by developing and reproducing *communicatively* "an ethical-political self-understanding of citizens." "What unites a nation of citizens, as opposed to a *Volksnation*, is not some primordial substrate but rather an intersubjectively shared context of possible mutual understanding."

46. Wayne E. Baker, "The Widening Cultural Divide," *Policy Newsletter of the Center for Society & Economy*, University of Michigan Business School, Spring 2000. Special issue on the euro. Electronic publication available at www.bus.umich.edu/cse.

47. Alexis de Tocqueville, *Democracy in America*, trans. George Lawrence, ed. J. P. Mayer (New York: HarperCollins, 1988); John W. Kingdon, *America the Unusual* (New York: St. Martin's/Worth, 1999); Lipset, *American Exceptionalism*.

48. Habermas, *The Inclusion of the Other*, p. 113.

49. Lipset, *American Exceptionalism*, p. 31.

50. Putnam, "Bowling Alone;" Putnam, *Bowling Alone*.

51. Amitai Etzioni, "Is Bowling Together Sociologically Lite?" *Contemporary Sociology* 30 (2001): 223–24.

52. See, for example, Pamela Paxton, "Is Social Capital Declining in the United States? A Multiple Indicator Assessment," *American Journal of Sociology* 105 (1999): 88–127. Everett Ladd argues that social capital is not declining but changing: new forms of social bonds are replacing old forms. *The Ladd Report* (New York: Free Press, 1999).

53. See, for example, the symposium on *Bowling Alone* in *Contemporary Sociology* 30 (2001): 223–30.

54. Etzioni, "Is Bowling Together Sociologically Lite?" p. 223.

55. Lipset, *American Exceptionalism*, p. 31.

56. Joseph S. Nye, Jr., "Introduction: The Decline of Confidence in Government," pp. 1–18 in Joseph S. Nye, Jr., Philip D. Zelikow, and David C. King, eds., *Why People Don't Trust Government* (Cambridge: Harvard University Press, 1997). Quote is from p. 18.

57. For example, the General Social Survey (GSS) and National Elections Studies (NES) offer longer time-series than the WVS. The earliest WVS is 1981, while the GSS started in 1972 and the NES started in 1952. However, the GSS and NES are U.S. surveys and do not permit cross-cultural comparisons. They do not include critical survey items, such as the importance of God in the respondent's life, materialism and postmaterialism, moral authority (apart from religion), and thinking about the meaning

and purpose of life. The GSS and NES data *are* appropriate for analyzing the "polarization claim," but this analysis has already been carried out by others, as discussed in chapter 3. The International Social Survey Programme (ISSP) and the International Social Justice Project (ISJP) offer cross-cultural data, but they are limited in scope and hence do not permit comparisons with a large number and wide diversity of societies. Without the WVS, for example, it would be impossible to know that the United States is as traditional as many developing and low-income countries—which is a major finding in the book. Moreover, both the ISSP and ISJP offer shorter time-series than the WVS. For example, the ISSP included only six countries in its first survey, conducted in 1985 (Australia, Austria, Germany, Great Britain, Italy, United States), and this number did not exceed ten countries until 1989. The ISJP's first survey was 1991, and it included only twelve countries (Russia, Estonia, Poland, Hungary, Czechoslovakia, Bulgaria, Slovenia, East and West Germany, United States, Great Britain, Netherlands, and Japan). The second survey, in 1996, included only six (Russia, Estonia, Hungary, Czech Republic, Bulgaria, and Germany).

Chapter Two: America's Values in Global Context

1. Inglehart, *Modernization and Postmodernization*.

2. For example, ibid., pp. 81–98.

3. Inglehart and Baker, "Modernization." We use data from the most recent available survey for the given country; most of these surveys are from the 1995–1998 World Values Survey, but some are from the 1990–1991 wave. The data for the following fifty societies are from the 1995–1998 wave: United States, Australia, New Zealand, China, Japan, Taiwan, South Korea, Turkey, Bangladesh, India, Pakistan, the Philippines, Armenia, Azerbaijan, Georgia, Great Britain, East Germany, West Germany, Switzerland, Norway, Sweden, Finland, Spain, Russia, Ukraine, Belarus, Estonia, Latvia, Lithuania, Moldova, Poland, Bulgaria, Bosnia, Slovenia, Croatia, Yugoslavia, Macedonia, Nigeria, South Africa, Ghana, Argentina, Brazil, Chile, Colombia, Dominican Republic, Mexico, Peru, Puerto Rico, Uruguay, Venezuela. Data for Canada, France, Italy, Portugal, Netherlands, Belgium, Denmark, Iceland, Ireland, Northern Ireland, Austria, Hungary, Czech Republic, Slovakia, and Romania are from the 1990 World Values Survey. The number of respondents interviewed in these surveys averages about 1,400. Most of the 1995–1998 surveys were carried out in 1996, but Ar-

gentina, Australia, China, Croatia, Ghana, Nigeria, Japan, Puerto Rico, Russia, Slovenia, Taiwan, and the United States were surveyed in fall 1995, while Armenia, Brazil, Bulgaria, Colombia, West and East Germany, Macedonia, Pakistan, and Poland were surveyed in 1997, and Bosnia, Great Britain, and New Zealand were surveyed in 1998. The data from these surveys are available from the ICPSR survey data archive.

4. See, for example, Ronald Inglehart and Pippa Norris, *Rising Tide: Gender Equality and Cultural Change around the World* (Cambridge: Cambridge University Press, 2003).

5. To avoid dropping an entire society from our analysis when one of these variables is not available, the nation-level aggregate dataset, but not the individual-level dataset, sometimes uses results from another survey in the same country. For example, the Materialist/Postmaterialist battery was not included in the 1981 surveys in the United States and Australia; but this battery *was* included in the 1980 national election surveys in both countries, and the results are used in these cases. When this option was not available, we ranked all societies on the variable most closely correlated with the missing variable and assigned the mean score of the two adjacent countries in this ranking. For example, the 1997 Bangladesh survey omitted V197 homosexuality, but did include V60 homosexuals, among the groups one would not like to have as neighbors. Nigeria and Georgia were the two closest-ranking societies on V60, so Bangladesh was assigned the mean of their scores on V197.

6. The items in each cultural dimension are highly correlated; together, the two dimensions explain 70 percent of the total cross-national variation among these ten variables, and 39 percent of the total individual-level variation among the ten variables. This holds true despite the fact that we deliberately selected items covering a wide range of topics. With the first dimension, for example, we could have selected five items referring to religion and obtained an even more tightly correlated cluster, but our goal was to measure broad dimensions of cross-cultural variation.

7. The correlation of fertility rates and traditional/secular-rational dimension in 1995 is −.75.

8. Robert William Fogel, *The Fourth Great Awakening and the Future of Egalitarianism* (Chicago: University of Chicago Press, 2000), pp. 176–77.

9. R. Shusterman, "Pragmatism and Liberalism between Dewey and Rorty," *Political Theory* 22 (1994): 391–413. Quoted by Fogel, *The Fourth Great Awakening*, p. 205.

10. Inglehart, *Modernization and Postmodernization;* Inglehart, *Culture Shift;* Inglehart, *The Silent Revolution: Changing Values and Political Styles in Advanced Industrial Society* (Princeton: Princeton University Press, 1977).

11. These maps are consistent with an earlier one by Inglehart in *Modernization and Postmodernization*, pp. 334–37, based on the 1990–1991 World Values Surveys. The overall pattern is strikingly similar to the cultural maps in Inglehart (see chaps. 3 and 11). The similarities of these maps demonstrate that these two key dimensions of cross-cultural variation are quite robust. The same broad cultural zones appear, in essentially the same locations, but some of them now contain many more societies.

12. Samuel P. Huntington, "The Clash of Civilizations?" *Foreign Affairs* 72, 31 (1993); Huntington, *The Clash of Civilizations and the Remaking of World Order* (New York: Simon & Schuster, 1996). An alternative strategy would be to use one of the many available clustering techniques to identify the groups of nations and draw boundaries. Inglehart and I preferred to use the theoretical classifications proposed by Huntington, and then to test for their explanatory power.

13. Daniel Bell, *The Coming of Post-industrial Society* (New York: Basic Books, 1973); Bell, *The Cultural Contradictions of Capitalism* (New York: Basic Books, 1976).

14. For example, Max Weber, *The Protestant Ethic and the Spirit of Capitalism* (New York: Charles Scribner's Sons,1904–1905; English translation, 1958).

15. Robert Putnam, *Making Democracy Work: Civic Traditions in Modern Italy* (Princeton: Princeton University Press, 1993); Francis Fukuyama, *Trust: The Social Virtues and the Creation of Prosperity* (New York: Free Press, 1995); Gary G. Hamilton, "Civilizations and Organization of Economies," pp. 183–205 in Neil J. Smelser and Richard Swedberg, eds., *The Handbook of Economic Sociology* (Princeton: Princeton University Press, 1994); Paul DiMaggio, "Culture and Economy," pp. 27–57 in Smelser and Swedberg, eds., *The Handbook of Economic Sociology;* Mauro Guillén, *Models of Management: Work, Authority, and Organization in a Comparative Perspective* (Chicago: University of Chicago Press, 1994); Charles Hampden-Turner and Alfons Trompenaars, *The Seven Cultures of Capitalism* (New York: Currency/ Doubleday, 1993).

16. Huntington, *The Clash of Civilizations;* "The West: Unique, Not Universal," *Foreign Affairs* 75, 6 (1996): 28–46.

17. Robert N. Bellah, "The Protestant Structure of American Culture:

Multiculture or Monoculture?" fall lecture in Culture and Social Theory, Institute for Advanced Studies in Culture, University of Virginia, 2000. Amitai Etzioni makes a similar argument in *The Monochrome Society* (Princeton: Princeton University Press, 2001).

18. This generates a dummy variable having sixty-two cases coded "0" and only three coded "1." With such an extreme skew, this variable is unlikely to explain much variance.

19. Some modernization theorists place heavy emphasis on the cultural impact of rising educational levels, but these results suggest that expansion of the educational system is not the crucial factor.

20. By controlling for economic development, we may be underestimating the impact of a society's historical heritage. For it is possible that Protestantism, Confucianism, or Communism helped *shape* the society's contemporary level of economic development. For example, Weber attributes a crucial role to Protestantism in launching economic growth in Europe, and it is a historical fact that—in its early phase, though clearly not today—industrialization was overwhelmingly concentrated in predominantly Protestant societies and among the Protestant population of mixed societies.

21. Based on various tests, such as one-way ANOVA and various multiple comparisons tests, there is no statistically significant difference ($p > .05$) between America's location on the traditional/secular-rational dimension in 1981 and 1995.

22. Based on one-way ANOVA and various multiple comparisons tests, there is a statistically significant difference ($p < .05$) between America's location on the traditional/secular-rational dimension in 1995 and 2000 (somewhat less traditional in 2000).

23. See also Inglehart and Norris, *Rising Tide*.

24. With only four time points in the World Values Surveys, statistically evaluating trends over time is subject to error; nonetheless, I include them here for heuristic value. I assess time trends by regressing year of survey on the position of the United States on the traditional/secular-rational scale in each year. OLS regression is generally not recommended for time-series analysis, as pointed out by Richard McCleary and Richard A. Hay, Jr., *Applied Times Series Analysis for the Social Sciences* (Beverly Hills: Sage, 1980). This is in part because OLS regression is very sensitive to outliers (pp. 33–34). The time-series analyzed here does not exhibit outliers. Given the availability of only four time points, simple regression is the best technique.

I report the p-value for year of survey (these are reported for heuristic value, since significance tests are not strictly applicable). There is no statistically significant linear trend from 1981 to 2000 along the traditional/secular-rational dimension ($p = .260$). There is a statistically significant ($p < .01$) and an almost perfect linear trend from 1981 to 2000 along the survival/self-expression values dimension.

25. Stability itself is not some quirk. Other societies, such as Italy, the Netherlands, and Spain, have not changed their positions on the traditional/secular-rational dimension. Further, loss of traditional values is not the only possible direction of change on this cultural dimension. The map in figure 2.4 shows that many societies have regained their traditional values, such as China, Bulgaria, Russia, Belarus, Argentina, Brazil, Turkey, and South Africa. Their national value systems have become more traditional and less secular-rational over time.

26. America's location in 2000 on the traditional/secular-rational values dimension may portend a loss of traditional values in the years ahead. Nonetheless, the evidence presented here shows that the widespread perception of a loss of traditional values over the past two decades did not coincide with an actual loss during the same time.

27. Hiroyuki Hasegawa, "Economic Crisis, Modernization, and the New Roles of Government in East Asia," *Policy Newsletter of the Center for Society & Economy* 2 (Summer 2001). Published electronically at http://www.bus.umich.edu/cse.

28. Fogel, *The Fourth Great Awakening*, p. 232. Fogel notes that Huntington sees the end of the cold war and the victory of American values as a threat. Because America is defined by its struggle against totalitarianism, winning the struggle means that the nation has lost its purpose. See Huntington, "The Clash of Civilizations?"; *The Clash of Civilizations;* "The West."

29. Tom W. Smith and Lars Jarrko, "National Pride: A Cross-national Analysis," National Opinion Research Center/University of Chicago, General Social Survey Cross-national report No. 19 (1998). America's rank as the most patriotic comes from the average ranking of two national-pride scales. The World Values Surveys also find that Americans have the highest levels of patriotism.

30. See also Inglehart and Norris, *Rising Tide*.

31. Ibid.

32. N. J. Demerath III and Yonghe Yang, "'Lambs among the Lions:'

America's Culture Wars in Cross-Cultural Perspective," pp. 199–219 in Williams, ed., *Cultural Wars in American Politics*.

33. See Inglehart and Norris, *Rising Tide*, pp. 53–59. Their religiosity scale derives from a factor analysis of the proportion of people in each nation who (1) say that religion is "very important" in their lives, (2) find comfort in religion, (3) believe in God, (4) identify as religious, (5) believe in life after death, and (6) attend religious services regularly.

34. Phyllis A. Tickle, *God-Talk in America* (New York: The Crossroad Publishing Company, 1998).

35. Karl Mannheim, "The Problem of Generations," pp. 276–332 in P. Kecskemeti, ed., *Essays on the Sociology of Knowledge* (London: Routledge and Kegan Paul, [1928] 1952); José Ortega y Gasset, "The Concept of the Generation," in *The Modern Theme* (New York: Harper and Row, 1961). See also Howard Schuman and Jacqueline Scott, "Generations and Collective Memories," *American Sociological Review* 54 (1989): 359–81. For an analysis of political generations and social movements, see Nancy Whittier, "Political Generations, Micro-Cohorts, and the Transformation of Social Movements," *American Sociological Review* 62 (1997): 760–78.

36. See, for example, the analysis and findings presented in Inglehart, *Modernization and Postmodernization*, chap. 5.

37. Ideally, we would want to have economic data since the first decade of the twentieth century, to coincide with the birth years of our oldest cohort. For technical reasons, comparable data from before 1950 are not available.

38. See, for example, the map in Inglehart and Norris, *Rising Tide*, p. 155.

39. Tocqueville, *Democracy in America;* Kingdon, *America the Unusual;* Lipset, *American Exceptionalism*.

40. Kingdon, *America the Unusual*, p. 23. Italics in original.

41. Ibid.

42. Lipset, *American Exceptionalism*, p. 19.

43. Ibid., p. 31. Italics added.

44. Ibid., p. 19.

45. Kingdon, *America the Unusual*, pp. 58–64. Kingdon notes that there were four categories of immigrants: (1) those who fled religious and political persecution; (2) those who migrated for economic reasons; (3) those who came against their will, such as enslaved blacks; and (4) the people who were here before the Vikings, notably those who crossed the Bering Strait. "Over the course of American history, the first two categories came to dominate American politics" (p. 59).

46. Ibid., p. 58. See also Lipset, *American Exceptionalism;* Fogel, *The Fourth Great Awakening.*

47. Kingdon, *America the Unusual*, pp. 59–60; David Hackett Fischer, *Albion's Seed: Four British Folkways in America* (New York: Oxford University Press, 1989).

48. Lipset, *American Exceptionalism*, pp. 19–21; chap. 2.

49. Kai T. Erikson, *Wayward Puritans* (New York: John Wiley and Sons, 1966), p. v.

50. Lipset, *American Exceptionalism*, p. 20.

51. Kingdon, *America the Unusual*, pp. 60–61. As Kingdon points out, all immigrants who came for economic reasons did not come for the same economic reasons. Some came to escape starvation; others were deported as criminals. But enough came for the reasons of economic advancement and achievement to push the center of American values and politics "in a more individualistic and antigovernment direction" (p. 61).

52. Many sociologists, political scientists, and economists favor the path dependence argument to explain technologies and institutions today, though, of course, the debates about path dependence continue. The argument for political path dependence in America is made, for example, by Kingdon, *America the Unusual*, pp. 79–84; it is a major thesis in Lipset's *American Exceptionalism*.

53. Kingdon, *America the Unusual*, p. 80.

54. Based on face-to-face interviews with 2,047 adults in January 1996. Hunter and Bowman, *The State of Disunion*. The quote is from the executive summary, p. 3. Hunter also summarizes key findings in his *The Death of Character* (New York: Basic, 2000).

55. Hunter and Bowman, *The State of Disunion*, executive summary, p. 3.

56. Bellah, "The Protestant Structure of American Culture."

57. Etzioni, *The Monochrome Society*.

58. Diana L. Eck, *A New Religious America* (San Francisco: HarperSanFrancisco, 2001), p. 42.

59. Andrew M. Greeley and Michael Hout, "Americans' Increasing Belief in Life after Death: Religious Competition and Acculturation," *American Sociological Review* 64 (1999): 813. They argue that the changing beliefs about life after death were *not* caused by contact with native Protestants (e.g., religious intermarriage or friendship). Rather, the trend is linked to religious competition. For example, Catholic institutions in America competed with other religious institutions to reach out to and hold onto Cath-

olic immigrants. These Catholic institutions were dominated by Irish Catholics, who strongly believe in life after death. The Irish Catholic-dominated institutions were very successful at retaining Catholic immigrants and their children in the church and socialized them to the belief in life after death. An exchange on these findings appears in the *American Sociological Review* 66 (2001): 146–58.

60. Eck, *A New Religious America*.

61. Inglehart and Baker, "Modernization."

62. Mauro F. Guillén, *The Limits of Convergence* (Princeton: Princeton University Press, 2001), p. 3.

63. Anderson, *Imagined Communities*. Habermas uses the concept and phrase in *The Inclusion of the Other*, p. 111.

64. Habermas, *The Inclusion of the Other*, p. 111.

65. Ibid., p. 113. Quoted in Lipset, *American Exceptionalism*, p. 18.

66. Lipset, *American Exceptionalism*, p. 31.

67. John Kenneth Galbraith, *The Good Society* (Boston: Houghton Mifflin, 1996), p. 1.

68. Emile Durkeim, *The Division of Labor in Society*, trans. George Simpson (Glencoe, IL: The Free Press, 1960); Durkheim, *The Rules of Sociological Method*, trans. by S. A. Solovay and J. H. Mueller (Glencoe, IL: The Free Press, 1958), p. 67; Kai T. Erikson, "Notes on the Sociology of Deviance," pp. 9–21 in Howard Becker, ed., *The Other Side* (New York: The Free Press of Glencoe, 1964); Erikson, *Wayward Puritans*. Quote is from page 4 of *Wayward Puritans*. His argument fits "all kinds of human collectivity—families as well as whole cultures, small groups as well as nations" (p. 9).

69. Roderick P. Hart, *Modern Rhetorical Criticism*, 2d ed. (Boston: Allyn and Bacon, 1997). The seminal study of this rhetorical function of the mass media is M. McCombs and D. Shaw, "The Agenda-Setting Function of Mass Media," *Public Opinion Quarterly* 36 (1972): 176–87.

70. As Erikson notes in *Wayward Puritans* (p. 12), the television, radio, and print media are important sources of normative information: "A considerable portion of what we call 'news' is devoted to reports about deviant behavior and its consequences. [The media] constitute one of our main sources of information about the normative outlines of society."

71. Lipset, *American Exceptionalism*, p. 108.

72. Shusterman, "Pragmatism and Liberalism between Dewey and Rorty."

73. All societies have a conception of human nature, ranging from in-

herently good to inherently evil, with "evil but perfectible" in the middle. See Florence Rockwood Kluckholn and Fred L. Strodtbeck, *Variations in Value Orientations* (Evanston: Row, Peterson, 1961). The Puritans viewed human nature as evil but perfectible, making the self a moral project of perfectibility.

74. Greeley and Hout, "Americans' Increasing Belief in Life after Death," p. 813.

75. Robert Wuthnow, *After Heaven: Spirituality in America since the 1950s* (Berkeley: University of California Press, 1998).

76. The decline of a "spirituality of dwelling" and a rise of a "spirituality of seeking" is a key thesis in Wuthnow, *After Heaven*. Wuthnow's thesis is limited to the United States. However, the results from our analysis of data from the World Values Surveys support his thesis far beyond the American context. Inglehart and Baker, "Modernization."

77. These data were compiled by Lisa Leneway, who was a research assistant on this project. I am grateful to Lisa for her dedication and meticulous work. The following is her description of the data collection effort. The research methods for this project can be broken into three main steps. The first task was to find the best-seller list for every year as far back as we could go. The book *80 Years of Best Sellers 1895–1975* provided much of this information. It used lists from the literary magazine *Publishers Weekly*, which began running best-seller lists in 1912. The lists include only books distributed by trade (books sold to bookstores and libraries) and exclude books sold by mail or by book clubs. In 1912 and 1913 *Publishers Weekly* published lists of the top ten fiction and nonfiction best-sellers. The nonfiction list was dropped in the years 1914–1916 and reappeared with the top seven titles in 1917. The reason was that the prices of nonfiction works were higher during this time, and the market was very small compared to the fiction market. In 1918 the nonfiction list contained ten titles, and in 1919–1921 it contained only six books. In 1921 the nonfiction list once again had ten titles, and it remained that way until 1978, when it was expanded to fifteen. During World War I, in 1917 and 1918, *Publishers Weekly* also published a special list of the top ten war books. Since *80 Years of Best Sellers 1895–1975* stops at 1975, for the years 1976–1997 we looked up the best-seller list in the appropriate issues of *Publishers Weekly* (in early spring the magazine publishes its list of the previous year's best-sellers).

Once all the lists had been found, we located summaries for each book, for the most part in *The Book Review Digest* (BRD). These volumes collect reviews that a book received from many different sources. When we could not find a summary in the BRD, we looked in *The Book Review Index*, which provided a listing of where reviews could be found—usually in a literary magazine or a newspaper such as the *New York Times Book Review*. For some of the more recent books, excerpts were also located by using the Internet, at an on-line bookstore. Summaries could not be located for about twenty books over the 1912–1997 period.

The third and most important aspect of the project was to code the books using our original coding scheme. Each book was fitted into one of the main genre categories. Then the subthemes were recorded under the more specific categories. While developing the coding scheme, we wanted to highlight all the advice books. We used a special advice category at the beginning of the coding sheet to highlight the advice books, and a self-help/guidance category under the main genres. Within the self-help category, there were twelve subcategories to further classify the self-help books into categories such as religion, cookbook, or psychology.

78. Inglehart and Baker, "Modernization"; Fogel, *The Fourth Great Awakening*, pp. 176–77.

79. As Inglehart and I argued in "Modernization," this pattern for ex-Communist countries "may reflect the impact of current circumstances: During the last decade most ex-Communist societies have been in turmoil, with the peoples of the Soviet successor states experiencing the collapse of their economic, political, and social systems. Life has been insecure and unpredictable, and life expectancy has actually fallen. This results in a complex pattern: Although we find a relatively steep intergenerational slope, suggesting that the long-term trend during the last 60 years in which peoples' lives became increasingly secure, the immediate reality is one in which the peoples of the former Communist societies now emphasize survival values even more strongly than the peoples of low-income societies. In other words, we find evidence of both cohort and period effects" (p. 45).

80. Societies with traditional values also have much higher fertility rates than those with secular-rational values, which enables traditional values to remain widespread despite the forces of modernization. Our traditional/secular-rational values index shows a strong negative correlation with the 1995 fertility rates of these societies ($r = -.75$), even controlling for economic development, education, and social structural variables. Today, most

industrial societies have fertility rates below the population replacement level. In Germany, Russia, Japan, Spain, and Italy, the average woman of child-bearing age now produces from 1.2 to 1.6 children (2.1 is the replacement rate). In contrast, low-income societies continue to have much higher fertility rates (due, in part, to the high rates of reproduction encouraged by traditional values). In Nigeria, for example, the average woman currently produces 5.5 children, and she has them earlier in life, making the span between generations shorter. The fertility differences between industrial and developing societies are so large that we observe two seemingly incompatible trends: (1) most societies are industrializing, and industrialization tends to bring increasingly secular worldviews; but (2) today, more people than ever before hold traditional values. In 1970, 73 percent of the world's population lived in developing countries, and 27 percent lived in developed countries. By 1996, the developed countries contained only 20 percent of the world's population; by 2020, they will contain an estimated 16 percent (U.S. Bureau of the Census 1996). The peoples of most developed countries have shifted toward increasingly modern values, but their societies contain a diminishing share of the world's population.

81. The data from 1981 to 1995 show a clear movement toward self-expression values (fig. 2.4). From 1995 to 2000, America moved even farther in this direction on the survival/self-expression dimension. There is an almost perfect linear trend from 1981–2000.

82. Though many Americans report that their sense of personal safety and security has been shaken, this appears to have resulted in only a temporary change in religious beliefs and national pride. (1) About half of the respondents in the first wave of the "How America Responds" poll, conducted at the University of Michigan Institute for Social Research (ISR) soon after the attacks, reported that their sense of personal safety had been shaken "a great deal" or "a good amount." The second wave of the survey, conducted six months after the attacks, revealed little change in Americans' perceived loss of personal safety and security. (Michael W. Traugott, Robert M. Groves, and Courtney Kennedy, "How America Responded: Public Opinion after 9/11/01," paper presented at the 57th Annual AAPOR Conference, St. Pete Beach, FL, May 17, 2002). (2) A survey conducted by Princeton Survey Research Associates soon after the attacks reported significantly higher levels of religious belief and national pride. Six months later, however, these had returned to their previous levels. (Pew Research Center for the People & the Press and Pew Forum on Religion

and Public Life, 2002 Religion and Public Life Survey, conducted by Princeton Survey Research Associates. Report available at the center's web site, http://www.people-press.org/.)

Chapter Three: Culture War

1. Hunter, *Culture Wars*, p. 42.

2. The first clear statement of the culture war thesis may be found in ibid. Hunter's thesis is sometimes called the "strong form" of the culture wars thesis, a distinction I discuss in detail below. See also James Davison Hunter, *Before the Shooting Begins: Searching for Democracy in America's Culture War* (New York: Free Press, 1994).

3. For those who believe in the culture war thesis, see, e.g., Guinness, *The American Hour*; Hunter, *Culture Wars*; Hunter, *Before the Shooting Begins*; Hunter, *The Death of Character*.

4. For those who disagree with this thesis either in whole or in part, see, e.g., John H. Evans, "'Culture War' or Status Group Ideology as the Basis of US Moral Politics," *International Journal of Sociology and Social Policy* 16 (1996): 15–34; Robert Wuthnow, "Restructuring of American Religion: Further Evidence." *Sociological Inquiry* 66 (1996): 303–29; Alan Wolfe, *One Nation, After All*.

5. Hunter, *Culture Wars*.

6. For example, see Orrù, *Anomie*, pp. 3–7; S. N. Eisenstadt, "The Axial Age," *European Journal of Sociology* 23 (1982): 294–314; Karl Jaspers, *The Origin and Goal of History*, trans. Michael Bullock (London: Routledge & Kegan Paul, 1953).

7. Joseph Fletcher, *Situation Ethics: The New Morality* (Louisville: Westminster John Knox Press, 1966). Fletcher describes the three approaches to decision making—legalism, antinomianim, and situationism—in chapter 1.

8. Ibid., p. 20.

9. Daniel Shanahan, *Toward a Genealogy of Individualism* (Amherst: University of Massachusetts Press, 1992), p. 20. Shanahan traces the rise of the belief system of individualism, in which the individual has become the final source of morals and moral judgment.

10. Fletcher, *Situation Ethics*. Fletcher might have disagreed with my categorization of "situation ethics" under "relativism" because he viewed "relativism" as one of four presuppositions at work in his moral approach (the

others are pragmatism, positivism, and personalism) (see chap. 2). Note also that the heart of his situation ethics is the absolute of "love" (*agape*). James F. Childress discusses this "supreme moral principle" in the introduction to Fletcher's book.

11. Fletcher, *Situation Ethics*, p. 22.

12. Peter Berger, *The Sacred Canopy* (New York: Doubleday, 1967), p. 19.

13. Fletcher, *Situation Ethics*, p. 22. A vivid example, one that Fletcher and others use, is "Jean-Paul Sartre's advice to the student who asked whether he should stay with his mother in France (his father was a Nazi collaborator) or join the French Resistance against the Nazis. Sartre answered: 'You're free, choose, that is, invent.'" From Childress, "Introduction," in ibid., p. 4.

14. Brent Staples, "Common Ground," a review of *One Nation, After All*, in the *New York Times Book Review*, March 8, 1998, p. 6; Wolfe, *One Nation, After All*.

15. The distinction between moral visions and religious beliefs is emphasized by Orrù, *Anomie*. He notes that society (Durkheim's view) and abstract ideas (Plato's view) are also sources of a transcendental moral authority. Moral visions and religious beliefs are often confused and conflated in theory and research on the culture war thesis, as I discuss later in this chapter.

16. George Lakoff, *Moral Politics* (Chicago: University of Chicago Press, 1996).

17. Ibid., p. 7.

18. The "harm" example comes from ibid., p. 8.

19. The "mother" example comes from ibid.

20. See ibid., chap. 1, for an introduction to the theory of radial categories.

21. Ibid.

22. Ibid., p. 13.

23. Ibid., p. 366.

24. Ibid., chap. 5, presents Strict Father morality.

25. Ibid., p. 127.

26. Ibid., p. 111.

27. Ibid., chap. 6, presents Nurturant Parent morality.

28. Charles Colson, "Will We Lose the Culture War? An Effective Battle Strategy," radio transcript no. 90908, Prison Fellowship Ministries, 1999. I am indebted to Paul DiMaggio for bringing this to my attention.

29. Compare with Berger, *The Sacred Canopy*.

30. Geertz, *The Interpretation of Cultures*, p. 126.

31. Nancy J. Davis and Robert V. Robinson, "Are the Rumors of War Exaggerated?" *American Journal of Sociology* 102 (1996): 769.

32. For example, see Guinness, *The American Hour*; Hunter, *Culture Wars*; Hunter, *Before the Shooting Begins*.

33. Hunter, *Culture Wars*, p. 42.

34. Himmelfarb, *One Nation, Two Cultures*; see also Himmelfarb, *The De-Moralization of Society*.

35. For example, Evans, "'Culture War'"; John H. Evans, "Worldviews or Social Groups as the Source of Moral Value Attitudes: Implications for the Culture Wars Thesis" *Sociological Forum* 12 (1997); Wolfe, *One Nation, After All*.

36. See, for example, Evans, "'Culture War'"; Evans, "Worldviews or Social Groups."

37. For example, see Martin Fishbein, *Belief, Attitude, Intention and Behavior* (Reading, MA: Addison-Wesley, 1975).

38. Paul DiMaggio, John Evans, and Bethany Bryson, "Have Americans' Social Attitudes Become More Polarized?" *American Journal of Sociology* 102 (1996): 691.

39. For a compendium of empirical work, see, for example, Rys H. Williams, ed., *Cultural Wars in American Politics* (New York: Aldine de Gruyter, 1997).

40. DiMaggio, Evans, and Bryson, "Have Americans' Social Attitudes Become More Polarized?" and Davis and Robinson, "Are the Rumors of War Exaggerated?" See also Nancy J. Davis and Robert V. Robinson, "A War for America's Soul: The American Religious Landscape," pp. 39–62 in Williams, ed., *Cultural Wars in American Politics*.

41. DiMaggio, Evans, and Bryson, "Have Americans' Social Attitudes Become More Polarized?" p. 738.

42. Ted Mouw and Michael Sobel reanalyze some of the abortion items in the DiMaggio et al. study, using different methods for ordinal variables, and do not find evidence of polarization over time. Ted Mouw and Michael E. Sobel, "Culture Wars and Opinion Polarization: The Case of Abortion." *American Journal of Sociology* 106 (2001): 913–43. In reply, Evans, Bryson, and DiMaggio note that Mouw and Sobel's approach, while an important contribution, "addresses only one of our four indicators of polarization in attitudes toward abortion. Moreover, using Mouw and Sobel's method and ad-

ditional years of NES data, we find support for our substantive conclusions about even this one measure of polarization with evidence indicating that polarization in responses to the NES abortion item increased between 1980 and 1998." John H. Evans, Bethany Bryson, and Paul DiMaggio, "Opinion Polarization: Important Contributions, Necessary Limitations," *American Journal of Sociology* 108 (2001): 945.

43. John H. Evans, "Polarization in Abortion Attitudes in U.S. Religious Traditions, 1972–1998," *Sociological Forum* 17 (2002): 387–422. Evans also found increasing polarization between black Protestants and both Catholics and white evangelicals. Further, mainline Protestants are polarizing internally, as are Catholics. He argues that demographic changes account for the internal polarization within mainline Protestants, while demographics changes have restrained polarization that could have occurred within white evangelicals. The cause of internal polarization within Catholics is yet to be determined.

44. David C. King, "The Polarization of American Parties and Mistrust of Government," pp. 155–78 in Joseph S. Nye, Jr., Philip D. Zelikow, and David C. King, eds., *Why People Don't Trust Government* (Cambridge: Harvard University Press, 1997).

45. John H. Evans, "Have Americans' Attitudes Become More Polarized?—An Update," *Social Science Quarterly* 84 (2003): 71–90.

46. Davis and Robinson, "Are the Rumors of War Exaggerated?" fig. 1, p. 770. This distribution is almost statistically normal.

47. Ibid., pp. 769–70.

48. According to results from the Pluralism Project at Harvard University, reported in Diana L. Eck, *A New Religious America* (San Francisco: HarperSanFrancisco, 2001).

49. Davis and Robinson, "Are the Rumors of War Exaggerated?" p. 780.

50. DiMaggio, Evans, and Bryson ("Have Americans' Social Attitudes Become More Polarized?") pioneered the approach used to test for polarization. Here, I use three of their measures: (1) The *variance* or *standard deviation* measures the dispersion of a distribution. (2) *Kurtosis* tests for the peakedness or bimodality of a distribution. Kurtosis is negative if the distribution is flatter than the normal distribution, and approaches −2 as a distribution becomes more bimodal. (3) *Skewness* tests for asymmetry in a distribution. Positive skewness occurs when the values in a distribution bunch toward the left of the distribution (lower values) and there is a long tail to the right (also called "skewed to the right"). Negative skewness occurs

when the values bunch toward the right (higher values) and there is a long tail to the left (also called "skewed to the left"). A normal distribution has a standard deviation of 1, kurtosis = 0, and skewness = 0. These statistics can be used to test for different aspects of polarization at one point of time; they can also be used to evaluate trends toward or away from polarization over time. With only four time points in the World Values Surveys, statistically evaluating trends over time is subject to error; nonetheless, I include them here for heuristic value. I assess time trends by regressing year of survey on the statistic of interest (i.e., standard deviation, kurtosis, skewness). I report the p-value for year of survey (these are reported for heuristic value, since significance tests are not strictly applicable).

These statistics for the traditional/secular-rational dimension are: 1981 (SD = .760, skew = .863, kurtosis = .776); 1990 (SD = .848, skew = .666, kurtosis = .006); 1995 (SD = .812, skew = .694, kurtosis = .304); 2000 (SD = .859, skew = .545, kurtosis = .064). (1) The standard deviation of the distribution traditional/secular-rational values is fairly stable over time, indicating that the dispersion of values has been more or less constant over the twenty-year period. The analysis of time trends supports this finding ($p = .26$). (2) Kurtosis is always positive in each year, indicating that the distribution of traditional/secular-rational values is as peaked as or even more peaked than the normal distribution. In fact, the distributions in 1981 and 1995 are significantly more peaked than the normal distribution (the measures of kurtosis are more than twice their standard errors). Over time, kurtosis exhibits fluctuations up and down, but there is no linear trend ($p = .23$). Moreover, the distribution of traditional/secular-rational values is never less peaked than the normal distribution. (3) Skewness is always positive in each year, indicating that values tend to bunch toward the traditional pole of the traditional/secular-rational dimension. In fact, the distributions in each year are significantly more skewed than the normal distribution (each measure of skewness is several times larger than its standard error). Skewness does exhibit a significant linear trend over time toward less skewness ($p = .06$). However, even the year with the least skew (2000) is significantly more skewed than the normal distribution (the measure of skewness in 2000 is eight times its standard error). The linear trend shows a tendency for less clustering toward the traditional pole, but values are still very clustered at this end of the dimension.

Based on these findings, I conclude that there is little evidence of polarization of traditional/secular-rational values. Rather, there is considerable consensus among Americans, who tend to cluster toward the traditional end of this dimension in each year of the survey. In contrast, consider that Americans tend to be clustered at the self-expression pole of the survival/self-expression dimension; further, there is a statistically significant linear trend toward self-expression values (in contrast to the lack of a significant trend for traditional/secular-rational values), and there is also a statistically significant *decrease* in the dispersion (measured as the coefficient of variation) of values on the survival/self-expression dimension (in contrast to the lack of a statistically significant change in the dispersion of values on the traditional/secular-rational dimension).

51. For example, see the various empirical studies in Williams, ed., *Cultural Wars in American Politics*, such as N. J. Demerath III and Yonghe Yang, "What American Culture War? A View from the Trenches as Opposed to the Command Posts and the Press Corps," pp. 17–38. One possible exception is Alan Wolfe's Middle Class Morality Project, an in-depth interview study of two hundred middle-class Americans (Wolfe, *One Nation, After All*). He administered a follow-up survey to his interviewees, in which each person used a five-point Likert scale to report the extent to which he or she agreed or disagreed with statements about various social attitudes. On several key moral issues, middle-class Americans are divided, for and against, with few taking the middle position of "no opinion." For example, 50 percent agree or strongly agree that "America has become far too atheistic and needs a return to strong religious belief," but 40 percent disagree or strongly disagree. Only 10 percent said "no opinion" (pp. 46–47). Overall, however, Wolfe rejects the culture war hypothesis: "I have found little support for the notion that middle-class Americans are engaged in bitter cultural conflict with each other over the proper way to live" (p. 278).

52. Based on face-to-face interviews with 2,047 adults in January 1996. Hunter and Bowman, *The State of Disunion*. Hunter summarizes key findings in his *The Death of Character*.

53. Hunter, *The Death of Character*.

54. Pie chart is constructed from data in table 90, Hunter and Bowman, *The State of Disunion*.

55. Orrù, *Anomie*.

56. Note that the middle category (disagree with both statements) had to be volunteered by the respondent; the interviewer did not explicitly state it as a choice.

57. Wolfe, *One Nation, After All*, pp. 46–47.

58. Ibid. Note that Wolfe equates absolutism with *religious* absolutism. There are also nonreligious types of absolutism, such as society and ideas, as I describe in this chapter and chapter 4. Nonetheless, even though Wolfe restricts his definition to religious absolutism, he finds a bipolar distribution of beliefs about moral authority. And his results were obtained using a Likert five-point scale, not a dichotomous scale (see the discussion in the text of dichotomous measures).

59. There are multiple sources of absolute moral authority, even though many assume that absolutism is associated with religion. As Marco Orrù points out in *Anomie*, society and abstract ideas are also sources of transcendental or absolute moral authority.

60. Davis and Robinson, "Are the Rumors of War Exaggerated?" p. 767.

61. Using formula 6–18 in J. Nunnally, *Psychometric Theory* (New York: McGraw-Hill, 1978).

62. Demerath and Yang, "What American Culture War?" p. 20. Their criticism is directed at Wuthnow's measures in *The Restructuring of American Religion*.

63. Northern Ireland is the only society in the first wave of the World Values Surveys that came close to a 50:50 split: 44.4 percent were absolutists, 51.0 percent were relativists, and 4.6 percent were intermediates.

64. Moreover, other questions in the World Values Surveys with the same response format (agree, disagree, neither) rarely produce a polarized pattern.

65. Kluckholm and Strodtbeck, *Variations in Value Orientations*.

66. As such, this item was never reworked, as survey items sometimes are, to create more variance in responses (which could have created a false appearance of polarization).

67. Hunter, *Culture Wars*, pp. 42ff. Hunter uses the labels "moral orthodox" and "moral progressives," which are the same as my absolutists and relativists.

68. See Jeni Loftus, "America's Liberalization of Attitudes toward Homosexuality, 1973 to 1998," *American Sociological Review* 66 (2001): 762–82. Using data from the General Social Survey, Loftus finds that Americans "distinguish between the morality of homosexuality and the civil liberties of homosexuals. Americans became increasingly negative regarding the morality of homosexuality through 1990, but since then their attitudes have

become increasingly liberal. The same 25-year period witnessed a steady decline in Americans' willingness to restrict the civil liberties of homosexuals" (p. 762).

69. Kluckholm and Strodtbeck, *Variations in Value Orientations*.

70. Davis and Robinson, "Are the Rumors of War Exaggerated?"

71. Lipset, *American Exceptionalism*, p. 19. Donald G. Mathews provides an explanation of how America became so religious, in his "The Second Great Awakening as an Organizational Process, 1780–1830," *American Quarterly* 21 (1968): 33–43.

72. Logistic regression is used to assess the relationship between moral visions and religious beliefs, controlling for sociodemographic characteristics. Moral vision is the dependent variable, coded as 1 = absolutist, 0 = relativist. (Intermediates, "don't know," and the few cases with responses that were not ascertainable are excluded from this analysis.) The logistic model correctly classifies 77 percent of absolutists and 56 percent of relativists. Overall, the model correctly classifies 67 percent of all cases.

73. DiMaggio, "Culture and Economy," pp. 27–57 in *The Handbook of Economic Sociology*, eds. Smelser and Swedberg.

74. Richard Swedberg, *Max Weber and the Idea of Economic Sociology* (Princeton: Princeton University Press, 1998). See especially chapter 5.

75. For example, certain goals, such as "monetary success," may be unattainable for some unless they "deviate" from acceptable paths to success. See, for example, Merton's theory of anomie. Robert K. Merton, *Social Theory and Social Structure* (New York: Free Press, 1968), pp. 190–91.

76. These scales were built using factor analysis to discover the dimensions underlying opinions about various economic and social acts. In some but not all waves of the World Values Surveys, respondents were asked about as many as twenty-four acts. From these, I selected the items that (1) were included in all four waves, and (2) were *not* used in the construction of the two dimensions of cultural variation (these are homosexuality and abortion). Note that these two scales exhibit acceptable levels of reliability, using Cronbach's alpha measure (see table 3.4).

77. I also examined the internal consistency of opinion domains by age cohort and by socioeconomic status. Almost all results show that attitudes are consistent within each category, consistent across categories (only minor differences in alpha between different age cohorts or between different SES categories), and consistent over time.

78. DiMaggio, Evans, and Bryson, "Have Americans' Social Attitudes Become More Polarized?"

79. Attitude inconsistency can be viewed as a measure of psychological "anomie," indicating the difficulty a person has evaluating actions or making judgments, or problems of making too many exceptions to principles. These results support the findings of the classic study of ethical relativism and anomie by Snell Putney and Russell Middleton. They found that relativists were not more anomic than absolutists, and that relativists did not have more difficulty evaluating actions or make too many exceptions to principles, compared to absolutists. Snell Putney and Russell Middleton, "Ethical Relativism and Anomie," *American Journal of Sociology* 67 (1962): 430–38.

80. These statements are based on examining the proportion of variance explained for family/life values and attitudes about church-state separation, as well as the summary of direct, indirect, and total effects.

81. For example, see Davis and Robinson, "Are the Rumors of War Exaggerated?"

82. Most analysts support the weak form of the coupling claim. See, for example, Evans, "'Culture War,'" and Evans, "Worldviews."

83. Evans, "'Culture Wars'"; Evans, and "Worldviews"; Berger, *The Sacred Canopy*.

84. Etzioni, "Is Bowling Together Sociologically Lite?"

85. See, for example, the literature review in Paul S. Adler and Seok-Woo Kwon, "Social Capital: Prospects for a New Concept," *Academy of Management Review* 27 (2002): 17–40; Wayne Baker, *Achieving Success through Social Capital* (San Francisco: Jossey-Bass, 2000), chap. 1.

86. Putnam, *Bowling Alone;* Putnam, "Bowling Alone"; see also "The Saguaro Seminar: Civic Engagement in America," which can be found at http://www.ksg.harvard.edu/~saguaro/.

87. See, for example, Paxton, "Is Social Capital Declining in the United States?"; Ladd, *The Ladd Report*.

88. See, for example, the symposium on *Bowling Alone* in *Contemporary Sociology* 30 (2001): 223–30.

89. Gabriel Almond and Sidney Verba, *The Civic Culture* (Princeton: Princeton University Press, 1963); James S. Coleman, "Social Capital in the Creation of Human Capital," *American Journal of Sociology* 94 (1988): 95–121; Coleman, *Foundations of Social Theory* (Cambridge: Harvard University Press, 1990); Fukuyama, *Trust;* Putnam, *Making Democracy Work*.

90. As we show in Inglehart and Baker, "Modernization," Americans are more trusting than the peoples of most societies, but less trusting than most historically Protestant nations. The level of interpersonal trust in the United States is higher than in all the historically Catholic countries except Ireland, higher than in all the Islamic countries, higher than in all the Orthodox countries, and higher than in all the countries that experienced Communist rule. However, the peoples of all other historically Protestant countries—Australia, Britain, Canada, New Zealand, Switzerland, Netherlands, Sweden, and others—are more trusting than Americans. The only exception is the eastern region of the Federal Republic of Germany, but this society's low level of trust comes from its years of Communist rule.

91. As compiled, for example, by Putnam in *Bowling Alone*, p. 140, Fig. 38, and p. 467, n. 26.

92. "Americans of all ages, all stations of life, and all types of disposition are forever forming associations. There are not only commercial and industrial associations in which all take part, but others of a thousand different types—religious, moral, serious, futile, very general and very limited, immensely large and very minute. Americans combine to give fêtes, found seminaries, build churches, distribute books, and send missionaries to the antipodes. Hospitals, prisons, and schools take shape this way. Finally, if they want to proclaim a truth or propagate some feeling by the encouragement of a great example, they form an association. In every case, at the head of any new undertaking, where in France you would find the government or in England some territorial magnate, in the United States you are sure to find an association." Tocqueville, *Democracy in America*, p. 513.

93. James E. Curtis, Douglas E. Baer, and Edward G. Grabb, "Nations of Joiners: Explaining Voluntary Association Membership in Democratic Societies," *American Sociological Review* 66 (2001): 783–805.

94. Ibid., p. 799.

95. Putnam, *Bowling Alone*, chap. 3.

96. Lipset, *American Exceptionalism*, pp. 280–81.

97. Wolfe, *One Nation, After All*, pp. 256–57.

98. Ibid., p. 257.

99. The four waves of the World Values Surveys include somewhat different numbers and types of voluntary organizations. The 1981 and 1990 waves, for example, included several more types than the 1995 wave. To ensure strict comparability over time, I analyze the six types of voluntary organizations that were included in every wave. Nonetheless, the wording of

the response categories was somewhat different in the various waves. In the 1981, 1990, and 2000 surveys, respondents were asked if they "belonged to" a list of voluntary organizations, and if they "did unpaid work for" these organizations. In the 1995 survey, respondents were asked if they were an "active member," or an "inactive member," or "don't belong" to each type of voluntary organization. I assume that the categories "active member" or "inactive member" in the 1995 survey are equivalent to "belong to" in the 1981, 1990, and 2000 surveys.

100. It is possible that the growth from 1990 to 1995 could be an artifact of the differences in wording in the survey questions (see note above). However, it does not seem likely that respondents would not interpret "belong to" as the equivalent of "active member" or "inactive member."

101. Consider that the ratio of relativists to absolutists in 1981 is 3:2. Forty-eight percent of relativists, and 62 percent of absolutists, belonged to a church or religious organization. Assume a population of 500 respondents, with 300 relativists and 200 absolutists (3:2 ratio). The number of relativists who belong to a church or religious group is 144 (300 × .48), and the number of absolutists who belong is 124 (200 × .62).

102. Ted G. Jelen, "Culture Wars and the Party System: Religion and Realignment, 1972–1993," in Williams, ed., *Cultural Wars in American Politics*, p. 149.

103. Demerath and Straight, "Lambs among the Lions," p. 207.

104. Lipset, *American Exceptionalism*, p. 65.

105. The results of the CBS News/New York Times poll were reported in many publications around the country, such as in the Reuters article by Deborah Zabarenko, "U.S. Marks 25th Anniversary of Abortion Ruling," January 22, 1998.

106. Reported by the Associated Press, January 29, 30, 1998.

107. Statistics collected since 1977 by the National Abortion Federation reveal the extent of disruption and violence against abortion providers: 6 murders, 14 attempted murders, 289 death threats, 37 bombings, 427 bomb threats, 150 incidents of arson, 355 invasions, 695 incidents of vandalism, 100 incidents of assault and battery, 45 burglaries, 3,755 harassing phone calls and hate mail, 19,761 incidents of picketing, 671 clinic blockades, and 33,809 arrests. Statistics from 1977 to 1997, compiled by the National Abortion Federation (NAF), available at http://www.prochoice.org/violence/97vd.htm. (I added one murder and one bombing to their numbers to reflect the January 29, 1998, bombing of an abortion clinic in Birmingham,

Alabama.) The number of arrests is the number of arrest incidents, not the number of people arrested (some blockaders are arrested more than once). The NAF started collecting statistics on stalkings since 1993; there were 330 incidents. The total number of "violent" acts is 2,092; the total number of "disruptions" is 23,765. The home page for the NAF is http://www.cais.com/naf/.

108. Leon F. Litwack, "Civil War, American," *Microsoft® Encarta® 96 Encyclopedia*. © 1993–1995 Microsoft Corporation, © Funk & Wagnalls Corporation.

109. Demerath and Straight, "Lambs among the Lions," p. 200.

110. *Vigilante Justice: Militias and "Common Law Courts" Wage War against the Government* (New York: Anti-Defamation League, 1997), p. 4.

111. Ibid., p. 4.

112. Felice J. Levine and Katherine J. Rosich, *Social Causes of Violence: Crafting a Science Agenda* (Washington, DC: American Sociological Association, 1996), p. 4.

113. Based on statistics reported by the U.S. Department of Justice, Federal Bureau of Investigation, Criminal Justice Information Services Division (CJIS), Uniform Crime Reports, Hate Crime—1995. These statistics are available at http://www.fbi.gov/ucr/hatecm.htm. "The incidents were reported by more than 9,500 law enforcement agencies in 45 states and the District of Columbia. Participating agencies covered 75 percent of the U.S. population."

114. Reported by Jean Merl, "City Still Viewed as Racially Split," *Los Angeles Times*, April 29, 1997. This special report is available at http://www.latimes.com/home/news/reports/riots/poll.htm. The sample included 1,560 randomly selected residents of Los Angeles interviewed by phone in English or Spanish.

115. Donald R. Kinder and Lynn M. Sanders, *Divided by Color: Racial Politics and Demoncratic Ideals* (Chicago: University of Chicago Press, 1996).

116. David Jacobs and Jason T. Carmichael, "The Political Sociology of the Death Penalty: A Pooled Time-Series Analysis," *American Sociological Review* 67 (2002): 109–31. Their key finding of the effect of the size of black populations on the retention of the death penalty holds even when other factors are held constant, such as the amount of violent crime, region period, and social disorganization. Other factors that matter include economic inequality, conservative values, and a Republican-dominated state legislature.

117. Subscription to www.gallup.com.

118. Williams, "Introduction," in *Cultural Wars in American Politics*, p. 12.

Chapter Four: Dynamics of Crisis

1. Barry Glassner, *The Culture of Fear: Why Americans Are Afraid of the Wrong Things* (New York: Basic, 1999).

2. On moral panics, see Nicola Beisel and Brian Donovan, "The Problem with Moral Panics," *Newsletter of the Sociology of Culture Section of the American Sociological Association* 12, 2 (Winter 1998): 1–3.

3. Lipset, *American Exceptionalism*, p. 267.

4. Based on Himmelfarb, *The De-Moralization of Society*, pp. 221–23.

5. See Steven Vago, *Social Change*, 4th ed. (Upper Saddle River, NJ: Prentice Hall, 1999), chap. 1.

6. Quoted Arthur M. Schlesinger, Jr., *The Cycles of American History* (Boston: Houghton Mifflin, 1986), p. 23. I base parts of my discussion in this section on his analysis and literature review in chapter 2, "The Cycles of American Politics."

7. Henry Adams, "The Rule of Phase Applied to History," *The Tendency of History* (New York, 1919), p. 167. Quoted in ibid., p. 23.

8. See, for example, Kenneth E. Boulding, *A Primer on Social Dynamics* (New York: Free Press, 1970); Pitirim Sorokin, *Social and Cultural Dynamics* (Boston: Porter Sargent Publisher, 1957); Stephen R. Barley and Gideon Kunda, "Design and Devotion: Surges of Rational and Normative Ideologies of Control in Managerial Discourse," *Administrative Science Quarterly* 37 (1992): 363–99. For a cross-cultural comparison of the rise and fall of managerial ideologies and practices, see, Mauro F. Guillén, *Models of Management* (Chicago: University of Chicago Press, 1994); Christopher Chase-Dunn, Yukio Kawano, and Benjamin D. Brewer, "Trade Globalization since 1795: Waves of Integration of the World-System," *American Sociological Review* 65 (2000): 77–95.

9. Schlesinger, Jr., *The Cycles of American History*, outlines his father's theory and its evolution in chapter 2, "The Cycles of American Politics."

10. Ibid., p. 24.

11. Ibid.

12. Ibid., pp. 24–25. Quote is from Arthur Schlesinger, *Paths to the Present* (New York: Macmillan, 1949), p. 93.

13. Schlesinger, Jr., *The Cycles of American History*, pp. 25–27; Albert O. Hirschman, *Shifting Involvements: Private Interests and Public Action* (Princeton: Princeton University Press, 1982). Schlesinger, Jr., also relates the dynamic of political alternation to the tension between democracy and capitalism noted by Herbert McClosky and John Zaller, *The American Ethos: Public Attitudes toward Capitalism and Democracy* (Cambridge: Harvard University Press, 1984).

14. See discussion in Schlesinger, Jr., *The Cycles of American History*, pp. 30–31.

15. Ibid., p. 30. Schlesinger bases his analysis of generations on the works of Karl Mannheim, "The Problem of Generations," pp. 276–332 in *Essays on the Sociology of Knowledge*, ed. P. Kecskemeti (London: Routledge and Kegan Paul, [1928] 1952); and José Ortega y Gasset, "The Concept of the Generation," *The Modern Theme* (New York: Harper and Row, 1961).

16. Schlesinger, Jr., *The Cycles of American History*, p. 30.

17. Samuel P. Huntington, *American Politics: The Promise of Disharmony* (Cambridge: Belknap/Harvard University Press, 1981).

18. This definition of the content of the American Creed comes from Lipset, *American Exceptionalism*, p. 19.

19. See discussion in Andrew S. McFarland, "Interest Groups and Political Time: Cycles in America," *British Journal of Political Science* 21 (1991): 257–84.

20. Stephen Skowronek, "Presidential Leadership in Political Time," pp. 115–19 in Michael Nelson, ed., *The Presidency and the Political System*, 2nd ed. (Washington, DC: Congressional Quarterly Press, 1988).

21. See review in McFarland, "Interest Groups and Political Time," pp. 258–59.

22. Ibid.

23. Ibid., p. 257.

24. Ibid.

25. Schlesinger, Jr., *The Cycles of American History*, p. 27.

26. Ibid., p. 28.

27. Ibid.

28. Ibid., pp. 28–29.

29. Sorokin, *Social and Cultural Dynamics*, pp. 680–82.

30. Ibid., p. 654.

31. Peter F. Nardulli, "The Concept of a Critical Realignment, Electoral

Behavior, and Political Change," *American Political Science Review* 89 (1995): 11.

32. Ibid.

33. Ibid.

34. V. O. Key, "A Theory of Critical Elections," *Journal of Politics* 17 (1955): 3–18.

35. Nardulli, "The Concept of a Critical Realignment," p. 14.

36. Walter Dean Burnham, *Critical Elections and the Mainsprings of American Politics* (New York: W.W. Norton, 1970), p. 10.

37. Respectively, Alan Abramowitz and Kyle Saunders, "Ideological Realignment in the U.S. Electorate," *Journal of Politics* 60 (1998): 635; Paul Allen Beck, "The Electoral Cycle and Patterns of American Politics," *British Journal of Politics* 96 (1979): 130.

38. Nardulli, "The Concept of a Critical Realignment," p. 10.

39. Ibid., pp. 10–11.

40. Ibid., p. 11.

41. Ibid.

42. Ibid., p. 10.

43. See, for example, William G. McLoughlin, *Revivals, Awakenings, and Reform* (Chicago: University of Chicago Press, 1978); Gordon Wood, *The Radicalism of the American Revolution* (New York: Knopf, 1992); Bernard Bailyn, *The Ideological Origins of the American Revolution* (Cambridge: Harvard University Press, 1967); Bailyn, *The Peopling of British North America* (New York: Knopf, 1986); Bernard Bailyn et al., *The Great Republic: A History of the American People*, 4th ed. (Lexington, MA: D. C. Heath, 1992); Richard Bushman, *From Puritan into Yankee* (Cambridge: Harvard University Press, 1967).

44. McLoughlin, *Revivals*, chap. 6; Fogel, *The Fourth Great Awakening*..

45. McLoughlin, *Revivals*, p. xiii. McLoughlin uses "world view" while I use "worldview" in this book. For consistency, I make this same edit in quotes from McLoughlin.

46. Ibid., pp. xiii, 8.

47. Ibid., p. 12.

48. Ibid., p. 11.

49. See ibid., pp. 12–16.

50. Ibid., p. 14.

51. Ibid., p. 17.

52. Ibid.

53. For example, Roger Finke and Rodney Stark argue that revivalist George Whitefield's role and impact in the so-called First Great Awakening have been greatly exaggerated. See *The Churching of America 1776–1990: Winner's and Losers in Our Religious Economy* (New Brunswick: Rutgers University Press, 1992), pp. 46–53.

54. McLoughlin, *Revivals*, p. 22.

55. Ibid., chap. 2.

56. Ibid., chap. 1. McLoughlin then devotes a chapter to each of the four.

57. Ibid., p. xiv.

58. Fogel, *The Fourth Great Awakening*, pp. 28–29.

59. Ibid., p. 29.

60. Ibid., p. 17.

61. On cultural lag theories, see, for example, Fred Spier, *The Structure of Big History: From the Big Bang until Today* (Amsterdam: Amsterdam University Press, 1996).

62. Fogel, *The Fourth Great Awakening*, p. 82.

63. Ibid., p. 20.

64. Ibid.

65. From Howard Zinn, *A People's History of the United States* (New York: Harper Perennial, [1980] 1990), chaps. 3 and 4. The statistics on the distribution of support are on p. 76. Zinn uses the estimate of "actively treasonous" from John Shy, *A People Numerous and Armed: Reflections on the Military Struggle for American Independence* (New York: Oxford University Press, 1976).

66. Fogel, *The Fourth Great Awakening*, p. 21.

67. Quoted from interview in tape 1 of the 1998 PBS series, "The American Experience, America 1900." See also the companion book, Judy Critchton, *America 1900: The Turning Point* (New York: Henry Holt, 1998).

68. Critchton, *America 1900*, p. 4.

69. Fogel, *The Fourth Great Awakening*, p. 23.

70. Thomas S. Kuhn, *The Copernican Revolution: Planetary Astronomy in the Development of Western Thought* (Cambridge: Harvard University Press, 1957), p. 192.

71. William F. Lawhead, "Religion, Relativity, and Common Sense: Einstein and the Religious Imagination," pp. 37–45 in Dennis P. Ryan, ed., *Einstein and the Humanities* (New York: Greenwood Press, 1987), p. 38.

72. Fogel, *The Fourth Great Awakening*, p. 23.

73. Lawhead, "Religion, Relativity, and Common Sense," pp. 38–40.

74. Richard Reeves, *American Journey: Traveling with Tocqueville in Search of "Democracy in America"* (New York: Simon & Schuster, 1982).

75. Manuel Castells, *The Power of Identity*, vol. 2 of *The Information Age: Economy, Society, and Culture* (Oxford: Blackwell, 1996); *The Rise of the Network Society*, 2nd ed., vol. 1 of *The Information Age* (2000); *End of Millennium*, 2nd ed., vol. 3 of *The Information Age* (2000).

76. Manuel Castells, "The Informational City Is a Dual City: Can It Be Reversed?" pp. 26–41 in Donald A. Schön, Bish Sanyal, and William J. Mitchell, eds., *High Technology and Low-Income Communities* (Cambridge: MIT Press, 1999).

77. Fogel, *The Fourth Great Awakening*, p. 44.

78. Ibid., pp. 74–79; Robert W. Fogel and Dora L. Costa, "A Theory of Technophysio Evolution, with some Implications for Forecasting Populations, Health Care Costs, and Pension Costs," *Demography* 34 (1997): 49–66.

79. For criticisms of McLoughlin's theory, see, for example, Timothy Smith, "My Rejection of a Cyclical View of 'Great Awakenings' in American Religious History," *Sociological Analysis* 44 (1983): 97–103; Jon Butler, "Enthusiasm Described and Decried: The Great Awakening as Interpretive Fiction," *Journal of American History* 69 (1982): 305–25. For a critical review of Fogel's book, see John Murray, "The Fourth Great Awakening and the Future of Egalitarianism," Economic History Services, Book Reviews, www.eh.net/bookreviews/library.

80. Butler, "Enthusiasm Described and Decried."

81. Bailyn et al., *The Great Republic*, vol. 1, p. 66; see also Bailyn, *The Ideological Origins of the American Revolution;* Bushman, *From Puritan into Yankee*, pp. 220, 286. Quotation and summary from Fogel, *The Fourth Great Awakening, p. 29.*

82. For example, see, R. C. Gordon-McCutchan's summary of a symposium on religious awakenings, "Great Awakenings?" *Sociological Analysis* 44 (1983): 83–95.

83. Fogel, *The Fourth Great Awakening*, pp. 31–36.

84. Ibid., pp. 31–33.

85. Smith, "My Rejection of a Cyclical View of 'Great Awakenings.'"

86. Fogel, *The Fourth Great Awakening*, p. 32.

87. I say "partial" because Fogel's use of quantitative methods and data does not pertain to religious phenomena but to congressional and popular voting behavior, economic growth, and biodemography.

88. Finke and Stark, *The Churching of America*. See also Roger Finke and Laurence R. Iannaccone, "Supply-Side Explanations for Religious Change," *Annals of the American Academy of Political and Social Science* 527 (1993): 27–39.

89. As shown, for example, by regressing year on rate of religious adherence, using data in Finke and Stark, *The Churching of America*, fig. 1.2, p. 16.

90. Ibid., p. 274.

91. Finke and Iannaccone, "Supply-Side Explanations," p. 28.

92. Ibid.

93. Summarized by Finke and Stark, *The Churching of America*, pp. 40–43.

94. Ibid., p. 42.

95. Ibid.

96. Ibid.

97. Ibid., see figure 3.1, p. 55.

98. Butler, "Enthusiasm Described and Decried," p. 306.

99. Schlesinger, Jr., *The Cycles of American History*, p. 47.

100. McLoughlin, *Revivals, Awakenings, and Reform*, pp. 18–19.

101. Reported in George Gallup, Jr., and D. Michael Lindsay, *Surveying the Religious Landscape: Trends in U.S. Beliefs* (Harrisburg, PA: Morehouse Publishing, 1999), pp. 10, 24.

102. A time-series process includes *trend*, the change in the level of a time series, upward or downward, and *seasonality*, any cyclical or period fluctuation that repeats itself in the same phase of a cycle. Trend is called *deterministic* trend to distinguish it from stochastic drift. See, for example, Richard McCleary and Richard A. Hay, Jr., *Applied Times Series Analysis for the Social Sciences* (Beverly Hills: Sage, 1980).

103. Schlesinger, Jr., *The Cycles of American History*, pp. 46–47.

104. Fogel, *The Fourth Great Awakening*, p. 40.

105. Ibid.

106. John F. Wilson, "Perspectives on the Historiography of Religious Awakenings," *Sociological Analysis* 44 (1983): 117–20, pp. 3, 7. Quoted in Gordon-McCutchan, "Great Awakenings?" p. 85.

107. William Strauss and Neil Howe, *The Fourth Turning: An American Prophecy* (New York: Broadway Books, 1997).

108. Schlesinger, Jr., *The Cycles of American History*, p. 45.

109. Karl Jaspers, *The Origin and Goal of History*, trans. Michael Bullock (London: Routledge & Kegan Paul, 1953), pp. 1 and 2, respectively.

110. Julian Jaynes, *The Origin of Consciousness in the Breakdown of the Bicameral Mind* (Boston: Houghton Mifflin, 1976).

111. S. N. Eisenstadt, "The Axial Age," *European Journal of Sociology* 23 (1982): 294.

112. Ibid., p. 296.

113. Adam B. Seligman, "The Comparative Study of Utopias," pp. 1–12 in Adam B. Seligman, ed., *Order and Transcendence: The Role of Utopias and the Dynamics of Civilizations* (Leiden: E. J. Brill, 1989). Quote is from p. 6.

114. Randall Collins, *The Sociology of Philosophies* (Cambridge: Harvard University Press, 1998). Quote from p. 877.

115. See, for example, S. N. Eisenstadt, *Tradition, Change, and Modernity* (Malabar, FL: Robert E. Krieger Publishing Co., 1983), pp. 179–83.

116. Mark Chaves, "Secularization as Declining Religious Authority," *Social Forces* 72 (1994): 749–74.

117. Peter Berger, *The Sacred Canopy* (New York: Doubleday, 1967), p. 26.

118. Max Weber, *The Sociology of Religion*, trans. Ephriam Fischoff (Boston: Beacon Press, 1964 [1922]), pp. 138–50.

119. Seligman, "The Comparative Study of Utopias," p. 7.

120. S. N. Eisenstadt, "Utopias and Dynamics of Civilizations: Some Concluding Comparative Observations," pp. 139–49 in Seligman, ed., *Order and Transcendence*.

121. David Maybury-Lewis, "The Quest for Harmony," pp. 1–17 in David Maybury-Lewis and Uri Almagor, eds., *The Attraction of Opposites: Thought and Society in the Dualistic Mode* (Ann Arbor: University of Michigan Press, 1989). Quote from p. 1.

122. Daniel Bell, *The Cultural Contradictions of Capitalism* (New York: Basic, 1978), p. 155.

123. Maybury-Lewis, "The Quest for Harmony," p. 12; Barley and Kunda, "Design and Devotion."

124. Orrù, *Anomie*, p. 156.

125. Ibid., p. 5.

126. Paraphrased and quoted material from Maybury-Lewis, "The Quest for Harmony," pp. 11–12. See also Lloyd E. Sandelands, *Male & Female in Social Life* (New Brunswick, NJ: Transaction, 2001); Barley and Kunda, "Design and Devotion."

127. Barley and Kunda, "Design and Devotion," p. 385.

128. Sandelands, *Male & Female in Social Life*, p. 89.

129. For example, see Kenwyn K. Smith and David N. Berg, *Paradoxes of Group Life* (San Francisco: Jossey-Bass, 1988); E. Jacques, "Social Systems as a Defense against Persecutory and Depressive Anxiety," in M. Klein, P. Herman, and R. E. Money-Kyle, eds., *New Directions in Psychoanalysis: The Significance of Infant Conflict in the Pattern of Adult Behavior* (London: Tavistock, 1955); Sigmund Freud, *Group Psychology and the Analysis of the Ego* (New York: Norton, 1959).

130. Smith and Berg, *Paradoxes of Group Life*, p. 77.

131. Lipset, *American Exceptionalism*, p. 63.

132. Smith and Berg, *Paradoxes of Group Life*, p. 79.

133. Orrù, *Anomie*, p. 158, notes that "anomie" itself can be considered a lens, though some (especially European sociologists) consider "anomie" to be a real "thing." "In the eyes of those who consider anomie to be a real phenomenon, not *a way of looking* at a phenomenon, there can only be *one* anomie, and only a careful study of Durkheim's texts can show the *real meaning* of anomie."

134. Ibid., chap. 1.

135. Ibid., pp. 19–29.

136. Ibid., p. 13.

137. Ibid., chap. 4.

138. This period is nicely described by Roger V. Gould in his analysis of the Paris Commune, "Trade Cohesion, Class Unity, and Urban Insurrection: Artisanal Activism in the Paris Commune," *American Journal of Sociology* 98 (1993): 721–54.

139. Emile Durkhein, *The Division of Labor in Society*, trans. George Simpson (New York: Free Press [1933] 1964). Quoted in Orrù, *Anomie*, p. 106.

140. Orrù, *Anomie*, pp. 100–101.

141. Orrù concludes *Anomie* by quoting from the sophist fragment, *Dissoi Logoi* (Twofold Arguments): "Twofold arguments on good and evil are made in Greece by those who philosophize. Some affirm that one thing is the good, another the evil; others, instead, affirm that they coincide, so that what for some is good, for others is evil, and for the same person, now good, now evil" (p. 162).

142. For example, see the discussion in Edward Rothstein, "Culture Wars Go On, but the Battle Lines Blur," *New York Times*, May 27, 1997, pp. B1, B4. On p. B4, he writes: "The Ancients have tended to be identified as right-wing conservatives, the Moderns as left-wing liberals. Now the division is

less clear: many conservatives have no problem with diversity if it is accompanied by rigor; many liberals have no problem with rigor if it is accompanied by diversity. And the view that something is amiss in contemporary culture is becoming increasingly widespread." See Orrù, *Anomie*, for an insightful analysis of the roots and lineages of absolutism and relativism as responses to anomie.

143. Orrù, *Anomie*, chap. 1.

144. Ibid., pp. 4–5; Jaspers, *The Origin and Goal of History*.

145. Sorokin, *Social and Cultural Dynamics*, pp. 680–82.

146. Sorokin (ibid., pp. 34, 35) notes that *truth of faith* is "associated with the values which are absolute, eternal, and everlasting." In contrast, systems based on *truth of senses* "are never absolute, but are always relativistic, varying 'according to circumstances and situations.' They can be modified, have no sacred, unalterable, eternal imperatives."

147. Ibid., p. 681.

148. Regressing cohort number on percentage of absolutists shows this modest tendency. There is a statistically significant (though small) increase in the percentage of absolutists for 1981 and 1990. There is no statistically significant difference between cohorts in the 2000 data. Note, however, that the multivariate analyses in chapter 3 show that age never has a significant effect on moral visions once the two cultural dimensions and other sociodemographic variables are included.

149. Note that these analyses do not control for upward or downward mobility from one survey to the next, due to lack of appropriate data. For example, the data are not available to tell us whether someone who was, say, lower middle class in 1981 was upper middle class in 1990 or 2000.

150. Jaspers, *The Origin and Goal of History*; Orrù, *Anomie*. See also Sorokin, *Social and Cultural Dynamics*.

151. Orrù, *Anomie*, p. 6.

152. Barley and Kunda, "Design and Devotion," pp. 384–87, 389–91.

153. The Index of National Civic Renewal (INCH) is complied by the National Commission on Civic Renewal. Report available at http://www.puaf.umd.edu/Affiliates/CivicRenewal/Default.htm.

154. Many indicators of "civic health" were declining in the years prior to the 1980s, but the pace of change accelerated in the 1980s.

155. Clem Brooks, "Religious Influence and the Politics of Family Decline Concern: Trends, Sources, and U.S. Political Behavior," *American Sociological Review* 67 (2002): 191–211. Brooks notes that rising concerns

were particularly concentrated among evangelical Protestants who attend church regularly.

156. Reynolds Farley, *The New American Reality* (New York: Russell Sage, 1996), p. 339.

157. Ibid. Farley summarizes key findings in chapter 8. See also Barry Bluestone and Bennett Harrison, *The Great U-Turn: Corporate Restructuring and the Polarizing of America* (New York: Basic, 1988); Donald L. Bartlett and James B. Steele, *America: What Went Wrong* (Kansas City: Andrews and McMeel, 1992). On rising wealth inequality, see Lisa A. Keister, *Wealth in America: Trends in Wealth Inequality* (New York: Cambridge University Press, 2000).

158. Farley, *The New American Reality*, p. 341.

159. Ibid., p. 339. Italics removed from original.

160. Maybury-Lewis, "The Quest for Harmony," pp. 11–12.

161. Orrù, *Anomie*, p. 19.

162. James S. Coleman, *Introduction to Mathematical Sociology* (New York: Free Press, 1964), pp. 492–514. In general, rates of social interaction are a function of heterogeneity and opportunities for contact. See, for example, Peter M. Blau, *Inequality and Heterogeneity* (New York: Free Press, 1977); Peter M. Blau and Joseph E. Schwartz, *Crosscutting Social Circles* (New York: Academic Press, 1982).

163. Eck, *A New Religious America*.

164. Tocqueville, *Democracy in America*, pp. 535–38. He attributed Americans' restlessness to the fact that Americans "never stop thinking of the good things they have not got" and to being "tormented by the shadowy suspicion that they may not have chosen the shortest route to get it" (p. 536). In this analysis, Tocqueville anticipated Robert Merton's theory of anomie as the result of a disconnection between the American success goal and the institutional means of attaining it.

165. George M. Beard, *American Nervousness* (New York: Arno Press, 1881). Tocqueville's comments, Beard's concept of American nervousness, and related works are discussed by Robert N. Bellah et al., *Habits of the Heart: Individualism and Commitment in American Life* (New York: Harper and Row, 1985), pp. 117–21.

166. Alan Trachtenberg, *The Incorporation of America: Culture and Society in the Gilded Age* (New York: Hill and Wang, 1982).

167. Hilkey, *Character Is Capital*, p. 10.

168. Jack London, "The Shrinkage of the Planet," in his *Revolution and Other Essays* (New York: Macmillan, 1910). Passage quoted in Critchton, *America 1900*, p. 5.

169. Quoted from interview in tape 1 of the 1998 PBS series, "The American Experience, America 1900." See also the companion book, Critchton, *America 1900*.

170. Hilkey, *Character Is Capital*, p. 1. The attributes of this cultural artifact attest to its importance and value. Many success manuals "were massive, elaborately bound works of 600, 700, even 800 pages. Even more modest versions of 300–400 pages has a look of authority and importance about them, with their gold-embossed titles, filigree designs, and leather or leather-like fabric covers in black or deep blues" (p. 28). They were very expensive, costing as much as several days' wages (p. 29).

171. Ibid., p. 8. Hilkey also argues that "the success manual can be seen as part of the cultural apparatus that helped legitimize and establish the hegemony of the new industrial order that emerged in the Gilded Age" (p. 7).

172. Statistics cited are from ibid., p. 21.

173. Walter Lippman, *A Preface to Morals* (New York: MacMillan, 1929), pp. 14, 139.

174. Bellah et al., *Habits of the Heart*.

175. Paraphrased from Kai T. Erikson, *Wayward Puritans* (New York: John Wiley and Sons, 1966), p. 4. See my discussion of the functions of crisis rhetoric and additional references in chapter 2.

Chapter Five: The Search for Meaning

1. See, for example, the analysis in John H. Evans, *Playing God? Human Genetic Engineering and the Rationalization of Public Bioethical Debate* (Chicago: University of Chicago Press, 2002). Evans does not explicitly use the concepts of absolutism and relativism, but they are clear in his analysis of debates from 1959 to 1995 about human genetic engineering (HGE). Early in the debates, eugenicist scientists attempted to use HGE to explain the meaning and purpose of human life, and to design the perfect species. Theologians challenged this stance of "man-as-creator," arguing for the supremacy of God's will, and stimulated public opinion and legislative action against HGE. Fearing a loss of jurisdiction, scientists and the new profession of

bioethics responded with a relativistic argument that is consonant with the American principle of individualism and the goal of self-realization: individual autonomy and decision making.

2. For example, the literature on "American exceptionalism" from Toqueville to the present has considered America in comparison to only a few societies (usually Western European, but occasionally societies like Japan as well). For example, see Seymour Martin Lipset, *American Exceptionalism* (New York: W. W. Norton, 1996). See notes for chap. 1 for discussion of alternative sources of data and some of their limitations for the analyses conducted in this book.

3. Daniel Bell, *The Cultural Contradictions of Capitalism* (New York: Basic, 1978), p. xvi.

4. Ibid., p. 15. Bell calls the self-expression value orientation "antinomian"—literally, *against* laws or norms (see discussion of antinomianism in chapter 3 above). This value orientation is antinomian, he argues, because "the individual is taken to be the measure of satisfaction, and *his* [*sic*] feelings, sentiments, and judgments, not some objective standard of quality and value, determine the worth of cultural objects" (p. xvii).

5. As discussed in chapter 2. Quoted by Fogel, *The Fourth Great Awakening*, p. 205, from R. Shusterman, "Pragmatism and Liberalism between Dewey and Rorty," *Political Theory* 22 (1994): 391–413.

6. Lipset, *American Exceptionalism*.

7. Standardizing each cultural dimension puts them on a common scale for comparability and construction of deviation scores. As expected, the distribution of deviation scores exhibits positive skewness in each survey (1981 = .533; 1990 = .424; 1995 = .281; 2000 = .479). As elaborated in note 50, chapter 3, skewness tests for asymmetry in a distribution. Positive skewness occurs when the values in a distribution "bunch" toward the left of the distribution. Here, this means that there is a tendency for individual Americans to hold traditional and self-expression values, rather than secular-rational and survival values. In other words, proportionately more Americans have internalized the mainstream form of value incongruence (traditional and self-expression values) than have internalized the other form of value incongruence (secular-rational and survival values).

8. Viktor E. Frankel, *The Will to Meaning*, expanded ed. (New York: Meridian, 1988), p. 83; *Man's Search for Meaning*, rev. and updated ed. (New York: Washington Square Press, 1998). Frankel founded the school of logotherapy, which is based on the assumption that the primary motivation in life is the

will to meaning. Logotherapy is called the Third Viennese School of psychotherapy, after Freud's psychoanalysis and Adler's individual psychology.

9. Thomas Luckmann, "Shrinking Transcendence, Expanding Religion"? *Sociological Analysis* 50 (1990): 127–38. Phillip S. Gorski discusses this concept in "Historicizing the Secularization Debate: Church, State, and Society in Late Medieval and Early Modern Europe, ca. 1300 to 1700," *American Sociological Review* 65 (2000): 138–67.

10. Robert Wuthnow, *After Heaven: Spirituality in America Since the 1950s* (Berkeley: University of California Press, 1998).

11. Robert Wuthnow, "Returning to Practice," *IONS: Noetic Sciences Review* 49 (August–November 1999): 32–38. Quote on p. 34. This article is excerpted from Wuthnow, *After Heaven*.

12. Gorski, "Historicizing the Secularization Debate," p. 162.

13. Fogel, *The Fourth Great Awakening*, pp. 176–77.

14. Luckmann, "Shrinking Transcendence, Expanding Religion?"

15. Inglehart and Baker, "Modernization."

16. See also Inglehart and Baker, "Modernization."

17. See also Wuthnow, *After Heaven*.

18. Gallup's higher numbers are not strictly comparable, due to differences in item wording. For example, Gallup asked, "How often have you thought about the basic meaning and value of your life during the past two years—a lot, a fair amount, or only a little." Fifty-eight percent said a lot in 1985, and 69 percent said a lot in 1998. See George Gallup, Jr., and D. Michael Lindsay, *Surveying the Religious Landscape: Trends in U.S. Beliefs* (Harrisburg, PA: Morehouse Publishing, 1999), p. 42.

19. The proportions are 50 percent in 1981, 48 percent in 1990, and 50 percent in 1995. See tables in chapter 2.

20. See chapter 2.

21. Wuthnow, "Returning to Practice," p. 34.

22. Ibid.

23. Swidler, "Culture in Action," p. 283.

24. Ibid., p. 277.

25. Roger Finke and Laurence R. Iannaccone argue that Americans have always had a taste for Eastern religions and ideas, and the increase of interest is a function of increased supply rather than increased demand. See "Supply-Side Explanations for Religious Change," *Annals of the American Academy of Political and Social Science* 527 (1993): 36–37. See also Roger Finke and Rodney Stark, *The Churching of America 1776–1990: Winners and*

Losers in Our Religious Economy (New Brunswick, NJ: Rutgers University Press, 1992).

26. Harold Bloom, *Omens of the Millennium* (New York: Riverhead Books, 1996); "New Age Movement," Microsoft® Encarta® 96 Encyclopedia, Microsoft Corporation, 1993–1995.

27. Wuthnow, *After Heaven*, observes that the rising spirituality in the United States is a mix of old and new spiritual and religious elements.

28. James Redfield, *The Celestine Prophecy* (New York: Warner, 1993).

29. According to a Gallup Mirror survey of 1,236 Americans conducted in June 1990; reported in Terence J. Sandbek, "Hungry People Who Buy Imaginary Food with Real Money: Psychology, Mysticism, Superstition, and the Paranormal," paper presented at the 1991 Annual Convention of the American Psychological Association, San Francisco, CA, 1991. Text available at http://www.mother.com/~sandbek/Psychology/HungryPeople.htm.

30. According to a 1986 poll conducted by NORC (National Opinion Research Center); reported in ibid.

31. According to the General Social Survey, V111B, 1988–1991. Sixty-three percent of those polled reported "once or twice," "several times," or "often."

32. According to ibid. Forty-two percent of those polled reported "once or twice," "several times," or "often."

33. According to a national Gallup pole of 1,005 adults taken October 21–24, 1999. Reported by the Associated Press, "Poll: Belief in Ghosts, Witches Up" (October 29, 1999). The results show that, in 1999, three times as many Americans believe in ghosts, and twice as many Americans believe in witches, compared with the results from a similar survey twenty years earlier.

34. According to the General Social Survey, V697C, 1993 and 1994 combined. Forty-six percent of those surveyed reported that the statement "astrology—the study of star signs—has some scientific truth" is "definitely true" (8.7%) or "probably true" (37.5%).

35. Susannah Feher, "Who Looks to the Stars? Astrology and its Constituency," *Journal for the Scientific Study of Religion* 31 (1992): 88. Believers "are also more liberal, less likely to be married, and less religious."

36. Kluckholn and Strodtbeck note that all cultures confront five basic problems: the character of human nature, the relationship of people to nature and the cosmos, the temporal focus of life, the focus of human activity, and the relationship of people to each other. Kluckholn and Strodtbeck, *Variations in Value Orientations*, p. 10.

37. Ibid.

38. Ibid., p. 17.

39. Redfield, *The Celestine Prophecy*, pp. 180–217.

40. Ibid., pp. 218–43.

41. Ibid.

42. Michael J. St. Clair, *Millenarian Movements in Historical Context* (New York: Garland Publishing, 1992), p. 352. See also Adam B. Seligman, ed., *Order and Transcendence: The Role of Utopias and the Dynamics of Civilizations* (Leiden: E. J. Brill, 1989).

43. David John Frank, Ann Hironaka, and Evean Schofer, "The Nation-State and the Natural Environment Over the Twentieth Century," *American Sociological Review* 65 (2000): 96–116.

44. Glenn Firebaugh, "Introduction to the *ASR* Millennial Issue," *American Sociological Review* 65 (2000): v–vi.

45. Swidler, "Culture in Action," p. 280.

46. "The current economic crisis causes, due to its brutality, the effects of panic and mental disequilibrium in different spheres of life. When the principle of rationality is diluted or dislocated, people are tempted to appeal to forms of prerational thought. They turn to superstition, to the occult, to illogic, and they are disposed to believe in magic wands capable of transforming lead into gold and toads into princes. Each time, more people are threatened by brutal technological modernization and impelled to adopt suspicious and antimodern attitudes. It can be verified that the current economic rationality, scornful of man, favors the ascent of a social irrationalism. In the face of so many incomprehensible transformations and so many threats, many are open to an eclipse of reason. And they are tempted by the escape to an irrational image of the world. Some turn to the artificial paradises of drugs or alcohol, or to parasciences and occult practices. Is it known that in Europe every year more than forty million people consult seers or quack healers? That one of every two people says he or she perceives paranormal phenomena? Ignacio Ramonet, *A Directionless World* [*Un Mundo Sin Rumbo*] (Madrid: Editorial Debate, S.A, 1997), pp. 117–18. Originally published in French as *Un Monde Sans Cap*. Spanish translation by Antonio Albiñana; excerpts translated from Spanish to English by me. The phrase "ascent of the irrational" (ascenso de lo irracional) is the title of chapter 5.

47. James Randi, *An Encyclopedia of Claims, Frauds, and Hoaxes of the Occult and Supernatural* (New York: St. Martins Press, 1997; Randi, *The Faith Healers* (New York: Prometheus Books, 1987). Information on Randi, his

foundation, and investigations can be found at www.randi.org. Victor J. Stenger, *Physics and Psychics* (New York: Prometheus Books, 1990); Stenger, "The Myth of Quantum Consciousness," *The Humanist* 53 (1992): 13–15; John Allen Paulos, *Innumeracy* (New York: Hill and Wang, 1988); Paulos, *A Mathematician Reads the Newspaper* (New York: Anchor, 1996). See also Sanbek, "Hungry People."

48. See also Bart K. Holland, *What Are the Chances? Voodoo Deaths, Office Gossip & Other Adventures in Probability* (Baltimore: Johns Hopkins University Press, 2002).

49. Geertz, *The Interpretation of Cultures*, p. 141.

50. Weick, *Sensemaking in Organizations*, p. 37. See also Varela, Thompson, and Rosch, *The Embodied Mind*, pp. 140–45.

51. Joseph Campbell, *The Hero with a Thousand Faces* (Princeton: Princeton University Press, 1949); Campbell, *Myths to Live By* (New York: Penguin, 1972).

52. William James, *The Will to Believe* (Cambridge: University Press, John Wilson and Son, 1896), p. 14.

53. Julian Jaynes, *The Origin of Consciousness in the Breakdown of the Bicameral Mind* (Boston: Houghton Mifflin, 1976 [1990]), pp. 303, 318, 337, 440–41. Jaynes argues that organized religions, cults, pseudosciences, magic, drug use, hypnosis, and trances are vestiges of what he calls the "bicameral mind."

54. Daniel T. Gilbert, "How Mental Systems Believe," *American Psychologist* 46 (1991): 107–19.

55. The absolutist impulse may be a response to the inevitability of death and the "anomic terror" it creates; as Berger and Luckmann argue, the "legitimation of death is, consequently, one of the most important fruits of symbolic universes." Peter L. Berger and Thomas Luckmann, *The Social Construction of Reality* (New York: Anchor Books, 1967), pp. 101–03; Becker, *The Denial of Death*.

56. Schlesinger, Jr., *The Cycles of American History*, p. 12.

57. Ibid., p. 14.

58. Reinhold Niebuhr, *Faith and History* (New York: Scribner's Sons, 1949), p. 31. Quoted by Schlesinger, *The Cycles of American History*, p. 19.

59. Schlesinger, *The Cycles of American History*, p. 19.

60. Quoted in Lipset, *American Exceptionalism*, p. 31.

61. Huntington, *American Politics*, pp. 158–59.

62. Lipset, *American Exceptionalism*, p. 63.

63. Tom W. Smith and Lars Jarrko, "National Pride: A Cross-national Analysis," National Opinion Research Center/University of Chicago, General Social Survey Cross-national report no. 19 (1998). America's rank as the most patriotic comes from the average ranking of two national-pride scales. The World Values Surveys also find that Americans have the highest levels of patriotism.

64. Hunter and Bowman, *The State of Disunion*, p. 3.

65. de Tocqueville, *Democracy in America*, pp. 452–54.

66. Kenwyn K. Smith and David N. Berg, *Paradoxes of Group Life* (San Francisco: Jossey-Bass, 1988), p. 79.

67. Maybury-Lewis, "The Quest for Harmony," pp. 11–12.

68. Ibid., p. 1.

69. Ibid., pp. 1–2. Even though dual social organization is "exotic," it does appear in modern societies. For example, Kenneth A. Frank and Jeffrey Y. Yasumoto document dual social organization among the French financial elite. See their "Linking Action to Social Structure within a System: Social Capital within and between Subgroups," *American Journal of Sociology* 104 (1998): 642–86.

70. See chapter 3 for discussion of evidence of increasing polarization between Republicans and Democrats.

71. Lipset, *American Exceptionalism*, pp. 176–77.

72. Smith and Berg, *Paradoxes of Group Life*, p. 77.

73. Allan Bloom, *The Closing of the American Mind* (New York: Simon & Schuster, 1987); Lawrence W. Levine, *The Opening of the American Mind* (Beacon, 1996).

74. As noted in chapter 4, intellectual life thrives on opposition. See Randall Collins, *The Sociology of Philosophies* (Cambridge: Harvard University Press, 1998).

75. Mary Douglas and Aaron Wildavsky, *Risk and Culture: An Essay on the Selection of Technological and Environmental Dangers* (Berkeley: University of California Press, 1983).

76. "Notes on the Sociology of Deviance," pp. 9–21 in *The Other Side*, ed. Howard Becker (New York: The Free Press of Glencoe, 1964); Kai T. Erikson, *Wayward Puritans* (New York: John Wiley and Sons, 1966), p. 19. See also Emile Durkeim, *The Division of Labor in Society*, trans. George Simpson (Glencoe, IL: The Free Press, 1960); *The Rules of Sociological Method*, trans. S. A. Solovay and J. H. Mueller (Glencoe, IL: The Free Press, 1958).

77. Erikson, *Wayward Puritans*, p. 20.

78. Ibid., p. 22.

79. Lipset, *American Exceptionalism*, p. 269. Based on Gallup poll conducted in 1993.

80. Weick, *Sensemaking in Organizations*, p. 56.

81. Sara McLanahan and Lynne Casper, "Growing Diversity and Inequality in the American Family," pp. 1–46 in *State of the Union: America in the 1990s, Volume Two: Social Trends*, ed. Reynolds Farley (New York: Russell Sage Foundation, 1995), p. 11.

82. Thomas D'Aunno and Thomas E. Vaughn, "Variations in Methadone Treatment Practices," *Journal of the American Medical Association* 267 (1992): 253–58; Thomas D'Aunno, Robert I. Sutton, and Richard H. Price, "Isomorphism and External Support in Conflicting Institutional Environments: A Study of Drug Abuse Treatment Units," *Academy of Management Journal* 34 (1991): 635–61; Richard Price, personal communication, June 1998.

83. See, for example, the editorial in *Science* (June 5, 1998) by Barbara R. Jasny and Floyd E. Bloom, "It's Not Rocket Science—But It Can Save Lives."

84. Kenneth Burke, *Permanence and Change* (New York: New Republic, 1936).

85. Thomas S. Kuhn, *The Structure of Scientific Revolutions*, 2nd ed. (Chicago: University of Chicago Press, 1970). "Can it conceivably be an accident," asks Kuhn, ". . . that Western astronomers first saw change in the previously immutable heavens during the half-century after Copernicus' new paradigm was first proposed? The Chinese, whose cosmological beliefs did not preclude celestial change, had recorded the appearance of many new stars in the heavens at a much earlier date. Also, even without the aid of a telescope, the Chinese had systematically recorded the appearance of sunspots centuries before those were seen by Galileo and his contemporaries" (p. 116).

86. Becker, *The Denial of Death*, p. xi.

87. Collins emphasizes the collective or "network" nature of intellectual life, development, and revolution. Collins, *The Sociology of Philosophies*.

88. Barney G. Glaser and Anselm L. Strauss, "Awareness Contexts and Social Interaction," *American Sociological Review* 29 (1964): 669–79. They note that this concept "can be used for the study of virtually any problem entailing awareness at any structural level of analysis" (p. 670).

89. Ibid., p. 670.

90. Sorokin, *Social and Cultural Dynamics*, pp. 680–82.

91. Jaspers, *The Origin and Goal of History*, p. 132.

92. Smith and Berg, *Paradoxes of Group Life*, p. 83.

93. For example, see Joshua Gamson's integrative analysis of the paradoxes and contradictions of the debate about "popular culture"—television sitcoms, game shows, cartoons, horror movies, sleaze TV, music videos, formulaic romance novels, etc. Joshua Gamson, "The Depths of Shallow Culture," *Newsletter of the Sociology of Culture Section of the American Sociological Association* 12 (1998): 1–6. See also Joshua Gamson, *Freaks Talk Back: Tabloid Television and Sexual Nonconformity* (Chicago: University of Chicago Press, 1998).

94. Collins, *The Sociology of Philosophies*, p. 381. Emphasis added.

95. As Lloyd Sandelands said when he read an early version of this book in manuscript, "Blessed is he/she who is able to embrace both the transcendental order of the living group *and* the immanent order of the living self; able to live two lives at once; and find each enriching the other" (personal communication, fall 1997).

96. Weick, *Sensemaking in Organizations*, pp. 70–71, 174; Bell, *The Cultural Contradictions of Capitalism*, p. 149. In the context of organizations, see James P. Walsh and G. R. Ungson, "Organizational Memory," *Academy of Management Review* 16 (1991): 60.

97. Habermas, *The Inclusion of the Other*, p. 159.

98. Campbell, *The Hero with a Thousand Faces*, pp. 387–91.

99. Ibid., p. 388.

100. Ibid., p. 391.

101. James, *The Will to Believe*, p. 61. Emphasis in the original.

Appendix A

1. Inglehart, *Modernization and Postmodernization*, p. 91.

✶ *Index* ✶